GW01454287

BLÓ

A ROARING IN THE

BLOOD

Edited by
Annie Proulx

Remembering
Robert F. Jones

A
ROARING
IN THE

Photography by Bill Eppridge

Published by *Sporting Classics*, Columbia, SC

A ROARING IN THE BLOOD

Remembering Robert F. Jones

A Roaring in the Blood is published by *Sporting Classics*. Copyright 2006.

Edited by Annie Proulx

Publisher: *Chuck Wechsler*
Art Director: *Ryan Stalvey*

Printed in the United States

First Edition

ISBN 0-9660212-9-0
978-0-9660212-9-5
Library of Congress Catalog Card Number 2006923875

DEDICATION

Thanks to Annie Proulx who created this book, Tom Davis who kept it alive, and everyone who contributed. – Louise Jones

ACKNOWLEDGEMENTS

The publisher wishes to thank Louise Jones for her assistance in proofing the text, for signing our Deluxe Edition books, and for allowing us to reprint the following: "Under the Volcano," "The Dead Man on Wendigo Brook," "A Day Afield with the Wee Scot," "Kunst," "The Guinea Worm," and "The Lost Fire."

Thanks to Chuck Peterson and Wilderness Adventure Press for allowing us to print chapters from *African Twilight*.

Tom Davis, senior editor for our *Sporting Classics* magazine, deserves recognition on several fronts: First, for introducing us to this exciting project, for writing introductions to the Robert F. Jones stories and author credits, for originating the book's title, and for helping to coordinate every facet of its production.

A special thanks to Lilly Golden and The Lyons Press for allowing us to reprint entire chapters and excerpts from their excellent books, *Dancers in the Sunset Sky, The Hunter in My Heart, Upland Passage* and *The Run to Gitche Gumee*.

Ryan Stalvey, art director of *Sporting Classics*, created the striking dust jacket design. – *Chuck Wechsler, Publisher*

FOREWORD

By Annie Proulx

Bob Jones was a rule-breaker, a tough guy with a big laugh, an appetite for life, the chase and good companionship, a man to whom loyalty and friendship meant something. Such vivid personalities are rare and not easily forgotten. When Bob died he left a scattershot of punctures in the lives of those who knew and loved him, from editors to appreciators of strong tales. This book came about because his family and friends missed him and wished to honor him and his work in a more lasting form than individual human memories. If we could, we'd haul him back, but instead believe that something of the man will come through to readers who never had the good fortune to know Robert F. Jones.

CONTENTS

I. STAND & DELIVER:

Tributes, Memoirs & Reflections

Jonesword

by Louise Jones

We're driving along a highway, Bob staring at the road, puffing a cigarette; I'm looking at the trees whisking past. Suddenly he flings the butt out the window and turns to me.

"Why 'human beings'? Why not 'humans'?"

"Huh?" I respond.

"Why 'beings'? It's redundant." And a conversation begins, part linguistic, part anthropological, part guesswork. Bob's mind worked at full speed all the time, the cogs in the gears the expression of ideas. Even asleep, his technicolor dreams turned on puns and wordplay. He loved to speculate: What if we did this or that, went here or there, thought one thing or another? Where would that lead? He'd imagine options, examine possibilities, or just wonder why people said and did what they said and did. Such as, why call people human beings when 'humans' is perfectly descriptive.

His mother loved words, too. Rose Pueringer Jones, a tiny wren-like woman, was an intellectual who spent most of her later years curled in her nest, reading and making notes. She loved to talk about books and ideas, and when Bob came home from college on vacation she would question him rigorously about what he'd been studying and, more important, what he'd learned. When he and I lived in Milwaukee briefly – Bob's first job after leaving the Navy was as a general assignment reporter on the Milwaukee *Sentinel* – she and I would spend hours drinking tea in her kitchen while our baby Leslie snoozed or crawled around the floor. We'd talk about philosophy, psychology and human behavior as well as novels we'd read and what they meant to us.

She was a child when her parents came to America in 1913 from Unter-Eggendorf bei Wiener Neustadt, a little town southeast of Vienna, where her father was a metal worker. Her domineering mother read the newspapers and was convinced that war was coming and that their part of the Austro-Hungarian Empire would again be in the middle of it. She talked her husband into leaving Europe for America. They moved first to St. Paul where they had landsmen, and a few years later to Milwaukee. In 1966 Bob was in Vienna as part of a trip through Eastern Europe for *Time* magazine. He took a day and visited Unter-Eggendorf, still a small town but now a suburb of Vienna. At the city hall the mayor told him about a very old retired school teacher who lived nearby. Sure enough, this man

1

had taught my mother-in-law's older brother Frank and recalled when the Pueringer family left for the United States.

"They were the only family in town with a piano," he told Bob, which was why he remembered them. Rose told us that many townspeople were jealous and scornful of their leaving. One asked Frank, "Do you think that in America golden geese will jump into your mouths from the streets?"

The experience was not entirely happy. During the war, Rose said that her schoolmates made fun of her accent. "I would rather have been a black girl than an immigrant," she said. She resolved to speak like an American and concentrated on vocabulary and grammar until her command of the language was perfect. She was so ashamed of those years that she told her children she was born in this country after her family came here; it was only when Bob was a teenager and discovered her naturalization papers that he learned the truth. By that time he was studying German in high school, and his mother finally consented to speak her first language with him, correcting his German grammar and vocabulary as she did with his English. Milwaukee in the 1940s and 1950s still had a large population of German immigrants, including his high school girl friend's parents. He expanded his vocabulary and learned several dialects from them, so when he visited Austria in 1966 he could communicate very well with his mother's former townspeople.

Although Bob acquired his love of words from his mother, he learned about telling stories from his fraternal grandfather. Francis Jones was born in Chicago where, as a child, he worked in the stockyards. His story was that he learned a new meat-packing process and was hired away by a company in New York. Since he was no more than 18 at the time he went to New York City, it's more likely that he just ran away from home. He embroidered the tale in later years, a practice that Bob admired (and acquired). In Manhattan, young Frank Jones lost his first job because the boss told everyone they had to vote the Republican ticket in the upcoming presidential election, probably the election of 1892. Frank, independent and iconoclastic all his life, quit rather than be dictated to, even though he was too young to vote anyway. Recounting the story on a streetcar a few days later, he was overheard by a Tammany pol who, thinking the young man a loyal Democrat rather than an apolitical free spirit, found him a job as a streetcar ticket collector.

Later, Frank and a friend earned money by market hunting for gamebirds in the New Jersey Palisades. They would take the ferry across the Hudson River with a cart and shoot grouse and pheasants all day, then bring them back across the river and sell them to Manhattan restaurants. By the late 1890s Frank was working for a photographer, and we have a portrait taken at the time of the handsome young man of about twenty staring boldly at the world.

Eventually he returned to the Middle West and became a wandering photographer.

"I used to be a kidnapper," he would say with a wink, waiting for his audience to gasp. The technique was to wait outside a school, take pictures of the children, follow them home to see where they lived, develop the pictures and return to the homes to sell the pictures to the parents. Nowadays he would be arrested on the spot on suspicion of everything from lurking to harassment to child molestation, but at the turn of the century he was free to follow this dubious trade.

He met Bob's grandmother in a rural Wisconsin village, and they made a home in Milwaukee where Bob's father, and Bob, were born. Frank set up a photography studio. Old Grandpa Jones was a tough cookie who died of colon cancer at the age of 87, eight years after he was told he had less than a year to live, and three years after he'd put a new roof on his house by himself. He told Bob many stories about his adventures and insisted that one of his brothers left Chicago for the West and became an outlaw. Bob's father, a conservative banker, pooh-poohed this story, but Bob chose to believe it, as he did all his grandfather's tales, the more outrageous the better. I loved to listen to him, which infuriated my mother-in-law.

"I've heard all of those stories so many times, I can't stand it any longer," she'd grumble. "Don't encourage him." She resented her father-in-law; when he was very young his father died and his mother remarried a man who wanted to adopt all of the children and give them his name. It was a much more mellifluous name than Jones, but Frank refused the offer. "That old man's been stubborn all his life," Rose would say, "and he saddled us with this common name of Jones just to be ornery."

Bob caught the story-telling tradition – or truth-stretching, as I called it. (Whenever he embroidered a tale, he'd wink at me, just as his grandfather did.) Bob was seven when the U.S. entered World War II, and he told me that he used to pray that the war would last until he was old enough to join up. He started writing then, mostly war stories, which he illustrated. (He won a first place prize for crayon art in 1947: "the most outstanding in the entire state among pupils in the Seventh Grade," the plaque reads.)

Bob was infatuated with words. When he was a writer for *Time* magazine in the 1960s, he kept a list of unusual words that he wanted to slip into his stories on the wall next to his typewriter. One that he never got past Otto Feurbringer, the managing editor, was "absquatulate." Feurbringer's scrawl in the margin of the typescript was "use 'flee,' dammit!"

In 1966 Bob and his fellow writer, punster non-pareil John Blashill, learned that the president of Upper Volta, now Burkina Faso, was to visit Lyndon Johnson at the beginning of April. They wrote an April Fool's Day story entitled "Upper Voltage," full of electricity puns, which they passed on to Ed Hughes, the World section editor. Hughes threw it back at them.

A year later Bob was assigned to write an article about a coup in Ghana. The army had overthrown the president and was occupying the palace grounds, which included a zoo. Bob and Blashill collaborated on 'Fangs Alot,' rich with fauna and flora puns, which Hughes okayed this time; it actually ran in the magazine. Unfortunately, in those days *Time* didn't run bylines.

At home, one of us would come upon an unusually delicious word in a book, magazine or newspaper, which would lead to an evening of searching through dictionaries, including the OED – in later years using the magnifying glass – phrase books and anthologies of rare, obsolete or foreign words and phrases, which Bob collected (although there were few words he couldn't define). He was elated with the appendix of Indo-European Roots in the 1969 edition of the *American Heritage Dictionary of the English Language*. He could spend an entire evening reading through, lifting his eyebrows suddenly and muttering, "Right, that's the connection." At one point he joined an organization and needed a "business" name. He came up with Jonesword, a perfect description; Bob was a man who used words the way a medieval knight used his sword.

Now alone, I sit in my kitchen nibbling on slices of Jerusalem artichoke which grows wild near the house where the flower border meets the meadow, and I hear Bob asking the first time we ate it, "What's this?"

"Jerusalem artichoke. It's the tuber of those yellow flowers growing over there," I answer, pointing out the window.

"It tastes a little like artichoke," I add, short-stopping his next question.

"Why Jerusalem – what's Jerusalem got to do with it?" he asks. And I pull out my culinary histories and encyclopedias and the dictionary, and we're off again.

Louise Jones is a journalist, book reviewer and bookseller at the Northshire Bookstore in Manchester Center, Vermont. She was married to Robert F. Jones for 46 years and still lives in their home in West Rupert, Vermont.

Out of Whack

by Leslie Ellen Jones

In the medieval Welsh story *Owein*, the hero acquires the companionship of a grateful lion. Owein has arrived at a castle, and when they go in to dinner, the text says that "the lion went between Owein's two feet under the table, and Owein fed it with every food that was given to him." When we got to that part in my translation class, the professor (owner, it should be noted, of two obstreperous poodles) said, "That just shows you how social mores have changed between the twelfth century and today, ha ha ha." I said, "Well, actually, I was just about to say that it sounds exactly like my father at the dinner table."

This is perhaps the most consistent memory I have of Dad: sitting at the table surrounded by dogs and cats watching every move of his hand between plate and mouth, waiting for him to pick off some tidbit to distribute among them. There was a lot about Dad that was not, strictly speaking, modern. Now you are supposed to love all animals with a fluffy joy or eat them from styrofoam and cellophane packages. The idea of working with some animals, killing others, eating some, eating with others, fighting for bed space and sharing the steak is just so medieval.

In the twenty years I have been living in Los Angeles, Dad only came out to visit twice, and so the people who know me here never knew him. In the months after he died, co-workers and acquaintances keep asking me what he was like, what my relationship with him was like. I get the sense that I am not performing grief in a socially acceptable manner. All I can tell them is that, throughout the highs and lows, I could not possibly be anyone else's daughter. And what I have been doing since he died is writing like a maniac.

Both of my parents raised me with a deep distrust of organized religion, particularly the "organized" part. Dad was the ex-est Catholic I've ever known, though I have long suspected him of being an animist. I remember decorating the Christmas tree in the living room in Somers, with the Beatles' *White Album* playing in the background, while Dad informed me and Benno that the Christmas tree was not a Christian symbol, but a pagan Germanic one (and therefore acceptable in our household). I was always flummoxed in school when we sang Christmas carols, because I didn't know any of them; the best I could do was "Deck the Halls with Boston Charlie" and "Good King Sauerkraut." Christianity filtered through *Pogo*. I think, though, that writing, for Dad, filled the same role that religion is

5

supposed to fill for other people. It explains why the world came to be: The world exists so that writers have something to write about. If you could be a writer, why would you want to be anything else? Writing gives meaning to life.

Not simply putting words on paper, though. Storytelling. One summer in the 1960s when we went to Cape Cod, Dad was reading *The Hobbit,* and each morning Benno and I would jump onto the bed and he would tell us the story of what he had read the night before. *The Hobbit* was a bedtime story Tolkien told his kids before he wrote it down; Dad turned it back into an oral performance. "*Gollum, gollum,*" he croaked like a bullfrog. And then there were the age-old folktales, *The Creature from the Black Lagoon* and *Them, Cinderfella* as well as *Cinderella.* The last time I was home, the weekend before he died, we watched a movie of *Remembrance of Things Past* and an episode of *Buffy the Vampire Slayer.* A good story can slip between genres or media, as long as it is told well.

So here is a story about Dad. It's probably been embellished in my mind over time and as I've told it to other people, but even if the facts are skewed, I think it's true:

Once Dad started working at *Sports Illustrated,* the idea of going into the city became increasingly repulsive to him. Either he was out of town covering something, or he was at home writing, and he only went into the office occasionally and under duress, and even then, only one day a week. But a time arrived when, for one reason or another, he was going to have to go down to New York two or three days in a row. When he returned home after the first day, he was in a seething fury. The traffic was horrible, the weather was horrible, the people were horrible, New York was the epitome of Hell. "I can still smell it on my fucking moustache!" he roared. "It's right there under my nose!" He seethed for a few more minutes and announced, "I can't put up with this anymore; I am going to shave off my moustache!"

I think of the next bit as a Gluyas Williams cartoon from the *New Yorker* along the lines of the classic "Tomato Surprise": "Father Shaves Off His Moustache." Dad stands in the small yellow bathroom upstairs in something of a fencer's stance, one hand grandly on his hip. The other holds a straight-edge razor poised at the outermost arc of the sweep that just dispatched one-half of the moustache, while the other half is still shaving-creamed on his lip. Around the edge of the doorframe can be seen the heads of Mother, Daughter and Son peeking in a row, each with a hand pressed to cheek or O-ed lips, eyes round in awe. In fact, he probably used a regular safety razor or else an electric, and the rest of us were milling around like, Okay, so he's shaved off his moustache, what next?

The next thing was that after shaving off the handlebar moustache, his hip, early 1970's sideburns looked really weird all by themselves, so he shaved them off, too. And then his straggly long hair looked completely dorky, so he drove into Yorktown and got his hair cut short. And then the next morning, when he had to go back to the office, his flared pants, workshirt and wide, psychedelic tie made him look like he was a banker going to a costume party dressed as a hippie, so he pulled out a suit from his *Time* days and unearthed a narrow, muted tie, and drove off into the city.

He got into an elevator at the Time-Life Building and two secretaries kept eying him like they knew his face but just couldn't place him. Finally, one of them asked, "Are you new here?"

"Why, no," he said. "I'm Bob Jones's brother, Frank Jones. I'm in town on business from Milwaukee and I've come by to see him. Could you tell me where his office is?"

As he got off the elevator, he heard one of the women say to the other, "I think Frank is much better-looking than Bob, don't you?"

So he amused himself for the rest of the day telling people he was his (imaginary) brother Frank, and seeing how long he could string them along. Finally he ran into Tom Vanderschmidt, who had heard what was going on, and Tom completely ignored the transformation, so the jig was up.

But here's the thing: I'm not sure whether "Frank" the conservative banker/businessman type was Dad's good twin or his evil twin. On the whole, I'm inclined to think evil. I once said to Mom, "It's a good thing Dad didn't become a banker like Grandpa wanted him to, he'd have been miserable." Mom gave me the idiot-child look and said, "If he had become a banker, he would have been one of those guys who comes into the office one day with an Uzi and mows everyone down before blowing his own head off." That would have been Frank.

It's been strange reading the obituaries that people have written of him in which they remember all the things that made him unique, because I read them and think, but wait, that's normal. That's the way things are supposed to be; it's the rest of the world that's out of whack. *Don't make an argument unless you can back it up. Don't buy the party line. Don't be a snob, and don't be an idiot. Don't expect anyone else to bail you out. Don't stop writing.*

Leslie Ellen Jones *is Bob Jones's daughter. She is a freelance writer with a Ph.D. in Folklore and Mythology, the executive editor of the quarterly journal* African Arts, *and the author of five books.*

Good Country

by Howard Mosher

Bob Jones had always wanted to explore Vermont's Northeast Kingdom. Finally we arranged to take a day to tour the region. We'd wet a line, maybe, but mainly we'd see the sights, do some hiking, ride through the summer hills of this remote fragment of northeastern Vermont.

I've lived in the Kingdom all my adult life so I drove, heading first for High Falls on the Mississquoi River, near North Troy, just south of the Canadian border. We left the car beside the dirt road paralleling the north-flowing river and walked through a small patch of woods to the falls. There'd been a warm rain the night before, and on the way in Bob remarked on some meadow mushrooms that were good eating, fried up with a steak, and some evil-looking pink ones that weren't.

We could hear the river well before we saw it. When we came into view of the rapids just above the falls, Bob said that here the Mississquoi had the character of the Gallatin, a Montana trout river we both loved to fish. The Mississquoi has some history as well, and Bob loved seeing where, according to several old-timers, a Model A loaded with Canadian booze had lodged on a rock outcrop partway down the High Falls after being run off the road by Prohibition-era revenuers. He stood looking at the ledge for a long time, imprinting the spot in his memory in case he wanted to write about it later.

What the Mississquoi doesn't have these days that Montana's Gallatin does is a large population of good-sized trout. Knowing this didn't prevent us from trying several likely-looking pockets in the swift water upriver, where Bob enticed a hefty brown trout – we could see his yellow belly and red spots – into rising twice for his deer-hair dry fly. Then we wandered up an icy little meadow tributary full of small brook trout and speculated how much these descendants of the char brought here by the glaciers ten thousand years ago had altered in that time.

Over sandwiches and cold beer Bob asked how my son, who'd recently moved to Montana, liked Big Sky Country. I told him that Jake was photographing mountain lions in trees where they often purred like big kittens. Bob remarked that big cats in Africa did the same thing, to reassure themselves that they weren't in danger. Bob knew things like that.

We spoke about the difficulty, these days, of finding a good home for serious anecdotal outdoor writing as opposed to hook and bullet stuff. Bob said that during his last years with *Sports Illustrated* "if it didn't bounce or you couldn't throw it or hit it with a bat," the magazine wasn't interested.

After lunch we walked up a hill through mixed woods where I'd missed a woodcock the previous fall by shooting too soon. Bob said that flushing woodcock usually stopped for a second at the top of their flight before winging off to the nearest thick cover; that was the moment to shoot. He had an unusually keen eye for grouse cover and marked a barberry thicket, a juniper bush, some thorn apples and a mature beech grove. He showed me where a bear had climbed a big beech for nuts and grooved the skin-smooth gray bark with its claws sliding back down. He wondered if turkeys had made their way into the Kingdom yet, and whether moose were competing with deer for browse. We each told a story about a moose encounter. Bob was interested in how, at night, car lights sometimes went right *under* the animals, their slender, dark legs not showing up against the pavement.

"Then you've got a damn moose in the front seat with you," Bob said.

Late that afternoon we drove up to the height of land above Lake Willoughby where Robert Frost had summered. The conversation turned to books. Over the years Bob had put me onto a good many fine ones, including *A River Runs Through It,* which he'd instantly recognized as a superb work of fiction (as well as a superb book about fly fishing). Rivers ran through much of what we talked about that day, even when the subject was literature. I mentioned that I'd like to visit Hemingway's Big Two-Hearted River near Seney, in the Upper Peninsula of Michigan. Bob grinned and told me that in fact, the river running through Seney is the Fox. Hemingway had appropriated the Big Two-Hearted for his famous story because it sounded better.

"I wish you could have seen the Kingdom thirty years ago," I said at the end of our day. It was twilight and we were standing beside the Clyde River where a big fish had just jumped out of the water.

"Yes," Bob agreed, as the ripples from the leaping fish spread out and out, "but you know, this is still good country full of wonderful rivers."

It was, and is, and there's also a wonderful river in Bob's last novel, *The Run to Gitche Gumee,* published in 2002 – quintessential Bob Jones: fast-paced, unfailingly entertaining, and as clear and pure as Bob's Firesteel River, where the canoe run of his title takes place. The Firesteel is a river of many wonders and not a few terrors. Like Hemingway's Big Two-Hearted, you probably won't find it exactly where Bob puts it. But it runs through good country, the kind of wild and beautiful places Bob understood and loved as well as any man I've ever known. So I'd want to give him the last word, because when it came to describing good country, he did it best, and also because what Bob Jones says near the end of his novel of running the Firesteel seems true of his own good run through life.

"A fast run with the power of the Firesteel fueling their arms and backs. Wind and rain slashed their faces. The salmon were running too, but against the current. The men could see them working along the bottom, dark bronze with the mating urge that would end in a tattered misshapen death. Brighter fish, too, bigger and stronger than the kings and cohos – steelhead. But a madness was in the men now, the fury of the river, and they could not pause for the cerebration required: fly selection, casting angles, knots and mends and retrieves. You move when the mood is upon you. All urgencies end in death. Upstream or down."

Howard Frank Mosher *is the author of eight novels, including* Waiting for Teddy Williams, Where the Rivers Flow North, The Fall of the Year *and* Disappearances. *He lives in Vermont's rugged Northeast Kingdom, which serves as the setting for much of his fiction.*

When I Think of Bob Jones

by Edward Hoagland

When I think of Bob Jones, it is immediately and primarily of his generosity – how attentively he listened to my project of going to Antarctica in 1994, or shared his own experiences in Africa a bit earlier (though aware that all writers are larcenous). A review he wrote of a book of mine in 1973 was so generous that we have been quoting from it ever since – a span of three decades.

I didn't actually meet Bob, however, till about 1988 when I had moved from New York to Vermont but was at that point two-times-legally blind. He had heard about this somehow and simply called and showed up at my door to find out whether my situation and circumstances were okay. When you go blind and discover that some friends or colleagues are simply "dropping" you as no longer valuable for networking purposes, a new friend such as Bob Jones immediately proves sterling.

I liked that he'd lain in old buffalo wallows on the prairie as a boy in Wisconsin, and then had become such a world traveler and consummate fisherman and conscientious conservationist in the years since. By chance, I learned he was sick in the last week of his life and I spent two vivid afternoons with him and Louise in the Bennington Hospital, witnessing again his resilient, amused, and resourceful bravery and *maleness,* and remembering our conversations at his house or at the Northshire Bookstore or cafes of Manchester.

I'll miss him.

Edward Hoagland is one of America's most acclaimed essayists and observers of nature. His many books include Compass Points, Balancing Acts, African Calliope, Heart's Desire *and* Tigers & Ice. *He lives in Bennington, Vermont.*

The Mettowee

by Craig Nova

One of the things about having a friend is that when you are in his presence, you are changed a little bit. The sensation of this change is that you become someone who is different from who you are when you are alone, just as you become someone who is more likeable, too. When a friend dies, you not only lose him, but that person you liked to be, too. In this way, it is safe to say that when Bob Jones died, he took some of me along with him.

The Mettowee is a small to moderate stream in southwestern Vermont, although I find it hard to believe that anyone who knew Bob didn't know the Mettowee, either by reputation or through actual experience. The stream has some flattish pools just below riffles, and then there are stretches of broken water. A couple of pools are very deep, such as those behind the cemetery, and then there is the deep one that is known as Butternut Bend.

I know almost all of this water because of Bob. My notebooks show entries, beginning somewhere around the first of May, that read like this: "Three good rainbows. The water-colored leader cutting down into the boils the fish make in a pool with a green and silver surface, etc." I lived on the eastern side of the state, about fifty miles away, and so I didn't have time to fish this water until I knew that conditions were right.

Bob liked to reconnoiter the Mettowee in the springtime, and there was something faintly military about it. My phone would ring somewhere around the first of May, and then I'd hear Bob's voice saying, "You better get over here."

We'd make an appointment to meet somewhere on the stream, mostly at the top or the bottom of a section behind the cemetery. Sometimes, if I recall accurately, we would leave my car at one end of this stretch and his truck at the other and then fish the entire thing. In those days Bob had thinning gray to silver hair, a face that looked as though he had put it into some of the world's trouble, and this knowledgeable appearance made him look distinguished. He also had keen green eyes. He liked to wear a grouse feather in his fishing hat.

His truck was part of his essential equipment, and while I think other people have an affectation about driving a pickup truck, Bob liked the one he drove with a frank sincerity. The cab was filled with paper, an old rug his dog liked to sit on, feathers, shotgun shell boxes with a few loose 20-

gauge hulls rattling around in them, and assorted stuff that I can't recall but which I remember as a kind of automotive/domestic clutter. After awhile, when the truck bed was rusting to a brown-colored lace, he had a carpenter rip off the old metal and build a bed out of pressure-treated lumber. The effect was to make the truck look like something out of a long, rough campaign in Yugoslavia.

So, we'd fish through the water behind the cemetery. Depending on what the weather was like or if the insects were coming off regularly, the fishing would be easy or hard, and when it was hard, Bob worked through those small pools with a nymph, painstakingly fishing it around every rock, in every seam, and doing so with a kind of relaxed and pleasurable attention. On the days when the fish were hitting Hendricksons or caddis flies, it was easier, and when we got to the end of the water, he'd say, "I hooked six. Or "Five," or whatever the number was. I don't think he ever told a lie about this.

He had a particular laugh, a kind of one tone *Huff*! I remember this as coming as a kind of exclamation after he saw that you understood a joke he had made or one that he had told. For instance, he told me a joke he had heard in Africa when the Congo was breaking away from Belgium. At this time, a lot of Europeans were getting eaten. The joke about this was that a man went into a butcher shop one day and saw the prices for various nationalities. An American was $4.50 a pound, a German was $4.00, a Frenchman was $6.30 a pound, an Italian was $4.80, and a Russian was $22.00. The man who had come into the butcher shop noticed how expensive the Russians were. He asked the butcher if they are really that much better. The butcher said "No, but have you ever tried to clean one?" Bob told me this joke and then made that *Huff*! as he looked out at the green water of the Mettowee.

After the fishing we'd hang around his truck for awhile, talking about publishers, agents, advances, the usual stuff, and then he'd get into the cab and say good-bye and drive off, up Route 30 toward Pawlet, the greenish tint of the pressure-treated lumber disappearing into the greenish light of the spring evening.

*Craig Nova is the author of eleven novels, including T*he Good Son, Trombone, The Universal Donor and Cruisers, *and an autobiography,* Brook Trout and The Writing Life. *He is the recipient of numerous awards, including a Guggenheim Foundation Fellowship and an Award in Literature from the American Academy and Institute of Arts and Letters. He is currently the Class of 1949 Distinguished Professor of the Humanities at the University of North Carolina.*

Death Becomes Spring — Saying Goodbye to a Friend

by John Holt

T he memory of that sound remains undiminished despite the expanding distance of sometimes-rough years. I wonder if my friend John Talia and I have figured things right this year. Timing, while not everything in this case, is of some import. Is this first week of May when we need to be here or are we already late? Maybe even a little early? Would we hear that insane noise again after all this time? What a dilemma. What inane and manufactured drama for an audience of nobody. Questions of no importance when I think about them a bit. The point is that we're here, back in the Breaks and it's spring.

We lurch along in Talia's '84 Suburban, The Great White, as we did ten years ago. The land moves upon us in leaps and jerks. Grassy swales grow large through the windshield then slide past us to be replaced by eroded rips in the land that drop for a hundred feet or deeper. Then these too are overtaken by still another emerald green wave of grass mixed with blue-green clumps of sage. Antelope and elk are everywhere – standing, resting, grazing. The place is alive.

Deep blue, crimson, yellow, pure white spread across the prairie – wildflowers. Sage grouse burst up with loud clucks and the hammering sound of wings beating frantically in escape. The air smells sweet, rich and pungent – of life. Small grasshoppers of early season bounce off the rig by the hundreds. Heavy weather moves with speed to the south and east, but it's clear that we're in the pocket here in the Breaks and will be as long as necessary. Luck and fate is with us on this one. Everything is exactly as I remember it from the first trip. No *déjà vu* jive. Only flat-out, reconstructed exactitude.

And now that raucous spring of our past, with its roar of millions of Chorus Frogs screaming their little lungs out in full-tilt mating frenzy and sounding like countless fingers running over the teeth of an infinite number of combs, is plugged into this present. The moment is fresh in my mind. It is part of right now. Maybe it always will be, like the first time with a woman or the first hit of some psychedelic drug I did long ago. In the heart of the Missouri Breaks many hours from pavement, neon lights or Bohemian Corners Café roadhouse coffee, those crazed amphibians had one thing on their collective mind and that was sex. Reproduction. Preserve the species. And they were damn loud about it. The sound would drop down a few decibels to around the roar of a mid-sized commercial jet and then began rising in intensity and pitch until the air hummed and vibrated with a high-pitched scream like a tree-top-level squadron of F16s flashing directly overhead, the air crackling and vibrating. Unbelievable.

A bald eagle takes flight, working enormous wings as it leaps from a weathered, solitary fencepost draped with gnarled strands of rusted barbed wire that drop in a tangle, the ends disappearing in the dead, matted grass of last year. For some reason the sight of this huge bird lends certainty to the idea that all those whacked-out frogs are down along the Missouri raising their raucous brand of procreational hell once again, even as we cruise along this rutted two-track slowly closing in on the secluded breeding grounds. I imagine that I can hear the wild noise drifting up from the river, over the tops of the dusty bluffs, down along the dirt path we're on and through the window opening.

I glance at Talia. He's focused on the road just as I remember him looking back when he, Bob Jones and I were doing this. And I think about the sound all those frogs were making back then and how I yelled "Unreal," Talia just throwing up his hands and laughing. Bob puffing on his smoke and staring at the river. Neither one of them could hear me from a distance of ten feet.

The Chorus Frogs rocked on unabated. The cacophony jumped, twisted and soared on the spirited, warm spring breeze. The truest song of being alive I'd ever heard ricocheted back and forth among the limestone cliffs, tore through the pines and sizzled across the already tall grass flanking the river. The frogs' frenzy gathered in intensity. The air became charged as what must have been a group orgasm within the Montana contingent of the species became so loud I could not sense anything but this sound. Forget millions. Try billions of these little one-inch animals. Gray-green with three dark stripes. The landscape rippled with their movement like a surreal snake. The land was very much alive.

We all looked at each other and laughed, and I must admit to a slight sense of fear mixed with awe and wonder at this natural outburst. The Breaks are magic. The kind of country the three of us have lived for all our lives. The day before on that trip we'd spotted an elk the size of a rhinoceros with a companion that would be a five-point in the fall but seemed a dwarf in juxtaposition.

The Breaks. Wild. Dangerous in the quickest and subtlest of ways – muddy roads dropping off into space, lightning storms with hundreds of strikes a minute, rattlesnakes and their enemies, the milk snakes. And a decade ago this country provided the clearest vision I've ever seen of spring exploded to full-scale riot. I remember looking up and watching flights of ducks and geese coming down from The North – Canadas, mallards, a few teal, workman-like mud hens. Farther out and way over by a serrated series of salmon, ochre and charcoal ridges and gullies, hawks and eagles circled in easy truce with each other as the large raptors scoured the grassland below for jackrabbits, prairie dogs and, for all I know, down-sized deer. Coyotes dashed along ahead of the Suburban, often turning back to face us, barking and yipping at the large rig before resuming their dog trot as though they were employed as our guides.

Rebirth after weathering the illusion of a slow-motioned, dark death of winter.

The three of us doing whatever we pleased, from floating the Bighorn to fishing the small ponds here for rainbows and bass to eating way too much Talia-grilled meat to drinking a lot of whiskey and brandy. Bob called the whole, self-absorbed fiasco our Spring Breaks Trip.

All of that seems like a very long time ago. I glance at Talia and he nods, no doubt thinking along similar lines. Bob died last December. When I told John, he suggested scattering some of our friend's ashes in this country. Bob's wife, Louise, agreed and sent us some. That's why we're here this spring. To say goodbye in a way we understand and Bob would appreciate. Unspoiled land. Late night fires. Talk. Freedom.

We eventually reach John's dry camp, dropping down from a brief rise and then moving along an expansive bench covered with prickly pear and clumps of native grass. A coulee looking like a serrated wound made in the land with a dull knife runs north-south not far from camp. The Little Rockies and scenic downtown Zortman are miles to the west, the tops of the island mountain range just visible as hazy blue mounds. A cluster of pines whose tops are bent from the constant harsh winds of the area dominate the site. A small rise provides shelter from the western gales.

Setting up camp doesn't take long. We've done it before. I look over and see a fire already burned down to coals. Several thick pork chops are sizzling on a grill. John's opening a couple of bottles of good wine. Ten years ago we had the same thing in this place that hasn't changed. Cooking meat smells mix with those of grass, sage and pine.

"Hey Holt. Anything look familiar?"

"We're missing your Avon raft," and we both laugh.

On the first trip in, we'd dragged along John's Avon after fishing the madhouse that is the Bighorn for three days. We'd had uncommon luck. By that poor over-worked river's standards, the floating was relatively uncrowded, perhaps only 150 drift boats and rafts per day. The browns were active, hammering a variety of nymphs we dredged down deep in front of them. Lots of trout over twenty inches, a number over two feet. Bob connected with one that was past twenty-seven inches. That fish tore line off as it fled downriver. Talia rowed in pursuit. The brown won the race when it snapped the tippet.

And I remember taking photos of Talia sitting in the raft as it rested on the trailer in camp here with Bob casting artfully to several prairie dogs. None of them took, but we've learned to take fishing as it presents itself. And I recall a biologist rolling past at sunrise on her way to study the ghost-prairie-dog-town that had been wiped out by the Black Plague. She roared by but caught site of the raft, slammed on the brakes, skidding with a cloud of red dust. She looked through the cab's rear window, started to drive away, hit the brakes again and looked back one more time before accelerating down the two-track and away from what was clearly an ugly situation waiting to happen.

I reminded John of this. We both laughed, then were silent thinking about our departed friend.

Bob and I had known each other for years. We'd met in the Paradise Valley at Chico one stormy early May night. Since that time we'd visited each other in Montana or Bob's home in Vermont with a frequency that frightened our editors, family and one or two friends. Fly fishing, gunfire, late nights around fires, a bit of booze and many road miles in the process. Over the years we killed trout, bass, sharp-tailed grouse, woodcock, antelope and bar whiskey. Talia had been along for a number of these excursions. All through the years Bob had been a staunch supporter of mine, both through good times and uncommonly bad ones. He'd connected me with writer friends of his like Howard Frank Mosher and Annie Proulx, and always had time to edit and critique my book manuscripts. We both grew up in southern Wisconsin, loved sports, the outdoors and were somewhat outspoken in our opinions on a few things.

We'd made a pact on the first trip in here that the last one standing would drink a bottle of whiskey in memory of all of it. I kept my word on the Jim Beam end of things. As for Talia, it was his slightly sodden suggestion that I write a collection of short stories about my experiences with fly fishing guides and that I should call it *Guide Wars*. This idea was offered with one of his characteristic wise-ass grins and a bunch of enthusiasm late one night on the Spring Breaks outing around the fire pit that the meat's browning on right now. I wrote and sold the book. His fault, not mine.

We talk about all of this as we eat our meal. Then the two of us walk away from camp and look out over the Breaks. The land is turning sunset pink, orange and soft gold. We walk around taking in the view from all directions when John suddenly bends over and picks up a large green, spent shotgun shell. Ten gauge. And we find another near my tent. Remnants of the night we fired off several rounds from an enormous shotgun we called Big Bob way back then. We look at each other and laugh. Some trips never end. Thick indigo shadows move across the grass, sage and small pines. We raise our glasses in remembrance of Bob and take long drinks.

"Tomorrow we go down to Garden Coulee and out to the overlook above those frogs and scatter Bob's ashes," said Talia. "He'll have good views of things from there. It's only a couple of hours. Maybe we'll fish one of the ponds along the way."

We walk back to the fire beneath a moonless sky that is going black in a hurry and filling up with maybe too many bright stars and galaxies – the stuff of serious brain fade.

Late afternoon. High overcast. The sun glowing behind high cloud cover casts a metallic glow across the land. Cool southwest breeze. We stand on the edge of the bluffs. The Missouri flows steel gray hundreds of feet below. Rafts of ducks hold tight to shoreline reed beds. Strings of geese tack across the wind. The grasses ripple like waves.

Earlier we'd cruised along these bluffs farther into the Breaks. We passed reservoirs and ponds. Fish rose in some of them. We didn't cast to them. We dropped down a crumbling, narrow cut, through blond then tan then ochre then gray rock, down to a path that twisted along the river. As we came around a turn that hugged a limestone outcrop, the blast of the Chorus Frogs nailed us. John stopped the Great White. We got out and walked closer to the water, pushing through what seemed to be palpable waves of amphibian racket. The frogs were everywhere. So much so that they appeared to be a moving extension of the earth. I started to miss Bob and wish that he were here to experience this madness again, but stopped. Hell, I could hear his gruff but patient voice in my head and I could smell the smoke from the Merits he liked to puff on. He was with us. Good friends never leave. Not really.

I walked a hundred yards through a storm-battered stand of Ponderosas. I approached the gravesite of long-ago homesteader Joseph Cook. The weathered headstone was guarded by a small rectangle of wire fence. This man had lived more than 100 years and died nearly as long ago. Ten years ago, as we stood here Bob had removed his ball cap, stepped between the strands of wire and placed it on the marker. The hat was gone now. I returned to the Suburban. We turned around and began the slow climb that twisted along the face of the bluffs. The river was soon well below us. The sun broke through briefly. Shafts of light cut across the water, through the pines and down brightly on the gravesite. We rolled on.

Down by the Missouri River I unscrewed the lid of the jar that held Bob's ashes. I handed them to Talia who moved downwind of me and spread some of them along the ground at the edge of a bright, grassy drop to the river. The sun had turned the day warm and bright. And then we climbed up above the river and pulled out to the edge of a flat expanse that held the river in both directions for miles. John walked away and gave me the room to spread the rest of the ashes. I tossed them in the wind then flung the jar that held the remains far out into the coulee. The light gray ash dispersed across the land, blowing to the northeast. And then I broke up and cried for some time. And John was right. Bob could keep an eye on things from here. The weather couldn't sneak up on him. John returned and smiled as an old friend and we headed back to camp.

I don't know how Talia felt about all of this, but I believe that we both knew that we'd done the right thing. That our friend would have approved, nodding with a wry smile. We were alive. Bob's spirit rode along with us as it always would. And death had come full circle once more. This time in the heart of spring out in The Missouri Breaks.

John Holt's 14 books include Coyote Nowhere, Arctic Aurora *and* Hunted: A Novel. *His work has appeared in such publications as* Men's Journal, The Denver Post, Rolling Stone, E – The Environmental Magazine *and* American Cowboy. *A columnist for* Big Sky Journal, *he makes his home in Livingston, Montana.*

On the Passion of the Man

by Lionel Atwill

Bob Jones's reputation arrived in Vermont a week or two before Bob. "He's a little crazy," someone said. "Hot-headed. I heard he went after an editor across a restaurant table. Tried to strangle the guy."

That made me like Bob from the get-go. Editor throttling should be an accepted postprandial ritual. Leave just enough life in the bastard to pick up the check. Nonetheless, I was on my guard. I had *been* an editor, which, for all I knew, might warrant a light thrashing.

When we met a couple of weeks later, I found Bob not the least bit crazy – at least not crazy in an evil sense. He simply was passionate: about words, sentences, paragraphs, stories and books; about family, friends, friends' kids, dogs and friends' dogs; about trout, bass, rods, flies, tackle and water, flowing or still; about birds, deer, rifles, bows, shotguns and all the accoutrements of the hunt; about fields, woods, mountains, swamps and weather; about whiskey, campfires, bullshit, serious conversation and stories well told.

His passion for these things was not subtle; he wore it like Superman wears his costume – from head to toe. Toss out a subject in which Bob had an interest (and there were few subjects in which Bob did not have an interest), and his eyes bulged out, his head tilted forward, the cords in his neck went taut, his shoulders tensed, and his torso leaned into you like a sailor leans into the wind. That poor editor simply aroused Bob's passion. He should have known better.

Fueling the flames of his passion was his insatiable thirst for information. Bob did not research a subject; Bob lived the subject until he had absorbed all its minutiae. Soon after he and Louise bought their farm in Rupert, Bob joined the wood-butchering movement that invaded Vermont in the fuel shortage days of the late '70s. We all sought to lift the yoke of oil dependency by burning wood to heat our homes. You couldn't go to a cocktail party and not talk about which wood splits best and which puts out the most BTUs, about how to sharpen a chainsaw, about the efficiency of hydraulic splitters, about the damn moral obligation of heating with wood.

Most of us were delighted a few years later when oil prices

dropped, and we could put up our Stihls and Echos and Olympiks, calling on them only for those annual blows that dropped a tree or two in the back yard. But not Bob. He became so immersed in wood that he not only continued to cut and split and stack for the rest of his days, he wrote a thriller about wood that had more information on forestry and wood heat and implements for reducing whole logs to manageable chunks than most loggers know.

His passion extended to simpler things, too, well beyond subjects that had an intellectual component, to anything that expressed a joy for life, particularly life in the outdoors. An example: When my daughter was about a year-and-a-half, I shot a deer (one of very few I've shot in Vermont, so I remember this incident well). Since my daughter was born in Vermont, I believed she should develop an appreciation for venison, an outsized appreciation. So I taught her to respond to the question of, "What would you like for dinner, Amanda?" with a guttural growl and the reply, "DEER MEAT!"

Bob came over to hunt grouse one day. When we finished, we returned to the house for a drink. My then-wife was fixing Amanda dinner. "Ask her what she would like to eat," I said to Bob.

He did. And Amanda, true to form, growled a throaty, terrifying growl that would qualify her for an immediate exorcism, and said, "DEER MEAT!"

Bob howled. And did it again. And again. In fact, had I not said, "Bob, the kid has to eat," I think Bob would have been happy sipping his Scotch and being growled at by my daughter for the rest of the evening. And for the next twenty years, almost every time I saw Bob, he mentioned "DEER MEAT!"

I did not see much of Bob over the last few years. The grouse hunting around Vermont went to hell, and I had some ups and downs in my life – as did he. But our friendship remained firm. We did run into each other last summer at a pig roast hosted by our friend Norman. Bob, I knew, had had a bout with prostate cancer. He looked drawn and tired, but I was glad to see his passion had not abated. As always, he had a book project or two in the works, and he spoke of them with great enthusiasm. I told him about my new dog, Dutley, a Boykin spaniel, who is the sort of character animal Bob admires (he hunted grouse with a Jack Russell terrier, after all). I told him about Dutley's obsession with retrieving, how he would chase a tennis ball, a soccer ball, a stick, a snowball, all day. I told him how Dutley had palled up with my female airedale, Annabelle, making them the oddest pair of brown dogs in the state. Bob loved it and promised to come over for a visit. Unfortunately, he never made it.

And I never saw him again.

Bob was a good friend, a mentor, and an inspiration. And he knew how to treat editors right. I miss him. I hope he is feasting now on DEER MEAT.

Lionel Atwill *worked for three decades in the magazine business. For the last 20 years, he was a staff writer for* Sports Afield *and, later,* Field & Stream. *A former over-the-mountain neighbor of Bob and Louise Jones, he is now retired and living in western Colorado.*

Robust, Engaged & Visceral

by Geoff Norman

Bob Jones and I used to take his pretty good retriever and my pretty good pointer, load them in my truck or his, and drive around southern Vermont looking for grouse and woodcock country. Some of Bob's favorite spots were up toward Middletown Springs, an hour from his house, and to get there we'd drive past places I thought looked just as good, if not better. Didn't mind, though, because an hour on the road with Bob was a very full hour. There were no long silences.

Bob loved conversation and considered it a contact sport. He knew an awful lot about a lot of things and his knowledge was not the disinterested, academic, trivial-pursuit kind. It was robust, engaged and visceral. When I once described Bob's intelligence and curiosity as "omnivorous," a friend quickly corrected me.

"More like *carnivorous,* I'd say."

Which was true. Bob devoured books and ideas and thoroughly enjoyed a good argument. When he saw one coming, his eyes began to glitter, his nostrils would flare a little, and he could have been a fighter waiting for the opening bell. We talked and argued about a lot of things – the Civil War, Africa, farming, Orwell, great fighters, falconry, firewood, big game fishing, even politics – during our rides along the back roads of Vermont, and I still consider those sessions part of my continuing education – tutorials at the non-denominational, no-bull Bob Jones U.

I sometimes actually forgot that this wasn't just my buddy, old Bob, talking as we rode the dirt roads. This was *Robert F. Jones* who had been a force of nature in magazine journalism before he moved up here and we became neighbors. Before I ever knew him, a Robert F. Jones byline was enough, all by itself, to make me read a story. I would read his stuff – me and a few million others—and think, *This man is the real goods.*

That byline became famous at *Sports Illustrated* during the time when the magazine came into its own. It was the late '60s and a flamboyant editor named André Laguerre had put together a team of gifted writers that included Dan Jenkins (who later wrote *Semi-Tough* and other novels), Bob Boyle, Tex Maule, Roy Blount Jr., John Underwood and . . . Robert F. Jones, the most versatile, hard-charging member of the bunch. He wrote about pro football, boxing, auto-racing, hunting and fishing among other things. If you wanted to call him a macho writer, well, he wouldn't have minded or apologized or even cared. You weren't going to insult Robert F. Jones that way.

When he heard that Jones had died, Terry McDonell, current editor of the magazine, said this: "Bob was not only a hero of mine, but with his great intelligence and style, one of the most important people in the history of *Sports Illustrated.*"

Before Bob went to *Sports Illustrated,* he had worked at *Time* where he wrote an astounding twenty-two cover stories for the magazine. The breadth of subject matter – everything from Vietnam to the counterculture – was even more impressive than the stamina and energy it took to write that much and that well on deadline. But Jones was the pro's pro. He could stay up through the marathon closings that were part of the Time Inc. culture, eat and drink lavishly at a Manhattan restaurant, go home to the family in Westchester, then recharge quickly and go do it all again.

In 1979 he moved up here, to Vermont, to write books and get away from deadline journalism. But unlike most of us flatlanders, Bob and his wife didn't look for something in comfortable proximity to town so they could count on getting a *Times* and a cable connection. Bob loved the place they bought, five miles up a dirt road, on thirty-five acres where he could walk his dogs, fish the brushy little trout streams, and stare up at the hillsides when he took a break from his work.

Bob soon looked like he was born wearing a red and black wool jacket and a pair of Sorel boots, but it was no act. He was as authentic here as he'd been in Manhattan and the world of magazine journalism. As he had been, I'm sure, growing up in small-town Wisconsin or serving as a Naval officer aboard ship in the Pacific. He was an enthusiast, in the best sense, and his enthusiasm was utterly contagious. Bob couldn't have practiced artifice any more than he could have played the harp and sung. It wouldn't have been him.

The books he wrote were full of a kind of stylized violence and he plainly liked whiskey and guns and dogs and a lot of what some of us consider the good stuff in life. But people who focused on the violence in his books tended to miss the humor, which was wild but extremely literate. Because, above all, Robert F. Jones was a literate man. And a sweet man, in the surest, most Shakespearean sense of the word. My daughters, he knew, liked puppies.

"Bring the girls over," Bob would say. "They can play with the pup while you and I drink and argue about books." It was one of those invitations you can't turn down.

When I was laid up for a few weeks in early 2002, Bob would come by every afternoon and visit me in my sickroom. He'd bring some books he thought I needed to read and we'd talk and argue about things. When I heard he was sick, later in the year, I wanted to return the favor. In the hospital, one afternoon, we talked about the Ali/Frazier fights.

The next day he was home. I went to see him and we talked about dogs. I didn't want him to get up so I fed his Lab for him. The dog was young and strong and plainly had the drive of the dogs we'd hunted back when we drove up to Middletown Springs on dirt roads, talking about Hemingway. We recalled those days, particularly an afternoon when we'd both limited out on woodcock in the space of about fifteen minutes, and we made some promises to take the young Lab out in the fall when the flight birds were in.

It won't happen and like all of Bob's many friends I find it hard to believe he is gone. He leaves behind many good books and more good memories but still, without his restless vitality, this world sure feels like a diminished and less interesting place.

Geoffrey Norman is the author of 14 books, among them Sweetwater Ranch, Two for the Summit, Inch by Inch, and, most recently, Riding with Jeb Stuart. *His long list of magazine credits includes* Men's Journal, Esquire, Field & Stream, Outside *and* Sports Illustrated. *He lives in Dorset, Vermont.*

Hard & Tough

by Tom Davis

I t was the prairie chickens that brought us together.

The first gamebird Bob Jones ever killed was a chicken, knocking it from the sky with a homemade flu-flu arrow loosed from an Osage orange bow, then chasing the broken-winged bird for a good half-hour as it scuttled through the remnant prairie bordering his home in what, at the time, were Milwaukee's westernmost suburbs. In his story "Rusty and Belle" – named for a pair of footloose Irish setters recruited as his clandestine hunting allies – he recalled that luminous moment:

I sat there in the prairie, with the bluestem towering over my head, my hands and bare forearms stinging from sweat and innumerable grass cuts, with hard, sharp grass seeds stuck in the blood that seeped from the slashes, holding her at last in my hands . . . I ruffled the transverse chocolate and white bars on her breast again and again, as I later would the short, thick, soft hair of the first girl I ever loved. Never in my life had I been happier than I was at that moment.

But I knew there had to be a better way.

That way was with a dog and a gun.

Like many people of similar age and interests, it's hard for me to remember a time when I wasn't aware of Bob. His by-line, Robert F. Jones, was among the most familiar of the latter 20th century; in fact, I'm reasonably certain I was reading him before I knew his name. We always had a subscription to *Time*, and as a kid growing up in Iowa in the 1960s it was my window onto the larger world. At some point, I suppose when I was around 12, my parents became concerned about my interest in the hippie lifestyle – the emergence of which Bob was among the first (if not *the* first) to report on at the national level. I have a very clear memory of my mother, undoubtedly haunted by the specter of reefer madness (and troubled by my precocious affinity for the Jimi Hendrix Experience), exacting a promise from me not to "run off and join the hippies."

It was a promise I honored, even though her worries were misplaced. You see, I wasn't attracted by the drugs – they scared the crap out of me. No, the part that made my antennae vibrate was the prospect of those flaxen-haired, free-lovin', invariably and deliciously braless hippie chicks.

Bob, I think, would have gotten a kick out of that.

It was during Bob's tenure at *Sports Illustrated* in the 1970s that I began to look for his by-line and get a sense of him as a writer. I read his football and auto racing stuff, but what really stuck out were his stories of hunting in Africa. (*SI* cast a wider editorial net in those days.) Bob's tales of safari were as spikily vivid as thorn trees raked by the equatorial sun, and they helped forge an identification – in my mind, at least – with Hemingway. Given Bob's stripped-down prose and appetite for adventure, this identification was not altogether undeserved, and it only became stronger with the publication of his novels, beginning in 1974 with that tour de force of unfettered imagination, *Blood Sport*.

Not long after I broke in as a writer in the mid-1980s, Bob's essays and articles on bird hunting and gundogs – the cornerstones of my "beat" – began to show up in some of the same magazines I was working for: *Gray's Sporting Journal, Shooting Sportsman,* et. al.

Now, I'd be lying if I said that a part of me didn't think *Shit! What chance do I have against fucking Bob Jones*! The bigger part of me, though – the part that appreciates writing on these subjects that is literate, passionate, knowledgeable and grounded in deep experience – was thrilled to see Bob's by-line. For one thing, it reflected credit on a largely (and often justifiably) discredited genre. For another, Bob's participation raised the standard for outdoor writing in general – and raised the bar for the rest of us who scribble about hunting, fishing and the sporting life. In a sense, Bob was returning to his roots, for despite his ragingly diverse enthusiasms – and as much as he loved Africa and what he called "the high tension and dark tragedy of big game" – bird hunting was the sport that, from those Wisconsin beginnings, always lay closest to his heart.

Which brings us back to the prairie chickens.

A few years ago, I wrote a story called "The Drummer of Love," on the arduous but ultimately successful effort to preserve Wisconsin's chickens – the last substantial population of this magnificent gamebird east of the Mississippi River. (Drummer of love is the translation of the prairie chicken's scientific name, *Tympanuchus cupido*.) These days the chicken is thought of as a "western" species, but originally the birds ranged as far east as Ohio and Kentucky, where in the 1820s a young John James Audubon reported them so numerous that "they were held in no higher estimation as food than the most common flesh."

Now, you have to understand that despite my longstanding admiration for Bob's work, I'd never communicated with him in any way, shape or form. Nor was I looking for a reason to. But one day shortly after my story came out, I was re-reading it when something fired in my brain, and I suddenly thought, *I should send this to Bob Jones. These are the birds he grew up with. I bet he'd appreciate knowing that they're still around.*

Ralph Stuart, the editor of *Shooting Sportsman* – the home of Bob's column "The Dawn Patrol"– kindly provided the address, and I mailed a copy of the magazine along with an explanatory note. A few days later I was at my desk when the fax machine hummed to life. The document it extruded was a letter from Bob Jones, a portion of which reads as follows:

"The Drummer of Love" was delightful. Many thanks for sending it to me. Those birds are truly a wonder and it's great to know that they're doing so well in central Wisconsin. They were all over the place when I was growing up west of Milwaukee in the late 1930s and early '40s, but with the postwar suburban metastasis they disappeared . . . When I doubled on that covey rise in South Dakota a few years back I felt like I'd died and gone to heaven – i.e., that I was back in the Wisconsin of my youth.

Thus began a rich and abundant correspondence, conducted primarily through the miracle of cyberspace, that I'll treasure for the rest of my life. I consider the Internet a decidedly mixed blessing – my teenaged stepdaughter is all but addicted to "instant messaging" – but if it weren't for the ease of e-mail, I'd almost certainly not be writing this. Bob and I might have exchanged a few traditional letters, but they wouldn't have turned over enough soil for our friendship to take root.

Bob's e-mails were as entertaining as everything else he wrote – as funny, wise and insightful, too – and while gundogs, gamebirds and "the writing life" composed our original *lingua franca,* soon our exchanges were roaming in whatever direction we felt like taking them.

For example, as someone who's convinced (or at least wants desperately to believe) that the petulant, overpaid athletes of today aren't fit to carry the jockstraps of the old greats, I got a huge kick out of it whenever Bob reminisced about the sports figures he'd known during his *SI* stint – which is to say, damn near every last one who made any kind of mark in those years, and many more who didn't.

My mention of seeing the movie *Ali* – and being especially impressed by Jamie Foxx in the role of Ali's chief acolyte, Bundini Brown – triggered a recollection of spending a "scary" afternoon in a Vancouver bar with Brown and trainer Angelo Dundee ("a really good guy") when Bob was there to cover Ali's fight with George Chuvalo. An inquiry about a siren-like brunette named Wanda in Bob's novel *The Run to Gitche Gumee* received the explanation that she was loosely based on a Wanda who was Ken Stabler's squeeze *du jour* when Bob was dispatched to hang with him at his off-season home on Alabama's Redneck Riviera. According to Bob, this assignment largely consisted of bombing around the Gulf of Mexico with the Snake at the helm of his cigarette boat while the lissome, bikini-clad Wanda worked on her tan.

When the sportswriter Dick Schaap died, Bob remembered him has another of the "good guys," and recalled that when they covered the same events in New York City they'd always get together afterward for a drink or two. If they were lucky, they'd find a watering hole where Howard Cosell – who according to Bob's wife Louise had a habit of attaching himself to Bob like a remora – was unable to ferret them out.

The longer I communicated with Bob, the more astonished I was by his erudition. He seemed to be conversant on everything – and not in an abstract, mustily academic sense. On the contrary, I've known few if any people so fully engaged with the world, so robustly participatory in their approach to living, as Bob Jones.

He also had an insanely inspired imagination. When I teased Bob that the author's photograph for *Blood Tide* made him look like a youngish Orson Welles, he responded with a hilarious riff on the summer Welles, age 17, supposedly spent among the Ojibwe of northern Wisconsin, living in an ersatz "wigwam" made of birchbark and deerskin and working on a play about John Brown. Among other scenarios – a nubile Ojibwe maiden figured into one – Bob envisioned a stoned and hallucinating Orson, having been indoctrinated by his Indian cohorts into the local peyote cult, encountering all kinds of totemic animals, from a "great, ancient Ur-Bear" to "The Grandfather of All Grouse."

One of the few things Bob and I *didn't* talk about, oddly enough, was the actual art of writing. The business of writing, yes. As a pro's pro who knew as well as anyone how difficult it is to wrestle thoughts into words and words onto paper – to say nothing of finding someone willing to pay you for them – Bob was always happy to lend advice when I asked for it. His opinion on a book contract I'd been offered strikes me as classic Bob Jones.

"The advance is pretty good," he wrote. "But you're getting screwed on the royalty."

Bob also took it upon himself to find a publisher for a collection of my stories and essays on bird hunting and gundogs. I'd never so much as broached the subject; one day Bob asked if I'd ever had a collection of my outdoor pieces published, and when I told him no he basically said, "Let me see what I can do."

I spoke to Bob less than forty-eight hours before his death, and the two things he wanted most to talk about were the Packers' chances in the upcoming playoffs, which we both assayed as dismal (we were proved correct), and whether I'd heard anything about my book. One of my greatest regrets is that Bob died before learning that Lyons Press had agreed to publish *The Tattered Autumn Sky* – although as a friend and fellow writer of a somewhat metaphysical bent assures me, "Bob knows."

Of course, there was really no need for Bob to address the subject of writing's nuts and bolts, because his example spoke volumes. He loved the great old fighters of the 1940s and '50s – guys like Carmen Basilio, "The Canastota Clouter" – and it's no coincidence that he wrote with that same kind of energy, conviction and directness. Nor is it any coincidence that his two favorite words, it seemed to me, were "hard" and "tough." As someone who always thought of Bob as *il miglior fabbro* – the greater craftsman – I was in awe not only of the visceral power of his lean, verb-driven prose, but of his knack for cutting straight to the heart with just a single, perfectly crafted phrase.

Bob happened to read a memoir I'd written about the drive-in movies of my youth, a piece in which I devoted a lot of copy to their utility as venues for my first halting, fumbling, groping attempts at romance. After complimenting me, he added, "I don't remember much about the movies I saw at the drive-in. The windows were too fogged up." Talk about halting, fumbling and groping: In two sentences, Bob said everything that I'd taken two pages to *try* to say – and said it a hell of a lot better to boot.

As you've probably guessed by now, Bob and I never met. I would have liked to have shared a bristling grouse cover or a stretch of quicksilver trout stream with him; I would have enjoyed, after a day of bird hunting or fly fishing, knocking back some beers together in a North Country tavern, one of those woodsy, Paul Bunyan-meets-the-Hamm's bear places adorned with antediluvian-looking mounted muskies and deer heads of a size and vintage that suggest a vanished race of megafauna, a place where the walls are impregnated with the briny residue of a century's worth of tall tales told by sportsmen. I have a hunch we could have added to that emulsion.

It never happened – and yet I feel strangely unimpoverished. As another friend of Bob's, Jim Harrison, once observed, when you are a writer your life is essentially "an act of language." There is no separation – or at least no qualitative distinction – between words and deeds. And through his books and stories as well as his e-mails, I'll always have Bob's words.

No matter how far afield our correspondence roamed, it always found its way back home: to the dogs that we were both crazy over and to the birds that are the media for their art; to our abiding partnership with the former and to our joyful yet often bittersweet pursuit of the latter; to the irrevocable claim of blood. Of all the things we had in common, this ran the deepest: By the glow of the huntsman's ancient fires, we recognized each other as kin.

In the fall of 2001, shortly after Bob had acquired a new Lab puppy, Black Bart, as the heir apparent to 12-year-old Jake, the third member of

Bob's canine entourage, a Jack Russell terrier named Roz, went off her feed. At first Bob attributed it to jealousy over the pup's arrival, but when the weight loss continued he took Roz to the vet for a look-see. The diagnosis was grim:

It looks like my lovely little Jack Russell, Roz, only nine years old, has pancreatic cancer . . . She's been a delight and a strange but wildly keen little bird dog, especially on woodcock. She won't eat, and I'm afraid I'll have to have her put down sometime soon. It will break my heart.

Roz succumbed just a few days later, but not before one last, glorious hunt, a hunt graced by the gift of a woodcock, its value beyond all reckoning.

As everyone familiar with Bob's novels can attest, no writer understood the random, chaotic, ephemeral nature of our earthly tour better than he did. At the same time, none was quicker to pick up on its spooky convergences and synchronicities. And certainly no writer addressed the prospect of death – "That old bald cheater," he once called it, borrowing the line from Ben Jonson – with more unflinching honesty than Bob Jones did.

Make of it what you will, but what got Bob – on December 18, 2002, at the age of 68 – was pancreatic cancer, the same thing that got little Roz.

My mother never learned of Rusty and Belle – not until I told her about them, years later, toward the end of her life.

"Where did you develop this unhealthy passion for blood sports?" she asked me one afternoon when I was visiting from my home in the East. "You never got it from me or your father."

I told her the story, just about the way I've told it here. Her eyes began to fill with tears, and suddenly I was sorry I'd confessed. I looked out the front window, across the street. It was wall-to-wall suburbia now, clear down to the river. Not an acre of native prairie left.

"If I'd known it meant so much to you, I would have allowed you to hunt," she said. "Better that than keep it hidden from me all those years."

Fat chance, I thought. Don't feel sorry for her, feel sorry for what's gone. She just doesn't get it. None of them do. They never will.

Note: An earlier version of this essay appeared in the July/August 2003 issue of Sporting Classics *magazine.*

A senior editor for Sporting Classics *and editor-at-large for* Pointing Dog Journal, **Tom Davis** *is the author of* The Tattered Autumn Sky, To The Point *and* Why Dogs Do That. *He lives in Green Bay, Wisconsin.*

The World's Greatest Snorer

by Benno Jones

Robert F. Jones was arguably the world's greatest snorer.
Anyone who has spent a night in my parents' house, or even within a mile or so of it, can attest to this. At night the walls would shake and mysterious gargling noises would drift though the air, but there were no ghosts in the 100-plus-year-old houses in Somers, New York and West Rupert, Vermont where I grew up, just my father and his nocturnal emanations.

One of my favorite memories of my father's snoring happened on a canoe trip we took along the Penobscot River in Maine in the early 1970s along with two other sets of fathers and sons. We had camped one night on an island in the middle of a lake. The group had set up our camp in a clearing near shore and after dinner and a bull-session around the campfire had retired to our separate tents and gone to sleep for the night.

I don't know why, but I am one of the few people who was immune to my father's nocturnal sounds. They may have kept me awake for a time, but eventually I would fall asleep and be unbothered the rest of the night. I did this while sharing hotel rooms, thin-walled houses and tents with him over the years. Nights when my mother was unable to sleep even after moving from their bedroom to the living room couch, I slept soundly in the room next to him. And this night on an island in Maine was no exception.

Bill Johnson and his sons were not as fortunate as I in being able to ignore the rumbling, gasping, roaring noises coming from our tent that night. Unbeknownst to the rest of us, they took down their tent and moved it a half-mile away, to a place where, they later said, my father's snores, while still audible, were no longer loud enough to keep them awake.

The next morning dawned in confusion as the rest of us awoke and emerged from our tents to find the Johnsons' tent missing. One member of the party looked at the empty spot where the tent had stood the previous evening and then looked up to the sky, perhaps thinking they had been abducted by aliens or carried away by some act of God. We were just starting to organize a search when they appeared through the woods with their story of how they had fled my father's snores in the night.

Stories of similar episodes on his trips around the world, from the Alaskan wilderness to the plains of Kenya, abound. His snoring was mistaken for earthquakes, rampaging elephants, roaring lions and other

37

forces of nature. While I am known as a fairly prodigious snorer myself, when I am awakened in the night by my wife shaking me to stop my own snores, I often think: *You ain't heard nothin'!*

Benno Jones *is the son of Robert F. Jones. His photographs grace his father's last book,* Gone to the Dogs. *Despite his education and training in theatre and photography, he does from time to time write as well. He lives in Seattle with his wife Shannon and their three cats.*

A Novel Man

by Thomas McIntyre

For those of us who came of age in the late 1960s and early 1970s, and who hunted, fished and read – and who harbored notions of someday writing – the literary terrain of the time was more than a little barren. Robert Ruark was gone, and the whole Hemingway renaissance that would one day culminate in a truly tasteful line of home furnishings had yet to commence. Among the avant-garde, matters of the indoors definitely took precedence over those of the outdoors.

The first glimmer of hope for serious writers concerned with the literary aspects of outdoor writing came not in a hunting book, but in one about fishing. Thomas McGuane's *Ninety-Two in the Shade* celebrated its thirtieth anniversary in 2005. This arch and surreal novel, set in Key West, concerns a reformed doper, Tom Skelton, who resolves to become a professional permit guide, even if it costs him his life in a rivalry with other guides of the area. The author understood both the disjointed sensation of the era *and* fishing – hard-core saltwater fly fishing. McGuane's novel also had the virtue of being hilarious and, at the same time, suggesting a literary current – one drawing unapologetically on outdoor experiences – that beckoned some of us, perhaps *too* beguilingly, to follow.

The book that really kicked out the jambs, though, was Robert F. Jones's discreetly titled *Blood Sport,* which appeared shortly before *Ninety-Two*. In Jones's novel, one that almost certainly used for its inspiration a yarn spun by angling writer Sparse Grey Hackle, a father and son set off by canoe up the Hassayampa River (any resemblance to the Arizona river of the same name being totally far-fetched). Along the way there were hunts for manticore and unicorns, an encounter with a bandit chieftain, a duel with fly rods tipped with poisoned flies, and a little sex. It worked for me, and still does.

Jones was a prominent Time-Life (not to be confused with AOL-Time Warner) writer. He was a combat correspondent, the first to popularize the word "hippie," and an eccentric fixture at *Sports Illustrated*, until his novels allowed him to say good-bye to all that. By 1981 he had written two more hunting novels, *The Diamond Bogo,* about an African safari, and *Slade's Glacier,* about hunting in Alaska. *Slade's* contains one of the most memorable lines in any hunting story, a guide's nine-word introduction to his recounting of his run-in with a grizzly: "Most of this (like my face) is a reconstruction."

Jones wrote any number of other novels – about buffalo hunters and the West, the sea and pirates – and nonfiction books about Africa, wingshooting and Labradors. *Blood Sport, The Diamond Bogo* and *Slade's Glacier,* though, formed a nonlinear trilogy about the sporting life and psyche of the post-World War II and Korea and pre-Vietnam generation of men (Jones was born in 1934, McGuane in 1939). The sporting life was particularly important to these men because it gave definition to their lives, with the generations that came before and after them being defined by history. In the Ozzie and Harriet '50s, the way quite a few of these men came to define themselves was not as a *Rebel without a Cause*, but as a "Rebel with a Model 70" . . . and very much a pre-'64 Model 70.

Some of the ways men like Jones found to define themselves were not unmitigatedly salutary, it should be noted. They grew up in an era when genuine concern was still voiced about the mounting "feminization" of American culture and society, and the Hemingway machismo cycle was at its blustering apex. Such influences could lead to, among other things, both an obligatory pugnacity and the occasional overindulgence in intoxicants.

The one time I actually met Jones in person was at the wedding of two people who had no earthly business marrying each other. At the reception, maybe to avoid the subject of the nuptials, we talked about our mutual passion for African hunting and the stopping power of certain calibers. Much later in the evening, after my wife and I had returned to our hotel room, Jones reportedly behaved very demonstratively, earning him the lifelong title of "Bad Bob."

Bad Bob, though, was ultimately a facade, or maybe a protective armor for an essentially kind and generous spirit. Bad Bob might wax grandiloquently about death or growl about the fundamental inferiority of certain types of game. The real Bob, though, had a bottomless heart for, among other things, dogs, wild birds and the true plight of Africa's game. He was supportive to a fault of other writers – he was, for example, unceasingly enthusiastic about an oddball novella I wrote that nobody has ever seen fit to print.

The real Bob was a visionary, writing about the wild and the chase in all its manifestations, a man who rode in just in the nick of time, rescuing many of us from creative-writing programs and the academy. It wasn't so much that with books like *Blood Sport* and his other novels he opened the cabin door of hunting literature a crack for us to peer out, as much as that he simply blew the damn thing off its hinges.

Hell, he was the writing equivalent of Albert Johnson, the Mad Trapper of the Rat River, kneeling in the smoldering, dynamite-blasted ruins of his cabin. He was firing back at the literary Mounties of the current epoch, "laughing wildly as he flagged them," to quote another politically incorrect bard, Kinky Friedman.

Of course, the end of the story is the end of all the stories. Bob beat prostate cancer, but he couldn't beat pancreatic. He went quietly, to everyone's bewilderment and totally out of character, though you have to know that his heart raged on. I received word in an e-mail, a thoroughly inappropriate medium, for surely as he lived and wrote, word of Bob Jones's death should have come via native runner bearing a letter in a cleft stick. For once in my life I didn't know what to say. The only thing I could think of to tell his widow and family was, "A lion sleeps tonight."

His roar still echoes.

In addition to an interminable career as a writer for magazines such as Field & Stream, Sports Afield, Gray's Sporting Journal *and many others,* **Thomas McIntyre** *is the author of five books on hunting and fishing, including the critically acclaimed* Dreaming the Lion *and* Seasons & Days: A Hunting Life. *He is also the editor of, and a contributor to, the anthology* Wild & Fair: Tales of Hunting Big Game in North America. *He lives with his wife and son in northern Wyoming.*

O'er the White Alps Alone

by Annie Proulx

For a few happy seconds I thought the December e-mail from the Jones address was a holiday greeting. It was not. And it was very difficult to imagine Bob Jones dead. I had not even known he was ill, not this time and not the year before when he battled prostate cancer. Some sort of mistake must have been made, for although he smoked, drank and tickled danger under the chin, Bob Jones was not the kind of person who died. But as the days went by and other friends voiced their grief and sense of loss, the bad news became real. Bob Jones had chartered a fishing boat to cruise the waters of an unknown sea. He was gone, without maps or charts, without loran nor GPS nor a cell phone, without laptop and without leaving a contact number – "O'er the white Alps alone" as John Donne put it in a poem Bob liked. Those of us left standing have vivid memories and stories of a writing dervish and sporting companion with a big laugh who loved the rough world and who was sometimes known as Bad Bob for his occasional socially unacceptable behavior, usually liquor-fueled, especially at pompous and best-behavior public rituals which he derided as horse-shit.

I met Bob through his writing sometime in the late 1980s. In that decade Ed Gray had started a new magazine that thrilled every frustrated outdoor writer in the country. It was *Gray's Sporting Journal,* a high-quality, handsome magazine that featured articles, fiction, photography, paintings and food related to the blood sports. The magazine borrowed the approach of the late 19th century *Field and Stream* that Ed discovered in Baker Library's basement stacks at Dartmouth. Serious writing, not dumbed-down hook and bullet stuff, and fine illustrations made up the content. And the magazine paid its writers unusually well – or at least gave the illusion of paying well. Ed's famous acceptance letters offering a thousand dollars for a story encouraged many scribblers, even when the checks failed to arrive. Because the magazine was so attractive, and because the company of outstanding writers was so exalted, most of us kept on writing for Ed, even when the wolf quit howling at the door and climbed into bed. I was one of the *GSJ* writers and so was Bob, and most of the people included in this little book. For *Gray's* contributors there was a sense of belonging to an exclusive private club, a sense that we were part of a golden age of outdoor writing.

When I lived in Vermont I loved going to the Jones house, several hours distant, despite the cigarette smoke, cat and dog hairs, for every horizontal surface was stacked with towers of books. Books, books and books and the bookcases sandwiched between trophy heads, bits of dog and gun paraphernalia and the occasional easy chair, books that surely began to overflow years ago, probably as soon as they moved in. Louise worked at the big bookstore in Manchester and brought home, armfuls of good stuff. She knew Bob's greed for information and good writing and kept him humming. Much of Bob's massive grasp of history, literature and the world came from Louise's choice of books to bring home, and Bob usually prefaced a description of a new and excellent book with the remark that Louise had discovered it.

Bob had his life in order; he deeply loved his wife Louise and his children Leslie and Benno, yet could get away from them all when he needed one of his other lives. How it was for Louise who had to run the household, care for the children, keep the spit revolving I do not know, but I think Bob, with place, family, love, friends, dogs, guns, seasons in balance was a happy man. He might sometimes have wished he could have been an African explorer or lived with the Plains tribes, but he was sharply aware of the erosion of the natural world in his own lifetime and rather than lamenting, sought out and savored the remaining good country.

Bob was a man with a big curiosity, and he and Louise were perhaps the most well-read persons I have ever known. He ranged effortlessly from the Metaphysical poets to Cheyenne grammars. He was wonderful on geography, too, and there were few places in the world where he did not know the local cuisine, quality of mosquito netting or nearest source of hooch. He could speak (and write) on an amazing number of subjects from philosophy, astrophysics, best techniques in skinning beaver, gold mines, dog behavior, current events, storms at sea, gunsmiths, tracking, history, maps, technological advances. Yet he remained buffaloed by at least one 20th century technology. While he was working on *Tie Her Bones to My Back*, I loaned him a rare tape of "The Buffalo Skinners," sung unaccompanied by a nameless ranch hand with an achingly bitter and stark voice. It was my only copy and I foolishly did not make a spare. Somehow Bob, for whom the intricacies of the tape player were a mystery, managed to erase much of the tape and then to get it wound up in some improbable manner until it stretched, broke and curled into a wrinkled rosette. He was not a good one to loan books to, either. At one point, after he mumbled about wanting town names for a western setting, I mailed him a book on Wyoming place names. It came back many months later in parlous condition – bloated, with the binding sprung, the pages stained, dimpled and flared. Clearly this book had spent some time immersed in a river or bathtub, and although dried out and still useable, it had been through some swampy hell. Bob claimed the Vermont monsoon had inundated the Jones' mailbox. I could almost see the muddy, cresting wave roaring down Kent Hollow Road. Most of Bob's friends have tales that match, few of them suitable for inclusion here, and though scratched, stained, torn and exhausted, those friends persisted, for most of them had bitten the coin and found it solid gold.

He was curious about writers as well as their books and somehow kept up with the flood. Shortly after the publication of *Oil Notes,* Rick Bass was on a book tour that took him to Vermont. Several of us were interested in meeting this writer and Bob arranged a lunch meeting in Middlebury at the Inn. It happened to be a day when a considerable number of local matrons were enjoying salads and the dining room was crowded with murmuring groups. Bob and Rick sat on the same side of the table. I have a memory of a dainty but incongruous trellis bedecked with paper flowers behind them and the feeling that at any minute something frightful could happen, should happen – the trellis trampled, a whiskey glass flung, a passionate denunciation. But nothing more outrageous occurred than Bob's big laugh which roared out several times; beyond that we were all as demure as the salad ladies and finally tottered out into the sunlight, some of us wondering if a great chance for mischief had been missed.

Bob was something of a man's man, and his circle was small and tight. I did not fish or hunt with Bob. We each had our long-time excursion friends, and it is so difficult and rare to find the right person as a companion in the back country that you don't mess with the set-up once you've got one going. But we talked about where we had been and what had happened there. I used to go up to Allagash Lake with my friend Tom every spring at ice-out, crashing through mud holes, dismantling beaver dams, getting as close as we could to the tiny stream that briefly connected Johnson Pond with the Allagash River, then canoeing down to Allagash stream and into the lake. I told Bob about the time that we arrived there in mid-afternoon, when a third of the lake was still covered with two inches of old ice. At our campsite Tom said he wished he had some ice for his drink. As though it heard him, the wind picked up and the ice in the lake began to come forward with a crinkling sound and, like an army of huge crystal crabs, climbed up onto the shore, creaking, rattling, clicking. The fragile plates of ice mounted each other in layers. There was a surge and the ice gulped backwards. Out in the lake channels opened up following the old winter cracks with a kind of ice memory, and the leads and channels reflected the sun's spring heat. The wind continued to drive the ice down the lake with a remarkable sound, the jostling clatter of moving ice hash. It went on for hours. So intense was Bob's listening that afterwards I had the impression he had been along on this trip. You could talk to Bob – and very few other people – about ice music.

The Japanese have an old tradition of writing a death poem when the end grows near. The poet Hakuro, who died in December of 1766, wrote:

An ailing mallard
Falls through the chilly night
And teeters off.

It's the kind of image Bob would have relished. But the Minnesota poet, Mark Vinz, could have known Bob, so well does his "Lost and Found" fit the case.

In the small café just off the Interstate
they've taken down the photo of the local boy
who pitched in the big leagues for awhile.
Tired farmers visit back and forth
among the table tops and wives –
Their round wives with flat accents,
high hair and deep laughs.
The special today is country roasted ham
with corn and bread and American fries.
What was his name, anyway –
the kid from here who used to be a star?
We'll never see another one like that.

Now, more than a year after his death, those who loved Bob Jones remain connected by the memory of friendship with a highly intelligent maverick who loved the blood sports and the rough country of th: world – Bad Bob, Good Bob, Robert F. Jones.

Japanese Death Poems, Yoel Hoffman, Charles E. Tuttle Co., Rutland, VT, 1986, p. 183.

Mark Vinz, *Minnesota Gothic,* Milkweed Editions, Minneapolis, MN, 1992, p. 18.

Annie Proulx *won the Pulitzer Prize and the National Book Award for her novel* The Shipping News. *The Academy Award-winning film* Brokeback Mountain *is based on her short story of the same name, from the collection* Close Range. *She lives in Wyoming.*

A Genius for A Friendship

by Steve Bodio

I turned on my e-mail on December 18, 2002 and saw, to my delight, a message from Bob Jones. But when I opened it, the message began: "Bob died quietly early this morning…"

It didn't so much stop me in my tracks as make me feel that I'd been standing on the tracks when the train slammed into me. I had talked to him six weeks before, the usual writers' conversation about works in progress, the mindlessness of publishers, the sloth of editors, punctuated by more pleasant talk of dogs, his new Lab, my new sighthound, good books we had just read. Since 1982 I had come to delight in and depend on these conversations. Bob occupied a space in my life somewhere between elder brother, admired mentor, chief cheerleader and, always, combative friend. How could he be gone without so much as a goodbye?

In 1982 I opened a package sent through *Gray's Sporting Journal* to discover a paperback horror novel titled *Blood Root,* with a cover featuring a gnarled tree with a hole in it, through which a monstrous face stared. Opening the first cover disclosed a second one, where the "tree" hugged a naked woman with his roots. The author's name was "Thomas Mordane." But on the title page was a long inscription announcing that writing such things kept the pot boiling, thanking me for kind reviews, offering to show me secret grouse coverts, and ending "Thomas Mordane, aka Robert F. Jones."

It was the first time I ever received fan mail from someone I admired. I wrote back immediately, and we commenced a long-distance friendship, soon cemented by a first visit to him in Vermont, that didn't end until that final e-mail.

By the time that he wrote *Blood Root,* Robert Jones was the author of three utterly original novels. But this was only the second career of a man who was already a legend in the world of magazine writing.

He was born in Milwaukee on May 26, 1934, and grew up in suburban Wauwatosa. In those days deer and grouse habitat backed up onto suburban lawns, and kids could hunt out their back doors and fish in nearby rivers. The World War raged during his childhood and fascinated him for the rest of his life, as did all field sports.

He went to the University of Michigan, where he met Louise, who would be his wife for 46 years. He graduated in 1956 with honors in journalism. From 1956 to 1959 he served as an officer in the Navy, out of

47

Long Beach California and all over the Pacific.

When he left the Navy he had a letter of reference from a journalism professor to *Time*. *Time* told him he needed experience on a small paper before they would hire him. He spent ten months at the *Milwaukee Sentinel,* winning a Page One award for a crime story in the process, and went on directly to *Time*.

He started in New York and shortly left for California, where he covered the aerospace beat. In '63 he returned to New York as a writer. He wrote about everything from Southeast Asia and politics to Africa, another lifelong love. His first trip there was on his thirtieth birthday, and he would return five more times. His legend had begun to grow. You will hear many stories from this time, some of them true. He was *not* Bob Dylan's "Mr. Jones" in "Ballad of a Thin Man"; Bob was too hip to not know what was happening! But he might well take another credit from those years. Though he didn't coin the word "hippie," he was responsible for its general usage. When an editor, looking for a tag to apply to the people of the counterculture for Bob's cover story, asked what they called themselves, Bob answered "Hippies?" among a couple of other suggestions. The rest is history.

Before he left *Time*, Bob wrote an incredible, still unmatched twenty-two cover stories. The natural progression there was from writer to editor, but Bob preferred to write. In 1968 his friend Bill Johnson, who had moved over to *Sports Illustrated*, suggested that he would be happier there. *Sports Illustrated* was then edited by a wild Frenchman named Andre Laguerre, who preferred horse racing and boxing to more conventional sports. Under Laguerre and, later the legendary Patricia (Pat) Ryan, Bob was to write a new and more vivid kind of sporting journalism.

It is hard today to believe the freedom that writers had at the Laguerre/Ryan *Sports Illustrated*. Jones, Tom McGuane, Jim Harrison, Dan Gerber, William Hjortsberg, Russell Chatham, William Humphrey and many others wrote stories that stretched all the boundaries. They wrote about hunting and fishing, now absent in such magazines, but also about car racing and bull riding and (in Bob's case) about going back with your old high school swim team to challenge the present-day team to a match. It was the glory days of the so-called "New Journalism," and all of life seemed fair game. The era was a short one, but I doubt that magazines like the original *Gray's, Men's Journal, Outside* or *Big Sky Journal* ever would have existed without it.

Bob was the insider's insider at *Sports Illustrated*. I believe the first hunting piece of his I ever read involved his killing a wolf on a sandbar in the Yukon, an act about which he would always be ambivalent. Shortly thereafter there was one on an elk hunt in Montana, graced with details like a guide's bad lungs and a backyard peacock that you would never see in, say, *Field and Stream*. He reported from a driven shoot at Lord Alexander Hesketh's in England, a piece with echoes of Waugh and Wodehouse, with a little motor racing on the side. Who was this guy?

He upped the ante in the early seventies with a surreal short story in *Harper's,* which along with *Esquire* featured the best contemporary writing. It began with this memorable line: "The Hassayampa River, a burly stream with its share of trout, rises in northern China, meanders through an Indian Reservation in central Wisconsin, and empties finally into Croton Lake not a mile from where I live in New York State." The story, in which a father and son catch an eighteen-inch cop car on a speeding Camaro lure, was the seed from which Bob's first novel, *Blood Sport,* grew. Louise tells me that the first image came to him in a dream.

He was to write eight novels and seven non-fiction books, and you should read them all. He was not a "safe" writer; his loves and hates, passions and furies are all right there on the page. But it is safe to say that some of his books are perfect, some uneven, and every one has something unique and worth reading in it.

A quick Jones primer for those who are interested; not everything, but enough to give you a taste. First, *Blood Sport*: utter surrealism with field sport, sex and private wars; the legendary bandit Ratnose, moving tattoos, mastodons, fried maggots, reincarnation and black humor. It will always be a connoisseur's favorite. The first edition has a cover by the guy who did the Carlos Castenada books; I have a Spanish one with a tyrannosaur on it, and an obscene inscription in Spanish by Bob.

The Diamond Bogo: African satire with intelligent priapic naked apes, true safari stories and a cast of characters, mostly real. Bob loved writing his friends into books. In this one the hero is an actual person, the safari guide Bill Winter, under his own name.

Slade's Glacier: Alaskan adventure, with Jones-esque details. This, to me, is one of the "perfect" ones. My review of it prompted Bob to send *Blood Root*, another *roman a clef*. Bob had a disconcerting habit of killing off his friends in books – in *Blood Root,* his Vermont neighbors.

Blood Tide: an over-the-top, blood-drenched modern pirate's saga, with hilarious pseudo-academic excerpts on the side. Too much for some, but Elmore Leonard loved it.

Tie My Bones to Her Back: my favorite novel of the buffalo hunters, ever. There is a scene of train tracks leading between two walls of buffalo bones that out-Cormacs McCarthy.

The Road to Gitche-Gumee: Bob's last, with humor leavening the chill of mortality and a freezing last line.

Non-fiction: my favorite has to be *African Twilight,* not just because it is dedicated to John Holt and me. Africa recollected with serenity but not dispassion; one of the best African memoirs of sport and nature in our time. Large parts of this book, on the devastation of wildlife in East Africa, took up nearly an entire issue of *Audubon* magazine in the late great version edited by Les Line. Readers, by then less "naturalist" than eco-activist, were horrified. Line lost his job. I still think he was right, and one of the last daring editors.

Dancers in the Sunset Sky is an anthology of his wonderful bird hunting writing. Bob loved bird hunting best. I remember an evening-long battle we had on whether the most exciting moment in sport was a perfect shot on a flying bird or a perfect stoop by a falcon. "With the hawk, it's by *proxy!* It's not the same thing!" insisted Bob, as only he could insist.

His dog books, one for all ages – *Upland Passage;* and one for kids: *Jake.* They contain the best man-and-his-dog photos, by Bill Eppridge, of any book I know.

And finally, *On Killing,* his anthology of works by himself and others on that never-resolved subject; and *The Hunter in My Heart,* his last, which ranges through his whole career.

Bob had a genius for friendship. Although he was one of the most combative humans I have ever known, his ferocity was driven more by his fierce intellectual intensity than any tendency to be a bully. Still, an argument with him could be as disorienting as a roller coaster ride. He attended a wedding of mine and nearly started fistfights with two guests, one who was defending and one who was against the Vietnam War – he considered them both to be sloppy thinkers. The next day, he announced it was "the best wedding I've ever been to."

Further on marriage: He once told John Holt that a writer's first dedication was to writing, and that if necessary he should "divorce his wife and leave his family." A year later John mentioned that he had done so. Bob's reply? "I didn't mean for you to take it that seriously!" Remember, he was married, happily, for 46 years.

After a long day's drinking, he once put a girlfriend and me out of his car at two in the morning, in rural Vermont, because I disagreed with, among other things, his interpretation of "The Midnight Special," but mostly because he was furious that I was not as angry at my treatment by a certain publisher as he was. We had to walk four miles to a motel, and convince them to let us in without bags. The next day he wrote me, "They don't call me Bad Bob for nothing. If you forgive me, I'll forgive you. With reckless abandon – Bob." The letter is still in my copy of *Blood Tide.*

That same girlfriend, who admired him and his writing, contemplated a shelf containing *Blood Sport, Blood Root* and *Blood Tide*, and sighed, "Bad Bob is the blood master!"

Yes, but: I also saw this hardest of men tear up when asked by one of my writing students, after a lecture he gave on African conservation, if he would ever go back. He had seen devastation in East Africa, and said, with a catch in his throat, "I don't think so. I'm not that tough." He was also a man who loved dogs as much as humans should; the only other time I heard his voice go rough was when he described to me the death of his Jack Russell terrier, Roz.

His erudition was formidable; he read and had read everything, not just novels and sporting stuff, but history, anthropology, science. He could hold forth on Colonel Richard Meinertzhagen in Kenya or the scalping practices of Plains Indians.

Above all, he was a rock, always there, loyal, ready with soft words or fierce partisanship, or a kick in the ass if needed. His opinions on writing and good counsel in life will remain with me after all our happy arguments have faded. Through various crises and disasters he was inevitably the one with the advice or quip that would get you through. Here's a letter excerpt, in full, for the flavor:

"When I'm down like you are now, I go out to the woods or on the water, Christ was no fool spending forty days and forty nights in the mountains or desert or the Dead Sea of his immediate hopes. Lay off the words for a while, go mute and thoughtless except for what it takes to stay alive. Nothing enhances the biodegradability of Deep Shit or shoos away the Black Dog like a little mindless survival. But I'd take a dog with me – someone to pack up with, hunt with, watch for the sake of mindless, pared-down-to-bare-wire perception, a critter to nod to and have it nod back."

In fact, despite his ferocity, it is this kindness that shines through. My wife Libby, who had been apprehensive to meet someone called "Bad Bob," always told people he was "a gentle man and a gentleman." He was. He sometimes gave his gifts by stealth. Modesty forbids my quoting the bio he wrote for me, without telling me about it, in his anthology *On Killing*. Suffice it to say that my editor and I agree it will be my jacket bio on my next book.

And now he's gone, and I still can't get used to the idea; that I can't pick up the phone and hear his easy hello, his deep chuckle at some all-too-predictable idiocy, his fertile suggestions. When I heard about his death, the first person I called was our old friend and sometime drinking partner Anne Proulx. She said: "I guess we'll just have to send smoke signals now." I called Holt and he told me that, "We had a vow that the last one standing had to drink a bottle of whiskey to dinosaurs past," and that he was heading out to the Missouri Breaks to do just that.

He lived a wonderful life – lived, loved, created, married, fathered, befriended, fought, played hard, battled cancer once and won, twice and couldn't. Louise wrote that "although it seemed likely that he would end up falling from a plane in New Zealand or being run through by a rhino in Africa, he died instead in the hospital of a disease over which he had no control."

In the last lines of *Gitche Gumee* he said of life, "It never ends in comfort." He would never yield without a fight to death, a figure he personified as "La Grande Puta." But always knowing it must end, he wrote an epitaph for himself when writing about a friend's death in *Hunter in My Heart*. Substituting his name for his friend's, let me end with Bob's own words.

"I'd like to think that sooner or later an atom of the force that was once Bob Jones may permeate every body of water on this wild planet he so dearly loved. The world will be the better for it, as the world is surely better for his having lived."

Stephen Bodio is the author of Eagle Dreams, Querencia *and* On the Edge of the Wild, *among other books. The originator of the legendary "Bodio's Review" in* Gray's Sporting Journal *and a devotee of falconry and coursing, he lives in rural New Mexico when not traveling in Central Asia.*

Jones

by Dan Gerber

We shared our love of dogs, fly fishing, Africa, motor racing, and behind it all, our love of good writing. However prominent our enthusiasms may have been at any given moment, they were, of course, nothing without the stories that fixed them in memory, stories which often improved our experiences and became, as Ezra Pound posited their proper function, the sustenance that fed our desire to go on living. In the best sense of the term Jones was a *puer eternis*. He seemed not to have lost the wild imagination of boyhood, which he limned with consummate skill.

It was a rainy evening in the autumn of 1972 in The Oak Bar at the Plaza. Jones had called because he wanted to meet Jim Harrison, with whom I was traveling, and Jim brought me along. Bob was familiar with my work for *Sports Illustrated* and knew I had a first novel coming out. He had begun covering motor sports for the magazine shortly after a bad crash had forced me to give up driving, so we shared a great many friends and a unique realm of experience. We began corresponding immediately, and the following spring Bob asked if I might like to join him at Indianapolis for the 500. The next year I began working on a book on the race and our Indy rendezvous became a ritual each May. That summer I accompanied Bob on our first magazine assignment together, a month-long safari in northern Kenya.

Bob's second novel, *The Diamond Bogo*, was a fantasy spun out of that trip, an *SI* story on "the last great safari." The characters of Bucky Blackrod, the crass, hard-bitten New York journalist, and Donn McGavern, hippie-poet, ex race-driver were, of course, our thinly disguised selves. Bob gloried in the tough-guy persona he used to mask the artist and behind which, especially with a few Scotches in him, he might buffalo a casual acquaintance, unless they'd seen him with his dogs.

Among all the passions we shared in our long-distance friendship, we were most often proud parents discussing our dog children. Luke was an old grey-muzzle the April I had to put down Lily, my beloved thirteen-year-old Labrador. I mourned for about two months and then began searching the ads in *Dog World*. Finally, after extended conversations with breeders in Kansas, New York, California and Georgia, discussing the sweet temper, broad head, soft eyes and affability I was looking for, I met Grace Morris, a Lab breeder less than two hours' drive from our farm in Michigan. I visited the sire and bitch, ordered a female from the prospective litter and called Jones to see if he was ready to consider a male pup to study under Luke in his last season.

In October, when the pups were eight weeks old, Bob drove out to Michigan and, after a night of reminiscing on the splendors and awfulness of The Marquesas, Lake Turkana and Watkins Glen, and all the friends shared and lost to unyielding retaining walls and ill-tempered cape buffalo, we drove to Grace's to pick up the two chubby, yellow, incipient bags of puppiness whose names were Willa and Jake.

We spent the next two days walking the pups in the rainy October woods, watching them loll on the kitchen floor and chew on their ears, and regularly taking them out to the soaked roots of one certain beech tree to begin their housebreaking. By the second or third visit to their rain-sodden rest room, Jake and Willa would squat like a couple of bookends the moment we set them down. A good sign, we agreed, as we mused on the decade-long love affair we were each beginning with our new best friend.

It was almost a year later when Bob came back to our farm in Michigan. He had immortalized Jake, Luke and Willa in a story in *Sports Illustrated* on the training of his new hunting companion. He brought along Jake and Bill Eppridge, the award-winning photographer whose heart-melting work had adorned Bob's story, to complete the photo-shoot for a two-book contract his piece had engendered. But perhaps because Bob had just lost Luke, he needed the road trip to air out his grief. Non-dog people simply aren't capable of comprehending that our dogs, in addition to being our most effective teachers of living in the moment, are our most constant and agreeable companions.

The June evening he and Bill arrived at our farm was the only time I ever saw Bob cry. It wasn't the beauty of the last light of the solstice filtering through the trees, or as far as I could tell, some spectral memory of Luke in this place where we had all spent so many happy times together. What brought the tears was the fact that within a minute of their arrival, after the leaps of excitement and an obligatory butt sniffing, Willa and Jake, as elegantly as if choreographed by Balanchine, turned, trotted off to the exposed roots of one certain beech tree, performed a doggy *plié*, and peed.

Copper Canyon will publish A Primer on Parallel Lives, **Dan Gerber's** *seventh collection of poems, in the spring of 2007. A novelist and journalist as well as a poet, his other books include* Grass Fires, Trying to Catch the Horses, A Second Life *and* A Voice from the River. *He lives near Santa Ynez, California.*

If I Kill Myself

by Tom Rosenbauer

ast winter I found a scribbled note on a piece of paper torn from a spiral notebook. It was tucked away in a box with a tumbled quartz pebble from Nauset Beach, the three tiny pearls I've found in oysters over the years, an alligator tooth, and a Snickers Bar from Kamchatka with Cyrillic writing on the label. In Bob Jones's erratic handwriting it says:

If I kill myself in a car accident tonight I will pay Tom Rosenbauer $10,000. Signed, Robert F. Jones.

I got the note from a drunken Bob at a book signing at Northshire Bookstore. The wine was free and Bob had arrived with a pretty good head of scotch. I had taken his car keys and when Bob made a scene about getting them back, I exchanged his keys for the note.

I didn't like Bob much at social functions. His discomfort with events in our sometimes-snotty New England town was exacerbated by alcohol. When I first met him, introduced by a mutual friend, I hadn't yet learned of his drinking problems. But I was intimidated by stories I'd heard of Bob throwing knives into the wall at New York literary parties. In his best state of mind, his erudite references were way beyond my scope. But once he began drinking, I was totally out of the picture.

Take Bob into his own world, for instance his writing room, and he was one of the sweetest, most generous souls I've ever known. I remember calling him once for some writing tips, for a talk I had to give to a bunch of fishing guides on how to break into the world of outdoor writing. Instead of a few offhand platitudes, Bob gave me an hour of his valuable writing time. His suggestions were like nothing I had heard of or read before, and one sticks with me like no other: "Write your rough draft, and then let it sit for two days. Go back and completely eliminate all the writing you think is really clever."

don't think anyone could have appreciated Bob to the fullest without spending time in the woods with him, at least that is where I felt I knew him best. And liked him best. Free Bob from the alcohol (I never once saw him drink while hunting or fishing), get him away from a cocktail party, dress him in his old red plaid jacket and hiking boots, and he became warm, cheerful, open, with none of the cynicism he had for much of the indoor world.

Grouse hunting with Bob and one of his Labs was a casual affair. There was no agenda, no planned route. Bird hunting with some people begins with "We'll start here, work through those briars for a half-mile, then swing up into the

55

pines above the apple orchard." Not with Bob. He'd drop the tailgate of his pickup, the dog or dogs would head off into the woods into whatever scent caught their fancy, and for the rest of the day it was a random tour of Vermont hillsides in October. We might hunt the same cover twice, or backtrack to grab a wild apple from a bountiful tree. The hunt would end when it was too dark to see or when we ran out of cigarettes.

Bob could and did fish all over the world, but I think he was happiest fishing the little – and I mean little – brook in front of his house. His modest confidence in his sporting abilities allowed no room for breast-beating stories of large trout, or in counting fish. I think it mattered to Bob that he caught fish. But it was the intellectual challenge of each fish fooled on its own terms, not a scorecard, that counted.

I had fished Bob's stream, farther down into the valley where it widened, years before I met him. I had always thought the water at the end of the hollow was too thin for anything besides seven-inch brook trout. I was right, but that didn't deter Robert F. Jones. He just scaled his game down, with a one-weight graphite rod and tiny Royal Wulff dry flies. Once I met Bob and learned about the fun he had in the tiny plunge pools carved from slate, encircled with mature oaks and sugar maples and fragrant with wild leeks in May, I preferred vicarious visits to his water. He'd pick up the phone to ask me about the Hendricksons on the Battenkill. I'd ask how he was doing, and the edge in his voice would soften as he described the three tiny brookies he'd taken in an entire afternoon of fishing, the morels he'd picked, the pileated woodpecker that surprised him as it flushed from a perforated dead elm.

Last spring, I fished this brook for the first time since Bob died. Jim Babb was visiting, and I knew that, unlike most people, he appreciated trout streams where your fly ends up more often in the trees than on the water. We began a mile below "Bob's" water. After working halfway up, I told Jim that Bob Jones used to love fishing upstream aways. There was a moment of mutual silence. I don't know what Jim was thinking, but I could see Bob in his ratty wool jacket and hip-boots, a Marlboro drooling ash as he concentrated on a pool the size of a soup bowl. The water winked, and Bob skipped a sleek fish, no bigger than a sardine, all blue and green and white and orange, to the gravel bar at his feet.

I said to Jim that the water was getting pretty thin. He agreed.

"Yeah, let's head back to the car."

"OK. Probably only some tiny brookies up there."

Tom Rosenbauer has been a fly fisherman for 40 years and has lived for 30 of those years in Vermont. He is the marketing director for Orvis Rod & Tackle and the author of a number of books on fly fishing, including Prospecting for Trout, Reading Trout Streams *and* The Orvis Guide to Fly Fishing.

Bob the Mentor

by Lilly Golden

Bob Jones was my mentor and friend.

I was his editor at the Lyons Press, and though I worked with him to help shape several books, it was he who was doing most of the shaping, and not only of his own words, but also of me and my sensibility as an editor. And I don't think he knew the full weight of his influence. He embraced his role as mentor to me about the natural world, but he might have been surprised to know that I learned more about the craft of editing from him than from anyone else.

His warmth radiated through telephone calls. He always said hello with a tone in his voice that had a sweetness I can hear now in my mind's ear. Our phone calls, which would begin with specific purpose to discuss something as mundane as a deadline, or as important as a character or plot development, would always wander into territories of his expertise, which were as vast as the Great Plains. The woods were often on both of our minds and I'd tell him strange things I saw walking in my upstate New York woods and he'd explain them to me, as though we were walking together. When a grouse crashed into my house, shattering a window, landing dead in my living room, Bob was the one I called to ask what the hell had happened. And he explained it to me. (Grouse have been known to make suicidal take-offs when they're hormone-crazed adolescents.) Our conversations would ramble with my questions and his ruminations about books, nature, the outdoors, creatures of all kinds. He was so unlike my own father, whose deep knowledge covers very different ground. It was as though Bob was my second father, who shared my quirky interests in animals and everything that lives in wild places.

His mind was so rich and his knowledge so deep, that at first I was intimidated to alter the words or phrases or structure of his writing. But his enthusiasm and graciousness welcomed me to take my best shot.

He was magnanimous in his enjoyment of being edited, when he agreed with me. But in the margins of the manuscript pages of his novel, *The Run to Gitche Gumee,* and in his two collections of articles and stories, *Dancers in the Sunset Sky* and *Hunter in My Heart*, we would sometimes spar, get into heated arguments, and even bicker. Many of our arguments were over his contempt for the trend to make all writings politically correct. Some of our bickerings would sound like this: I'd write something to the effect of, "Bob, this makes you sound like a jerk." And he'd write back something that I'd interpret to mean, "You nancy, prancy editor, what are you, a *baby*?" He seemed not to care who he offended with his writing. But I wanted to protect him from having people think he was chauvinistic, or hard-hearted, because he was so far from those things.

There was also the grave and shameful error I once made of attempting to introduce an adverb into one of his essays. I had wanted to change what seemed to be an ill-used adjective into an adverb. I received a scouring lecture on the foolishness of overusing adverbs. Bob Jones became thereafter responsible for the salvation of several other writers' novels and memoirs, which have had (nearly) all their adverbs extracted.

At his best, no one can write better. His range is virtuosic. Bob wrote thrillers, a horror novel, he was one of the earliest contemporary novelists to use magical realism, and his outdoor writing set a standard that inspired a generation of writers. He could write with humor, silliness, beauty and astonishing violence. His opening pages to *Tie My Bones to Her Back* are some of the most unnerving I'd ever read:

"The buffalo herd moving through time: big ugly shaggy smelly louse-ridden powerful animals, black-humped, black-horned, huge heads and tiny feet, bellowing, roaring, grunting, pursued by wolves, ridden down by Indians, gunned in their milling millions by hide men, shot and puking blood, hundreds of them pouring into rivers and over cliffs, breaking their bones and dying, or drowning and dying, or doomed to starve with broken backs and legs, and the rest running right over them, through them, with no compassion, no concern, driven mindlessly, as are we, by their nature, our nature.

"These lives, our lives, are merciless – they will make you cry out for emptiness – cry out for a single redeeming message.

"You'll not get it here, unless . . .

"The Human race is vile, unthinking Nature best, and Prayers won't help us anyway.

"The plains go on forever."

Bob had a wonderful sense of irony. Some of his earlier books held a surreal power. *Blood Sport* is considered a classic today, wherein a father and son fish a mythical river in the wilderness, using a tiny yellow New York City cab as a lure:

"Inside a minute, he had three wiggling pedestrians on the hook, none of whom put up much of a fight. One was a girl in a patent-leather suit, hooked lightly through the lip, so we released her. The other two – a banker and a hippie – we put on the stringer. On the next three casts, we added a spade pimp, an elevator inspector, the clubfooted editor of a monthly insurance-company newsletter and three prostitutes, all of them plump and well over the legal size limit."

Lesser known is one of his earliest novels, a horror novel, *Blood Root,* which he sent to me when my husband and I had bought an old abandoned farm in the Catskills. On our weekend trips to the farm, I read it in the car, reserving the most chilling parts to read out loud to my husband on the hours-long pilgrimage. It was an eerie echo of our own plunge into the unknown of rural life, and Bob had written it when he and his wife had made their move to the country. In *Blood Root,* the trees are deities, a fitting theology for someone like Bob whose temple was the forest.

And no one wrote with more tenderness about his dogs. As in *Upland Passage:*

"Old Luke died the following spring. A sudden cancer, but one that apparently caused him little pain. He was thirteen years old, and he'd had a good run in the course of his life. He'd gone the distance with style and enthusiasm. It's hard for me to realize he's dead. Now and then I still hear him scratching at the back door, asking to be let in. But it's only the wind in the trees.

"For days after his death, every time I let him out, Jake hunted the fields behind the house, looking for Luke. I walked with him sometimes, with tears in my eyes. 'He's not there, boy. He's gone away.' "

One of my regrets is that I didn't have my beloved dog, Burt, in my life until after Bob had died. Bob would have also been my dog mentor. I had had the honor of meeting his legendary Jack Russell, Roz, and his eminent Lab, Jake. But I couldn't share with him Burt's joyous puppyhood. (I was glad to be able to tell Louise. I asked her the questions I would have asked Bob, such as: Are puppies always so . . . *flatulent?*) Then, when Burt died before he was a year and a half old, I felt desperate to share with Bob my unbearable pain. He would have understood. He would have known what to say. It took me months before I could tell Louise. She had suffered too much heartbreak already. She'd gone through Roz's abrupt death, and then Jake's, and then the big one, Bob's.

In our telephonic ramblings, Bob and I would discuss, among many other things, hunting. I'm not a hunter, and Bob was a hunter to his core. He taught me everything positive that I know about hunting and hunters, to moderate the unflattering observations I had made myself, in my own woods wanderings. I vicariously hunted with him and feasted on his take, the grouse, duck and woodcock, through his writing, as did all his many fans. I celebrated the achievements of Jake and Roz, and much, much later, Bart. And his readers and I watched as Bob's thoughts about killing underwent a shift in the last few years of his life. In his final collection, Bob decided to add several essays. One was on his decision to no longer kill woodcock.

"For a number of years I've been caught up in an agonizing internal debate: Should I or should I not swear off killing woodcock? No bird has given more pleasure, through a long, satisfying lifetime of bird hunting, than *Scolopax minor*, the plump, pint-sized, russet-clad, long-billed, bug-eyed solitary of the uplands. As Jorrocks, the rough-and-ready fox hunter who graced the works of nineteenth-century English sporting writer Surtees, often said of wily Reynard and his kin, "I loves 'em, I loves 'em, I loves 'em . . . and I loves to kill 'em." For years I've shared that emotion, but lately it's been eroding, at least as it applies to woodcock. Now when I pick one up after a successful shot, cup its warm musky body in my palm, and watch those big dark eyes begin to glaze, I feel mostly sorrow. These wings will no longer whistle…"

Bob made a vow to hold his fire on woodcock, but it was a promise that the hunter in his heart would not let him keep, though he renewed it many times in his last season.

But in hunting, bloodlust was never what Bob sought. Killing for sport alone didn't seem to set well with him. In his book *African Twilight*, he writes about the horrible mistake he made in killing a zebra. This zebra, which he shot by accident, had a foal, whose death Bob was now also responsible for, because the baby zebra would not escape death by a lion or hyena that night. He told me he cried like a baby when he realized what he'd done, and he knew that someday, somewhere, those zebras would be waiting for him . . . . I hope they have forgiven him.

In *The Run to Gitche Gumee*, Bob created the characters Harry Taggert and Ben Slater, two friends who each embodied different aspects of himself. In the second half of the book, they are Bob's age at the time he was writing it. Harry has been diagnosed with prostate cancer, about the time of Bob's own diagnosis. Harry, late at night, drinking, contemplates his fate, thinks of suicide and ponders the afterlife:

"Where I'd be able to hit every clay off the trap within ten yards, and every grouse that ever flew, and cast a streamer – a 4/0 Lefty's Deceiver – the length of a football field, with pinpoint accuracy.

"With only one backcast!

"And the wahoo would take it every time…

"But none of the fish I caught would ever go belly up after the release."

But none of Harry's perfect imaginings of heaven amount to what seems right to him. I don't think Bob sought perfection, as much as he sought saturation. He lived his life with bravado and kindness, and killing and healing, and love and passion. Well, only Bob really knows. I imagine him reunited with his dogs, no matter what else.

Perhaps his afterlife is something like the one he created in his short story, "In the Drowned Lands," wherein a cynical old man is notified that he's inherited the estate of his uncle (the Colonel). He is driven to his uncle's country home by a lawyer, and is left there for the weekend. Examining his inheritance he finds a comfortable stone cottage without electricity, along with two clumber spaniels, a library of the great classic outdoors writers, good cigars and fine sherry, and an exquisite antique firearm. The old man goes out with the dogs in pursuit of woodcock, in beautiful countryside and woods. He marvels at the perfect ease and joy with which he slides into the life of the bird hunter. He understands this paradise will never end; he will not be picked up and returned to his stressful city life at the end of the weekend. In fact, he will never be.

"Ahead of them lay the unspoiled mornings, crisp and cool and bright with the fire and steel of eternal autumn, punctuated only by brief white clouds of burnt powder, the slow cough of his smooth, steady barrels. Francis Cargill knew now that he would hunt all day, forever. The powder flask would never need refilling, the shot pouch would never go slack, nor would the birds ever cease to fly. It would rain only at night, of course. In his mind, as the mists blew clear, he could see the endless covert opening before him – the tight-laced woodcock brakes, the spongy snipe bogs, the sharp-thorned partridge lies, the grass-topped hills where he and his steadfast companions would pause to drink the cool breeze. Somewhere along the way, he was certain now, they would meet the Colonel. Together, dogs and men, they would push on into a world of blurred wings and broken rainbows.

"Forever and ever, amen."

Lilly Golden is a book editor. In addition to Robert F. Jones, she has worked with Stephen Bodio, Tom Davis, Mike Gaddis, Edward Hoagland, John Holt, Tom McGuane, Jay McInerney, Geoffrey Norman, Dan O'Brien, Annick Smith, William Tapply, Guy de la Valdene, and Joy Williams, among many other fine writers. Golden lives in the Catskill Mountains of New York with her husband, Garth Battista, and daughters Isabel and Rose.

He Was the Best

by Terry McDonell

I am writing this the way Bob Jones would like it – overnight, on deadline – the way he wrote so very many fast words before he jump-shifted into his literary life. And like Bob, I will probably be unhappy and hurt if mine is not the lead piece in this book. Just letting you know, the way Bob always did. I didn't know Bob in those days, but everybody who was around then and is still around now says there was no one better at the newsweekly style. That he was the best. *The best.* This is what Bob's colleague Roy Blount Jr. was referring to when he said what he learned in the business was that "if you have to write 5,000 keep-it-hopping words overnight in a bad hotel room with a couple of drinks already in you, you can."

Bob was a national correspondent for *Time* magazine for most of the 1960s, covering Nixon and Vietnam and all the rest of it, and knocking out twenty-two cover stories. Counting cover stories is how you kept score, by the way. Still do, and twenty-two puts you right up there. But my favorite detail from those days is that Bob introduced the word hippie into the national press lexicon in a 1967 *Time* cover story called "The Now Generation." Everybody tells that story, but *Time* was so relentlessly unhip back then, I can't help wondering what it took for Bob to pull the magazine along from Golden Gate Park to communes in the New Mexico mountains. The answer, of course, is that he was relentless.

Bob got to *Sports Illustrated*, where I work now, sometime in 1969, and that's where his journalism soared. He wrote college football, the NFL and motor sports, salted with a little hockey, golf, boxing and baseball, and rose to prominence next to the aforementioned Blount Jr., George Plimpton, Frank Deford and Dan Jenkins – an editor's dream team of eccentricity. What Bob brought to the party was his far-ranging knowledge and a voracious enthusiasm for books and the outdoors. His so-called outdoor writing set a standard for the *SI* Bonus pieces that still run at length in the back of the book.

Then there was Africa, where Bob found an almost spiritual relationship with words. This is from "The Game Goes On," which he wrote for *SI* in 1978:

"Swahili, the lingua franca of black Africa, is a language of fatalism, of the dying fall, of the story in which cruelty and beauty meld into a swift, soft sunset. Leopards cough at night on the kopje; the stars are like shattered sapphires; a baboon screams in death. Lions rip at a wildebeest's gut while zebras browse placidly nearby."

He could pin your ears back.

I didn't know any of the above in late 1976 when Will Hearst and I were starting a magazine called *Outside* out of the *Rolling Stone* offices in San Francisco and I picked up the mind-blowing *Blood Sport: A Journey Up the Hassayampa*. You can look it up online today and read it described as a "pathbreaking, surreal novel of the outdoors." No shit. I never told Bob this, but that first novel of his informed almost everything we did during the start-up of *Outside*. Just like rock and roll was about a lot more than the music, the "outdoors" we were doing a magazine about was about a lot more than Sierra Club cups. We too were hunting unicorns and manticore on our way up the river. I don't know why I didn't call him then, except that maybe Ratnose scared the hell out of me.

Bob and I finally met when I was at *Esquire* in the early 1990s. By then I was very aware of Robert F. Jones as a literary figure and, to borrow a phrase from P.J. O'Rourke, a "pants-down" environmentalist in a time when the environmental movement looked like a goldfish tank of irrelevancies. We had drinks and I think some caviar at a midtown hotel and decided to try to work together, which we did in a minor way. The trouble was, Bob was busy with his novels. And his bird hunting (read dogs) and his fishing.

Years blew past. When I was fired from *Esquire,* Bob called me up and told me that getting "canned" as he put it was a badge of honor. And then he said that one time or another he hated every boss he ever had, but he didn't put me in that category because I had a nice "touch." The truth here is that he made me feel like a much better editor than I probably was.

In 1994 I talked Bob into a piece for *Sports Afield* about, as we said in the subhead, "How Fishing for Records Will Make You Crazy." Bob said it was pretty much a bullshit idea but agreed to concoct a piece he insisted on calling "Wampus Cats & Oyster Toads." In it he told fishing stories, but they were about a lot of things besides the fish – like love. My favorite language described the fishing of a friend who had just broken up with a longtime girlfriend "as knitting up with fly rod and feathers the raveled sleeve of his care." But mostly the stories were about competition in the great tradition of "mine's bigger than yours."

He ended the piece with an explanation of his own "personal best for ugly, as well as big, weird and hazardous." It was back in the early 1960s when Bob was writing what he called "the post-Uhuru stuff" for *Time*. He was stuck in Nairobi waiting for an interview with Jomo Kenyatta and drinking too many chota pegs at the Long Bar in the New Stanley, so he decided to charter a small plane and fly up to Kenya's Northern Frontier to what was then Lake Rudolph (now Lake Turkana) for some fishing. It was harsh. Sandstorms, 120 in the shade, fifteen-foot crocodiles in the shallows and gangs of wild-ass Somali bandits called shifta roaming the surrounding desert with Kalashnikovs.

One night, Bob pulled in a Nile perch that weighed 187 pounds, 8 ounces, a record that would have held for twenty-seven years if he had bothered to submit it, which he didn't. Instead, he ate it (no catch and release in East Africa) with the affable Guy Poole, who ran the makeshift fishing camp; his mechanic, an ex-POW from World War II named Tony; Priya Ramrakha, a *Time-Life* photographer who was killed by a sniper in Biafra a few years later; and some friendly local *El Molo* tribesmen. All Bob's kind of guys, one way or another. That night was his 30th birthday and he lay happy and full under mosquito netting while hyenas whooped him to sleep.

I have been paraphrasing Bob's story up to now; this is his language:

"Eighteen months later shifta fell upon the camp, tortured and killed Guy Poole and a Catholic priest who was there to fish (Poole's wife and children had gone to Nairobi for supplies), shot up the radio, generator and three of the trucks, and burned the camp. They disappeared into the desert in the fourth truck, the *El Molo* said later. Tony was driving with an AK pointed at his neck, once again a POW. But not for long.

"They were bound for a well called Gus, the *El Molo* said. When they got there, they filled their water bottles, burned the truck, banged Tony on the head, and skinned him out like a catfish. They took the hide for a trophy."

Now that's a fucking fishing story.

To borrow a movie cliché, Bob could handle the truth.

Bob's world was large, but also disarmingly small as I found out in Kenya last August with my sons and our old friend from *Outside,* Will Hearst. We were outfitted and guided by the Bill Winter Safari Company, which was the same outfit that Bob had spent much of his time with in Africa and is pretty much the same, except that it was now run by Bill Jr., who grew up in the bush learning from his father's tracker, Lambat, a Dorobo from up in the Mukogodo country. Lambat was still with him, tall and dignified, with a good watch and the patience that comes from years of hunting. It was unnerving when he smiled so broadly when Bob's name bubbled up with the coffee one morning at breakfast. Bob was *rafiki,* friend. That simple.

Bill Winter Sr. was Bob's first guide in Africa and they became close friends, especially after Bill Sr. was shot in the right leg by a client while following up a wounded buffalo. The .357-caliber bullet shattered his leg a few inches above the ankle. After twenty-one operations and months of delirium in a Nairobi hospital, the foot was saved, but his right leg was two inches shorter than the left and the foot itself is virtually boneless. Bob wasn't there, but he understood what it meant to Winter not to be able to get around like he once had. They even laughed about it.

Bob said that to travel Africa with Winter was to have Linnaeus, Dickens, Darwin and Monty Python at your elbow. Not to mention Allan Quartermain. We heard all about it on our safari, hitting many of their spots – the Masai Mara, Funzi Island, Lewa Downs. We heard about the time on the Washinaro River that Lambat saved *SI* photographer Bill Eppridge from the spitting cobra; and the night the elephants stampeded through the camp ("at least sixty or eighty of them"), but Bob and Winter somehow avoided being "squashed as flat as hammered tin cans"; and the time the lioness came after them; and could it possibly be true that a drowned elephant came crashing down Adamsons' Fall?

When I returned from Kenya I sent a package of Bob's more recent books to the Bill Winter Safari Company and heard from Bill Sr., who for a number of years has been tethered to the family house in Karen, outside of Nairobi. He said he wished we could all go on one more safari together but since that wasn't going to happen he was looking forward to joining his "dear old bush-loving chum . . . in that great pristine wilderness in the sky." But the note didn't feel sad at all, just defiant, which made me think of Bob. At the bottom, Winter had written, "I can't wait!"

I have in front of me on my desk a journal I kept over that safari. It is full of rough notes, drawings and maps, with bits of feathers and grasses and leaves pasted on them. Next to the journal is a faded red folder I found in the *Sports Illustrated* Library. It is the Robert F. Jones file, and it feels to me like a heavily weighted counter-balance to the crude journal. It is as if the journal would never have existed without the file. In it, in a 1978 story about the end of the game in Kenya, Bob wrote this:

"A yellow and blue agama lizard crept out on a rock to bask in the heavy-hitting sun; as if in some strange counter-balance, the crocodile across the way slid into the roiling water, out of sight."

Terry McDonell's peripatetic career as an editor has included stints at Outside, Rolling Stone, Esquire, Sports Afield, Men's Journal *and* Us Weekly. *He is currently managing editor of* Sports Illustrated.

II. A BOB JONES PHOTO ALBUM

Photography by Bill Eppridge

Bob Jones was passionate about many things, but particularly his dogs. Here, he works with Jake, who quickly formed a strong bond with his loving master.

Jake and Bob would go out twice a day to play with the retrieving dummy, sometimes enjoying each other's company late into the evening.

Bob demonstrates his left-handed casting technique to an instructor at the Orvis Fly Fishing School. Bob was there to research an article for *Sports Illustrated*.

Bob would take his dogs hunting even as puppies. Jake, then only ten weeks, seems to be wondering why he's been plunked into the middle of the north woods.

From top, clockwise: Bob and Jake on a warm autumn day in the grouse woods; Jake as a pup, trying his best to keep up; Bob and the marvelous Luke.

Top: Bob, Louise and Luke and below, in their Vermont home with Jake controlling the chair, Luke dreaming of the hunt and Spike taking a cautious drink.

Jake and Bob on one of his favorite trout streams. Above: Seated in front, Bob watches Mont Arenal erupt while fishing Lake Arenal in Costa Rica.

III. THE SOUND & THE FURY:

Selected Works by Bob Jones

Rusty & Belle

How a boy growing up in the Milwaukee suburbs in the 1940s became a hunter – and how a pair of footloose Irish setters showed him the way. (It didn't hurt that there were prairie chickens literally across the street.) First published in the anthology *A Breed Apart* (1993), it also appeared in *Dancers in the Sunset Sky* (1997).

In the best of all possible worlds, a boy should start hunting with his father, or perhaps with a kindly uncle. But my dad, though he was a keen angler, didn't care much for the shooting sports, and my only hunting uncle happened to be in jail during my formative years. (That's another story.) So my education as a budding Nimrod took a different course. In fact, like Mowgli in Kipling's *The Jungle Book,* I was taught how to hunt by the wolves.

Well, okay . . . so maybe they weren't wolves, exactly. But a brace of half-wild, hell-for-leather Irish setters is probably the next best thing. How Rusty and Belle sniffed me out as a candidate for on-the-job training, I really don't know. I never even knew who actually owned them.

And yet, during a single glorious, murderous, never-to-be-forgotten autumn just after World War II, I found myself hunting behind them, gradually learning the nuances of the chase, gunning my first gamebirds over them, and developing under their rude tutelage a lifelong love of upland shooting. First times, as they say, are always the best.

Ever since my family had moved, in the fall of 1941, to the far western reaches of Wauwatosa in southern Wisconsin, I'd been mesmerized by gamebirds. Across the road from our newly built home lay a broad belt of virgin tallgrass prairie, stretching nearly a mile down to the Menomonee River. That reach of the Upper Middle West is part of what scientists call the Prairie Peninsula, islands of grassland studded across the great, dark green sea of the northern forests. This configuration provides lots of "edge," and the region was therefore rich in wildlife. Bison had roamed these prairie islands, as far east as Pennsylvania and New York, but the last of Wisconsin's buffalo were killed in 1832. Gamebirds remained abundant, though. Ruffed grouse, sharptails and prairie chickens, woodcock and snipe, clouds of ducks, and later the newly introduced ringneck pheasant – all proliferated on or around these grassy islands. In that time and place, it was almost inevitable that a boy should become an upland hunter.

That first winter in the new house, I began noticing clusters of large, brown, football-shaped birds scuttling around in the field across the road as they fed in the snow on grass seed knocked down by the wind. I was not yet seven years old, but something ignited in my heart. I wanted to hold one in my hands, maybe study its feathers up close, perhaps even pluck them out – though I knew the bird would have to be dead for me to do that. Okay, so I'd kill it first. And then when it was plucked . . .

And then what?

I'd eat it!

Yes, hunting is instinctive with us, despite the arguments of the antis. *I had to have one of those birds.*

"What are they, Dad?" I asked one afternoon as my father and I were shoveling snow in front of the house. He looked across the street. A dozen of the big birds were feeding busily in the field near the road.

"Prairie chickens," he said.

I stared longingly at them, less than a hundred feet away.

"They don't make good pets," he said.

"I don't want one as a pet," I said. "I want to kill one. We could cook it up for supper tonight."

He laughed.

"Don't let your mother hear you say that," he said. My mother was a sentimentalist, weeping quietly whenever a songbird snuffed itself against a storm window, or at the mere thought of a dead raccoon on the road.

One of the birds was feeding toward us, well away from the rest of the flock. "See if you can hit him with a snowball," my dad said.

I packed a good one, small and heavy and tight and round as I could make it. I crossed the road directly toward the bird. Not even looking up, he scurried back to the flock. I kept going. With every step I gained on them, they edged away deeper into the wind-bent grass. I couldn't get within range this way. I sprinted toward them in nightmare slow motion, the metal clasps of my heavy galoshes rattling as I ran. They scuttled a bit faster. Finally, panting, I hurled the snowball. They avoided it with ease and kept on feeding. By the time I'd had enough, I was a quarter of a mile into the prairie, knee-deep in snow, red-faced and slick with sweat, and my arm ached from futile throws at unhittable targets. I plodded back to my father, who was gentleman enough to hide the grin that was threatening to erupt into a boy-shattering guffaw.

"A snowball's no good," I said.

"Guess not."

"Dad, could I have a bow and some arrows?"

"We'll see," he said.

For Christmas that year I received a lemonwood longbow of fifteen pounds' pull. I was a big kid for my age, but the bow was too strong for

70

me at first. I persevered, shooting at snowmen in the backyard during the winter, or hay bales or bushel baskets or (when the grown-ups weren't looking) the occasional pumpkin in the neighborhood's communal Victory Garden across the road the following summer; and by fall I felt I was ready. I wasn't. Oh, sure, I could shoot a Pound Sweet apple out of the neighbor's backyard tree, and once I grazed a fat robin tugging a worm from the earth after a rainstorm, but I couldn't hit a prairie chicken that first autumn to save my wretched soul. I lost arrow after arrow, shooting at birds on the ground, and never nicked a one. They dodged the arrows as readily as they had my first snowball, and the arrows inevitably slithered off beneath the matted grass, rarely to fly again.

I began making my own arrows out of the long pinewood dowels my mom used to support leggy garden plants, fletching them with brightly dyed turkey feathers from a cheap Indian warbonnet that one of my aunts had given me for my eighth birthday. In hopes of saving arrows, I arrived independently at the principle of the flu-flu, in which the fletching is glued around the tail of the shaft in corkscrew fashion to slow down the final flight of the arrow, and learned how to stalk in quite close to the flock before shooting – sometimes as close as thirty feet.

Finally I hit a prairie chicken, a young one, just as the flock was rising in panic from my best stalk ever. I broke her wing, and it took me half an hour of frantic chasing through tangles of the low-lying sawgrass we called "ripgut" before I finally batted her flat with the bow. I fell on her like a fumbled football and wrung her rubbery neck.

I sat there in the prairie, with the bluestem towering over my head, my hands and bare forearms stinging from sweat and innumerable grass cuts, with hard, sharp grass seeds stuck in the blood that seeped from the slashes, holding her at last in my hands. She was hot, dusty smelling, heavy, limp and dead as a doornail. I ruffled the transverse chocolate-and-white bars on her breast again and again, as I later would the short, thick, soft hair of the first girl I ever loved. Never in my life had I been happier than I was at that moment.

But I knew there had to be a better way.

That way was with a dog and a gun.

My grandfather, Frank Jones, had led a peripatetic life as a young man, before the turn of the twentieth century. Born in 1871, he'd run away from home in Chicago at the age of fourteen after smashing a slate over a schoolmaster's head when that man falsely accused him of whispering to a classmate. He'd bummed around the Midwest, working on farms, becoming a dab hand with horse teams. He drifted into the small towns occasionally, working as a shop clerk, a hackney driver, and, once, an

71

assistant to an undertaker, among other odd jobs, but finally fetching up back in Chicago. There he became a foreman on the production line in a packing house. The company he worked for, maybe it was Swift or Armour, I can't remember, had developed a revolutionary new canning process, and a New York packer pirated him away to steal the new technique. He went to New York in 1890 and remained there for nearly ten years. When his boss at the packing plant told him that all employees would be expected to vote for the Republican incumbent, Benjamin Harrison, over Grover Cleveland in the upcoming 1892 presidential election, my grandfather quit his job, though he was still a few months shy of twenty-one and couldn't have voted if he'd wanted to. He was damned if anyone would tell him how to vote.

Out of work, he and an unemployed partner pooled their resources, bought an old breech-loading 12-bore W.W. Greener hammer gun, rented a team and a buckboard, and went across the Hudson River to the Jersey Palisades to hunt for the New York restaurant market. They brought along a stray dog they'd befriended, a lop-eared, curly coated, liver-colored pooch named Fred who may have been an American water spaniel.

"I didn't care what breed he was," my grandfather used to say. "Old Fred was good at his job and that's all I cared about."

"What did you hunt for?" I asked him.

"Mud bats, pa'tridges and prairie hens," he told me. I later deciphered those names to mean woodcock, ruffed grouse, and – of all things – heath hens, the last-named being the eastern equivalent of my beloved greater prairie chicken (*Tympanuchus cupido*). The heath hen died out in the early years of this century, almost simultaneously with the last of the passenger pigeons that once darkened the skies of nineteenth-century America during their spring and fall migrations, both birds the victims of unbridled habitat destruction and wanton American bloodlust.

But while it lasted, the hunting was superb, too easy the way my granddad told it. One of them would drive the wagon through the little pockets of open country back of the Palisades while the other walked ahead, with the dog and the gun, popping whatever got up. "We'd cross the river on a Friday night and come back Monday morning with the spring wagon groaning. We got two bits apiece for the bigger birds and a nickel each for the little fellas."

To me, at the age of ten, it sounded like heaven on earth.

"Do you still have that shotgun?" I asked hopefully.

"No," my granddad said, rolling another cigarette. He was a lean, leathery old man already in his seventies, with hard gray eyes, a thin scar of a mouth, nicotine-stained fingers, and a great, gritty fund of stories. He would live to be eighty-seven and to rise up from his deathbed on the final morning of his life to shave himself with a cutthroat straight razor, having reshingled his roof, unaided, only a few weeks before. "And even if I did still have that old iron," he added, "I'd dassent give it to you. Your ma would never forgive me."

Clearly I would have to seek elsewhere for a shotgun, and when I found it, keep any knowledge of the gun or of my hunting adventures from my tender-hearted, gun-hating mother. The few birds and rabbits I'd killed so far with the bow, I'd cooked and eaten out in the fields where I shot them. My friends and I filched lard, salt and matches from home, a little bit at a time, and kept them hidden in a "fort" we had dug on the prairie. We dug it into a sidehill, roofed it over with scrap lumber we swiped from a nearby building project (already the prairie was being nibbled to death by postwar housing development), and laid thick slabs of bluestem sod over the boards. We salvaged a rusty old frying pan from the town dump, cleaned it up with bootlegged Brillo pads, added an old-fashioned stoneware coffeepot one of the gang found in his attic, hauled water-smoothed rocks up from the river to build a fireplace, and were snug as jolly plainsmen in our splendid hideaway. It had everything a boy could desire – including a huge stack of moldy comic books. Everything but a gun and a couple of bird dogs.

Enter Rusty and Belle.

They came trotting up to the hidden entrance of our fort one hot September Saturday when a couple of us were boiling some crayfish we'd caught in the river. Crayfish were called "crabs" in those parts, and they were a pretty big subspecies, some of them six or eight inches long. We caught them with a hunk of liver tied to a piece of butcher's string and dangled near their holes in the shallows, under the river rocks. You let them glom on, hoisted them gently up near the top of the water, then netted them with your baseball cap. We boiled them up in an old Maxwell House coffee can after letting them soak for about an hour or so in clear, cold water to clean the mud out of their systems. When they were done, they turned red as lobsters. We cracked them open with stones, sprinkled salt on the pieces, and ate them, sometimes with Saltines and peanut butter for dessert.

Snuffle, snuffle, snuffle. We saw two big square, wet noses poking into the doorway. Nostrils big as gun muzzles, flexing open and shut as they sniffed the delicious smells.

"Cripes, it's a couple of dogs."

"I know them," Danny said. "They're Rusty and Belle. I think they're called Irish setters."

My ears perked up. A setter was a hunting dog. I'd never seen the Irish variety, though.

"Hand me my bow and quiver," I said.

"You're not gonna shoot 'em, are you?"

"No, asshole. I'm gonna see if they know how to hunt."

I brought out some crabmeat and a handful of Saltines for the dogs. They accepted the snacks eagerly and looked up for more.

"You've got to earn it," I told them. I strung the bow (I'd graduated to a 35-pound Osage orange longbow by this time), nocked a homemade flu-flu arrow, and headed off at a trot toward where I'd seen a small family of prairie chickens only about an hour before. We were hunting into the wind, so the bird scent would blow back down to the dogs. The only trouble was that they stayed right at my heels. *No good,* I thought. *I want them out in front.* I stopped. Rusty stopped too, and looked up at me. His eyes held the big question.

"Go ahead," I said, gesturing with my free hand. "Hunt 'em up!"

Belle responded first to my command, suddenly lighting out and hunting forward on a zigzag line with her head high, sucking in the hot autumn wind. Rusty took off after her, quartering in counterpoint to her course. Whenever they got more than fifteen yards ahead of me, I whistled them back, then sent them out again. I don't believe they'd ever been trained to this, but they must have had at least a smidgen of hunting instinct left, though I've read since that the breed had gone almost exclusively to bench stock by then. The red gods were certainly feeling benevolent that day, to send me by sheerest chance these eager, alert, glossy-red bird dogs.

Suddenly Belle stopped. Her broad-feathered tail went up. Her head poised flat and rock-steady, almost snakelike, angling slightly downward and ahead of her. By God, she was on point!

Foolishly, I ran in ahead of her in my eagerness, and the whole flock of chickens erupted at once, a great rattling blur of brown and white. I snapped an arrow after them but missed miserably. The birds flew on, fast and low, a few strong wingbeats, then a long gliding pause, then a few more wingbeats, until they were just dots at the far end of the prairie.

I could barely bring myself to look at Belle, who I was sure must be furious at me for blowing the shot. But she wasn't. She looked delighted with herself, smirking and pirouetting like a wanton minx. She and Rusty hunted on. We pushed through the tall, golden grass toward where the birds had pitched in.

About halfway there, Belle pointed again. This time I kept my head, walking in slowly ahead of her with the arrow nocked firmly and the bow held crosswise at waist height. A large, long-tailed bird suddenly scuttled ahead a few steps and took wing. A pheasant! A big slow, green-headed, white-necked, bronze-gleaming cockbird, cackling metallically as he lifted off. I drew, fired, and hit him, and he tumbled end for end into the grass as feathers drifted off downwind. Rusty, who had been to one side, was on him like a flash. I ran up quickly, not knowing if Rusty would run off with the bird to eat it, and while he was still wrestling with it, got it away from him and wrung its neck. I praised both dogs to the skies and they wagged their tails in delight. It was my first ringneck ever, and only a lucky hit at the base of the left wing accounted for our bagging it. On the way back to the fort, Belle jumped a rabbit, which I also managed to kill. A great day! I rewarded my newfound friends with a fair share of the rabbit meat when we fried it up that afternoon in our underground hideaway.

Later that fall, I arranged to buy a beat-up old single-barreled, 28-gauge Savage Model 220 from a kid in my grade at school. The gun was choked improved-cylinder and had a 28-inch barrel. Ron's dad was a wealthy doctor who spoiled his son rotten, and had just bought him a 16-gauge "Eagle Grade" L.C. Smith. I gave Ron eight dollars for the Savage – money I'd been paid by neighbors for mowing lawns and shoveling snow, hard-earned every penny of it. Ron threw in three boxes of low-base 7-1/2s and one of high-brass 6s, along with a can of Hoppe's nitro solvent and a cleaning rod. No contemporary gun deal in the streets of Miami or Harlem ever went down more surreptitiously.

I couldn't bring the gun home for fear my parents would discover it – my mom was an inveterate snoop, always poking around in my room while I was at school to see what I'd been up to. So I wrapped the Savage in oily rags and kept it, during the week, in the fort. That didn't work for long, though. Every minute of every day, I was afraid some tramp would wander up from the Milwaukee Road right-of-way just across the river and find the fort. He'd swipe my gun and hold up a bank, or something. It was driving me nuts. My schoolwork also suffered.

I had a friend named Harry who lived near the grade school, and I prevailed on him to let me hide the shotgun in his garage. There were fields across the road from the school, just like the ones across from my house, and I figured to do some hunting there after school, or on the weekends. Rusty and Belle had taken to following me to school that fall, hanging out in the playground during class hours and playing "keep away" with us during recess or the noon hour. Once they saw, smelled and heard the gun go off, they were even more strongly bonded to me. I've often wondered what their rightful owners thought they were up to during those long, long absences from home.

It took a lot of trial and error – more of the latter than the former – to perfect a decent shooting style with the Savage. But my experience in wingshooting with the bow stood me in good stead. The bow had taught me how to swing with a rising bird, and keep swinging as I released the shot. With the shotgun, I had a tendency to overlead birds – especially rising woodcock, which have a disconcerting habit of pausing at the top of the rise before zigzagging out on the level through the tops of a covert. Pheasants were easy, though – slow, loud, straight-away fliers. Ruffed grouse were harder, startling me to the point of paralysis in the racket they made getting up, then lining out low or with a tree between them and the gun, denying me a shot either way.

I wouldn't shoot at a really low bird for fear of hitting one of the dogs. I also swore off rabbits for the same reason. I could never break Rusty and Belle of tear-assing off after every bunny they jumped, like greyhounds at a dog-track. Once, Belle ran a bunny into a long piece of drainage pipe, wide enough for the rabbit but not for the dog. Rusty figured out instantly what was happening and leaped to the far end of the pipe, just in time to intercept the panicky rabbit when it emerged a moment later, still at full gallop. The gluttonous mutts quickly ripped it apart and ate it. I figured this must have been the way they hunted before they took up with me. Old habits die hard.

No, they weren't perfect gundogs by any means. In addition to eating perhaps one in every five birds I killed, they had a tendency to take off suddenly for parts unknown in the middle of a hunt, sometimes not returning until the next day. Rusty was a car chaser and Belle a cat chaser. They inevitably took on any skunk they happened across, with predictably malodorous results. Fortunately, we lived too far south for porcupines. Once they tackled a big boar raccoon, though, and before they learned their lesson, both of them had deep gashes in their noses, flanks and bellies that put them out of action for the better part of a week.

But now and then they were splendid. I'll never forget a double point that occurred one November afternoon in the fields across the railroad tracks. We'd been puddle-jumping mallards along the river, with only sporadic success, when Belle – who had the better nose – suddenly lit up. I followed her into the wind, away from the river, across the tracks, and into a low, damp swale that gave way to cattails before rising again to a farmer's planting of field corn. At the edge of the swale she froze on point. Rusty pussyfooted up behind her, then looked to his left. Sniffed a couple times. He angled over in that direction about ten yards and locked up.

Could be the same bird, I thought. A runner, moving ahead of Belle's point. But when I went in ahead of Belle, a woodcock got up right under her nose. As I mounted the gun, I heard and then saw from the corner of my eye a big cock pheasant vault skyward from Rusty's point – no doubt flushed by the piping of the woodcock's wingfeathers. It was one of those bright, cold, cobalt blue Wisconsin afternoons – no wind, sunlight gleaming on the dogs' rich mahogany-colored fur, the field corn pale yellow in the background, the cock pheasant resplendent in full flight.

"I'll kill 'em both!" I thought as the flight paths of woodcock and ringneck momentarily crossed. I shot in that instant. Both birds fell.

That's gunning at its best.

Rusty and Belle disappeared from my life that winter with the arrival of the first deep snows, which put an end to the bird shooting. I have no idea what became of them. Maybe their owner moved away. Maybe they died – both of them were reckless enough. Whatever it was, though, I'm sure it had nothing to do with a loss of interest in hunting. I've rarely met a keener pair of gundogs, nonstop indefatigable. I'll always be grateful to them for infecting me with that enthusiasm when it counted most.

My mother never learned of Rusty and Belle – not until I told her about them, years later, toward the end of her life.

"Where did you develop this unhealthy passion for blood sports?" she asked me one afternoon when I was visiting from my home in the East. "You never got it from me or your father."

I told her the story, just about the way I've told it here. Her eyes began to fill with tears.

"If I'd known it meant so much to you, I would have allowed you to hunt," she said. "Better that than keep it *hidden* from me all those years."

Suddenly I was sorry I'd confessed. But then I looked out the front window, across the street. It was wall-to-wall suburbia now, clear down to the river. Not an acre of native prairie left. *Fat chance,* I thought. *Don't feel sorry for her, feel sorry for what's gone. She just doesn't get it. None of them do. They never will.*

The Royal Macbob

There's sport . . . . and then there's *sport*. Jones' high-spirited account of a red-letter day afield (and presumably elsewhere) originally appeared in his long-running column "The Dawn Patrol" in *Shooting Sportsman* magazine, and was later collected in *The Hunter in My Heart* (2002).

Tired of the same old same-old? Here's a thought from our British cousins: Jaded outdoorsmen might consider spicing up their sporting lives by attempting to score a "Great Macnab," i.e., catching a salmon, shooting a stag and bagging a brace of grouse, all in the same day. The truly bored could add a fourth element to the challenge – bedding the cook at the shooting lodge to cap the day's performance. This feat, according to Britain's foremost outdoor magazine, *The Field*, elevates the accomplishment to the status of a "Royal Macnab."

Ungodly sexism aside, I found the notion interesting on two counts. First off, the source of the Great Macnab challenge stems from one of the most delightful sporting yarns I've ever read: John Buchan's 1925 novel *John Macnab*. The Scots-born Buchan (1875-1940), best known today for his thriller *The Thirty-Nine Steps*, which was made into a popular 1935 film by Alfred Hitchcock, was a sportsman, soldier, barrister, member of Parliament, prize-winning author and, later in his eventful life, governor-general of Canada.

The novel is purportedly based on a real-life feat performed in 1897 by a Scottish sport named Captain James Brander Dunbar. Buchan's version, embroidering on the actual event, deals with the merry misadventures of three eminent – and eminently bored – British sporting gentlemen who, in an attempt to shake their ennui, journey to the wilds of Scotland, where they issue written challenges to the lairds of three game-rich but closely patrolled estates. "Sir," reads one such missive, "I have the honour to inform you that I propose to kill a stag" – or a salmon as the case may be – "on your ground [on a specified date]. The animal, of course, remains your property and will be duly delivered to you . . . . In the event of the undersigned failing to achieve his purpose he will pay as a forfeit one hundred pounds to any charity you may appoint. I have the honour to be, your humble servant." All three letters are signed with the nom de chasse "John Macnab."

In other words, "Catch me if you can!"

The ensuing pages are filled with stalking lore and poachers' tricks, hair's-breadth escapes and wonderful descriptions of the bleak, beautiful, heather-clad Scots Highlands in all kinds of weather. In the course of the narrative, one of the adventurers falls in love with the lissome daughter of a victimized laird, which must be what gave the editors of *The Field* the idea for the final fillip of the Royal Macnab.

Though Buchan didn't include grouse in the prey his poacher-heroes sought, *The Field* wisely did. Most Scottish grouse, of course, are shot from butts after having been "driven" by beaters until they take flight well in advance of the line of guns. They come through high and fast, very challenging targets. What the Brits call a "rough shoot" – where the individual gunner and his dog walk up the birds, American-style – is considered déclassé, so perhaps that's why Buchan, who was an avid and accomplished wingshot but a bit of a snob (he later became Baron Tweedsmuir of Elsfield), did not include a grouse challenge. A single furtive gunner couldn't very well hire beaters to drive the birds to him without giving himself away. But *The Field*, by adding a brace of grouse to the challenge, made its version of the Macnab far more difficult an accomplishment, especially in the course of a single day.

I know because I tried it.

Some years ago, shortly after I'd first read Buchan's novel, I found myself in a position to go for what was later to be termed a Macnab. I was still bowhunting at that time – in those years before the woods began to fill up during the early arrows-only deer season with neophytes carrying compound bows and shooting at everything that moved – and one crisp, bright October morning in Vermont I managed to drop a buck within the first hour of hunting. My "stag" was nothing spectacular – a fork-horn that dressed out at 115 pounds – but through arduous preseason scouting I'd anticipated its habitual feeding patterns, got in the right position on opening day, and killed it with a close, clean neck shot. But by the time I'd "gralloched" it, shifted the carcass out of the woods, hung it from the meat pole in the cool, shady barn, skinned it and covered it with cheesecloth to discourage blowflies, I still had the whole day ahead of me. And energy to burn.

On my way out of the woods with the deer I'd crossed Oven Brook, a quick little mountain stream – what the Scots would call a burn – and noticed a decent-sized brook trout holding in a clear, cold, spring-fed pool not far from my back door. The "native" was in full spawning colors, red, black, green and ivory, and looked to go about fourteen inches, which was big for this little rivulet. Okay, so it wasn't a salmon fresh in from the salt, with the sea lice still on it – I'd have to travel to Maine or the Maritimes for one of those – but it was America's best-tasting and most beautiful salmonid, our classic coldwater fish, revered in song and story since colonial times. I decided to emulate John Macnab and have a go for it. And with an ultralight fly rod at that. Orvis had recently developed a short 1-weight rod, which the company was touting for small-stream fishing. I strung mine up and, disdaining waders, proceeded to stalk my prey á la mode de Macnab.

Creeping through the ferns on hands and knees, I approached the shadow-dappled pool. Was the trout still there? The floor of the pool was paved in broken chunks of marble, flaked off the bedrock of Bear Mountain over the 12,000 years since the retreat of the last glacier, and – coupled with the lacy amoeba-shaped whorls of foam that danced on the surface – that made the viewing difficult. A fortuitous caddis hatch was occurring, and when one of them fell on the water, struggling, my trout appeared as if by levitation from the depths to inhale it.

Heart pounding like a schoolboy's, I tied on a Henryville Special and had at him. To stand up would give the game away, so I was forced to cast from a squatting position, and with a very short line at that. But on the third drift of the fly down the pool, the brookie rose and took it.

I'd like to describe for you a monumental battle, line screaming off the reel, the trout taking me deep into the backing, wading upstream after him over spillway after spillway, finally gaining on him, socking the gaff home just as the hook was about to tear free. But the whole fight lasted thirty seconds at best and I certainly didn't need a gaff. Still, it had been a delicate stalk and a difficult presentation, and the fish, once I had him on the bank, was drop-dead gorgeous. He'd taste even better than he looked, poached in white wine and bay leaf, chilled, then served cold over a bed of watercress with a little of my wife's homemade mayonnaise on the side.

I looked at my watch. Not quite 10 a.m. The way to crown these successes, of course, would be with a brace of plump, sidehill ruffed grouse, the royalty of North American upland gamebirds. My black Labrador Luke was an eager accomplice. One of our most productive beats at that time of year lay across the gravel road from my home. There, on the over-grown lower slopes of Shatterack Mountain, an old, abandoned apple orchard trailed steeply uphill through young aspens and collapsing stone walls for half a mile. Grouse congregated there in the fall to feed on windfallen apples, most of them varieties no longer grown commercially. This was a good apple year, tree limbs heavy with red and yellow fruit, and the spring had been kind to grouse broods as well. If we were unlucky with the birds, I could always fill my game pockets with apples, which my wife would convert into the best applesauce I'd ever tasted.

We crossed the road, hiked through the meadow, crossed Oven Brook and a rusty barbed-wire fence that divided my land from that of a friendly neighbor, and suddenly Luke got birdy. His black coat gleamed as the guard hairs came erect. His tail came up. His nostrils opened wide to the scent of game. "Hunt 'em up, boy," I whispered. He broke toward the first big apple tree. Three grouse roared out from under it, using the tree for cover. What with the leaves still clinging green to the branches, I had no shot. Thus it often is in early season. But I got a good line on the birds, and we pounded uphill, hoping for a reflush.

A hundred yards farther on we came into a cluster of aspen whips interspersed with old apples. Again Luke got birdy. This time one of the grouse flew straight through a break in the trees. Big mistake. I dropped the partridge in a halo of feathers – a bird of the year, young and naive. He'd be tender and juicy. *This is too easy,* I thought. *It's not even noon. I'll be home in time for lunch . . .*

Like hell I would. The sidehill ruffs of interior New England are a cagey lot. All the dumb birds were killed out of the gene pool years ago by hungry hardscrabble farmers and market hunters, who thought nothing of shooting them from bare tree limbs, where the birds came to eat apple buds and popple catkins of an evening or early morning. The daily bag limit on Vermont grouse is four, and I'm not at all embarrassed to admit that in twenty years of hard pounding, I've never filled it. I certainly didn't that day.

Luke and I worked Shatterack from bottom to top and then back down again, getting flush after flush with no shot possible. The grouse had an uncanny knack of flying low, to keep a stone wall between them and the muzzle, or exploding behind me, going the other way, or waiting until I was bent over, ducking a tree limb, before launching themselves into blurred invisibility. My game journal shows twenty-two grouse flushes in the course of that hard, hot, leg-deadening six-hour day. I missed four shots along the way. We got up a number of woodcock as well, and I killed a limit of three, but I wanted – needed – that final grouse to complete my "brace."

As so often happens, we got the bird only after I'd pretty much given up and shaped our course homeward. We were pushing heavy cover to the edge of the field when Luke – who was nearly as weary as I was – perked his ears, lifted his tail, and lunged into a tussock of grass concealing a fallen barbed-wire fence. A ruff rattled out into the open field, a clear straightaway shot. I missed with the right barrel, cursed myself and the whole race of *Bonasa umbellus,* hit the back trigger, then exulted as the left barrel knocked the bird tail over tip, to fall with a gratifying thump some forty paces out from the wire.

That final bird revitalized us. When we got back to the house my wife was home from work and already preparing dinner. "I saw the buck in the barn," she said, smiling as she put a casserole in the oven. "Nice work."

"Did you see the trout in the refrigerator?" I showed it to her, then emptied my game pockets. She was duly impressed.

"Looks like you had a great day," she said.

"I know how to make it even better," I said. "Come on up to the bedroom. There's something I want to show you."

She grinned. "I guess I have a few minutes to spare," she said. "Catch me if you can."

It was one of the best days of my sporting life – the day I scored the Royal Macbob.

A Field Dog's Education

From *Upland Passage: A Field Dog's Education* (1992, reprinted in 2004): Based on a *Sports Illustrated* story, *Upland Passage* recounts the passing of the torch from Luke, Jones's veteran Labrador retriever, to Jake, the boisterous, stunningly precocious pup. In this excerpt, Jones traces the Lab's remarkable history, explains why he prefers the breed to all others, and shares his philosophy of training.

Why, you might ask (and many have), would a dedicated upland bird hunter prefer a Lab to the more surefire pointing breeds? Wouldn't a more traditional dog such as an English setter or pointer, a German shorthair or a Brittany spaniel – actually the dog of choice in my part of New England – produce more birds for you? Of course it would, but not the way I like to hunt them. I certainly admire the control and walking-on-eggs caution a good pointing dog exercises in his craft, but I'm not out for a high body count. I much prefer the spontaneity of hunting behind a flushing dog. There's a kind of existential rhythm to pounding along fast behind your dog, seeing him get birdy, tail going like mad, then having him check back to make sure you are ready before he plunges in to flush the bird. It all happens so suddenly. The birds seem to materialize out of nothingness, already moving fast, and are as quickly gone, or dead. You learn to shoot from any position. You may not get as many shots or hit as many birds, but you never lose any wounded ones that might elude a less effective retriever than a Labrador.

And, anyway, I just love Labs. The ones I've known over the years have had a greater sense of fun and retained it longer after puppyhood than any other breed I'm familiar with. I can see many moods in a Labrador's eyes – seriousness, resentment, anticipation, anxiety, sometimes gravity, sometimes even scorn or contempt, but most often love and its jolly twin, playfulness. Am I being anthropomorphic – attributing human emotions to a creature incapable of them? Perhaps, but then, I'm an anthropoid.

I'm not the only Lab fancier to find a nearly human quality in these dogs. In his *Recollections of Labrador Life,* first published in 1861, a traveler named Lambert de Boilieu had this to say of the breed: "The Labrador dog, let me remark, is a bold fellow, and, when well taught, understands, almost as well as any Christian biped, what you say to him."

Where did this paragon of dogdom come from? Zoologists recognize about four hundred breeds of domestic dog (*Canis familiaris*) throughout the world, all of them apparently derived from one of the small, wild subspecies of wolves found in southern Eurasia – perhaps the Indian wolf (*C. lupus pallipes*) or the Chinese wolf (*C.l. chanco*). Fossil finds from places as widely separated as Idaho and Iraq show that the dog was domesticated at least eleven thousand or twelve thousand years ago, while a specimen found more recently in the northern Yukon dates man's best friendship to twenty thousand years' standing. Early humans tamed the dog for many purposes: as a hunting partner, a draft animal, a guardian of camps and later flocks, for war, and even used them as a food source. American Indians ate their dogs during hard times, and dog meat is still a great delicacy in China and other Asian countries. But it's as a hunter that the dog most gladly assists mankind – and in my opinion, none more so than a Lab.

Richard A. Wolters, the foremost American champion of the breed, traces the Lab's origins back to sixteenth-century France, where a breed known as the Saint Hubert's hound was used to track "farre straggled" wounded game – in short, as a retriever. In his 1981 book *The Labrador Retriever: The History . . . The People*, Wolters cites an English text by one George Tuberville published in 1576, *The Booke of Hunting*, and contains a chapter entitled "Of blacke hounds aunciently come from Sainct Huberts abbay in Ardene." A woodcut accompanying the text shows a lop-eared, strong-tailed, wide-eyed, smooth-coated black dog with the distinctive Labrador head and gaze, even down to the questioningly furrowed brow peculiar to the breed today – though no Labs I've ever seen look quite as sheeplike as Tuberville's hound.

Wolters argues from this evidence that the ancestral Labrador retriever was already common to the West Country lowlands of Devonshire, where men subsisted by waterfowl hunting and fishing. Seamen from Devon, he continues, would logically have brought these superb water dogs with them to the New World when they began fishing the Newfoundland banks in the early sixteenth century, if only to aid them in their fishing and in hunting the abundant game they found ashore.

British sea captains and fishermen in the early 1800s saw black dogs of the Lab's general description being used by commercial fishermen on the Avalon Peninsula around St. John's, Newfoundland, and recognized their potential as a sporting breed, mainly for retrieving waterfowl shot over their home marshes. The Avalon fishermen, who knew the breed as the "St. John's dog" or the "Newfoundland water dog," took the dogs with them in their dories when they were working longlines. Fish sometimes came off the barbless hooks of the shorter drop lines attached to the longlines as they were pulled into the boat. The "water dogs" would leap overboard on command to fetch the escaping fish. They would also swim out from a dory to pick up net floats and bring them back for hauling.

Clearly this aptitude for working in frigid, storm-wild waters could be suited to a sport hunter's benefit.

By 1814 the appelation "Labrador" began to be used for this breed – Labrador being a part of the province of Newfoundland, and certainly its wildest, most game-rich region. In his *Instructions to Young Sportsmen*, published in that year, the British hunting authority Colonel Peter Hawker calls the Labrador dog "by far the best for every kind of shooting . . . Their sense of smelling is scarcely to be credited. Their discrimination of scent, in following a wounded pheasant through a whole covert full of game, or a pinioned wild fowl through a furze brake, or warren of rabbits, appears almost impossible . . . For finding wounded game, of every description, there is not his equal in the canine race; and he is a *sine quâ non* in the general pursuit of wildfowl . . .

"I have tried poodles, but always found them inferior in strength, scent and courage. They are also very apt to be seasick."

Richard Wolters, in the course of twenty thousand miles and two years spent researching and writing his history of the Labrador retriever, tracked down and visited what he believes to have been the last two surviving representatives of the original "Newfoundland water dog." Unfortunately both were males, then aged thirteen and fifteen, when he located them in the remote fishing village of Grand Bruit, on Newfoundland's bleak south coast.

"He looked much like a Labrador in every way," Wolters wrote of his first meeting with Lassie, the ironically cross-named thirteen-year-old male. "The white on his chest and feet still comes through in some of our Labs today. He was the missing link. His ears were small just like a Lab I used to have. His head was not square as some of today's show stock but you couldn't miss him for a Lab; as old as he was, he had that brainy look." And despite his age, he remained playful. "Lassie is still very alert," Wolters added, "is an excellent retriever and will come to life just like a puppy when the stick is thrown in the water."

In many respects, the most important quality handed down from the Saint Hubert's hound through the Newfoundland water dog to the Labrador retriever of today is this unquenchable spirit of playfulness. If handled correctly, it can be turned to a dog owner's advantage in training. And dogs must be trained, at least in civil behavior, whether they're to be hunting partners or simply good companions around the house.

Dogs that develop their own games – garbage-can dumping, car chasing, playing a steam shovel in a neighbor's tulip bed or howling all night at the moon – not only can bring bad blood to a neighborhood (even a remote one, like mine) but can themselves end up dead: under the wheels of a car, by poisoning or as the result of a neighbor's carefully administered "lead headache," a bullet through the brain.

But by using a dog's desire to play – truly, its *need* to play – to teach it worthwhile "games" such as sitting on command, walking at heel, and hunting and fetching, the dog's owner will keep his canine companion both happy and out of trouble. All dogs, even a tiny terrier or Pekingese, want to have jobs. Any job will do. Once they're shown what it is, what's expected of them, they will perform that function to the best of their ability, with class and style and an unmistakable pride. Unlike humans, however, they don't expect remuneration – only praise for a job well done, or correction if it isn't.

I don't believe anything more than the human voice is needed in correcting a dog's errors. Labs are particularly sensitive to tones of voice, even looks of approval or disapproval. Keep your eyes on your dog whenever you can, and talk to him as you would a person. None of this baby talk – dogs deserve better than that. Don't be surprised if your dog, as he matures, develops at least a listening vocabulary. Words such as "out" and "walk," "suppertime" and "bedtime" should be quickly understood, along with "no" and "good dog." I once calculated that my yellow Lab Simba had a vocabulary in excess of one hundred words. My wife and I had to resort to Spanish or German when debating if and when we were going to take him for a walk/hike/stroll/jaunt/perambulation/constitutional/promenade/saunter/ ramble/traipse or stretch of the legs. Even at that, it took him only a week to equate *paseo* and *Spaziergang* with all of the above.

"I think I'll remove the *perro amarillo* from the premises for a brief *paseo* before retiring."

Arf, arf, whine, whine – and a whirlwind dash toward the back door.

Luke on the other hand, could read my mind, I swear. I'd be sitting upstairs at the typewriter in my office, with a few hundred words painfully pecked out, when my thoughts would stray to the bird covers: which ones should we hunt today? Better give the ridge a rest – we hit it pretty hard yesterday. Maybe Dorset Mountain? No, it's Saturday – could be flatlanders in there. How about the Woodcock Islands up the road; we haven't been there in a while, and flight birds may have arrived.

Heavy breathing from the foot of the stairs, followed by a tentative moan. Then the slow clump of footsteps up the stairway. Luke's head peeks around the corner of the banister. His eyes lock on mine, then shift to the gun cabinet across from my desk. His eyes hold the question. Mine answer, involuntarily . . . And he's dancing on the carpet, lit up like a hunk of anthracite, his eyes sparking with joy. Drumming up enthusiasm.

I could say "No!" and he'd slink away to mumble and mutter

downstairs, doggy curses at the unfairness of it all, the birds are there, he knows it from the weather, from the cocky tang in the air, the hum of the planets, the stare of the moon last night. How can I deny him? I take down the shotgun and reach for my boots . . .

Luke's job and mine are one: together we kill gamebirds. Nothing else matters: not sex or food or comfort, not sleep or warmth, water or love. We're not merely a "team," man and dog, but a single being with a single-minded mission: to pound the hills forever, through briers and cold and muck and barbed wire, putting birds up in a roar of wings and knocking them down again with a bang and reek of gunpowder, fetching back the warm bird and stuffing it into a cold game pocket stained black with bird blood these many years. Later we eat them. (Yes, I always give Luke a few table scraps, especially when we eat gamebirds.)

At moments like this, Luke is all business, and so am I. We're driven by the same gods or demons: the wolf is revealed in all his cruel glory. Without Luke I'd be a dilettante. With him I'm a hunter. We transcend ourselves – he's more than a dog. I'm more than a man. Hunting alone, I would leave most of these birds unharmed, unseen perhaps, certainly unflighted. Left to his own devices, he would fly them, all right, but they'd never fall. Together we both fly them and fell them, interrupt the arc, break the rainbow, prove the Second Law of Thermodynamics and yet disprove it at the same time.

These birds we kill fly on in my dreams, and in Luke's dreams, too. In sleep, our legs twitch in synchrony, old muscles now, bone-stiff and bone-weary. Blood crusts on his thorn-ripped nose, blood scabs on my thorn-ripped hands.

Yes, I love Labs for their playfulness.

Under the Volcano

Fly-fishing for sailfish and tarpon in Costa Rica – until the earthquake comes and the tsunami hits. An unpublished story from a fishing book Jones was planning at the time of his death.

Whenever I find myself growing grim about the mouth, whenever it's a damp, drizzly mud-season in my soul, I account it high time to get to sea as soon as I can and pull big fish on a fly rod. I mean *really* pull them, putting back and heart into it, the long muscles fully in play, breaking rivers of winter-stale sweat under a tropical sun, legs braced and the rod bent to the max, pumping and reeling until I see color at last – the electric blue of sailfish or marlin, the silver flash of a tarpon – and some psychic color comes flooding back into my life as if in reciprocation.

Melville called this his substitute for pistol and ball.

"If they but knew it," he wrote in the opening paragraph of *Moby Dick*, "almost all men in their degree, some time or other, cherish very nearly the same feeling towards the ocean with me."

The Bat Islands rise sharply from the Pacific about 28 miles northwest of the lodge as the frigate bird flies. They're rough, wet miles in the prevailing seas. Our boat, the *Swordfish*, was not the fastest, most comfortable or spacious sportfishermen ever built – a single-screw, 31-foot deep-vee hull not unlike a miniature Rybovich, powered by a 250-horse Volvo turbine – but she's a legendary Siren at teasing up billfish.

Porpoises crisscrossed our track to the Bats, flirting up alongside to flash their frozen grins, then surging ahead to frolic in our bow waves. From time to time we spotted green turtles, big as manhole covers, bobbling and paddling in the spine-jarring chop. You don't want to hit one at speed. They can shatter a fiberglass hull as effectively as a mortar shell. But Captain Calin, our skipper, had a sharp eye for such hazards. *No problema.*

Surf crashed high on the oddly-canted, mustard-yellow rocks of the islands. Squadrons of *tijeretas* – frigate birds – swung black on their crooked wings against a bright blue sky. Already half a dozen other sportfishing boats were trolling conventional tackle in random patterns off the Bats, chumming up sailfish with dipnets full of live anchovies. But we were fly fishing – no live bait allowed.

The standard deployment of teasers for sailfish on the fly rod is two bonito bellybaits trolled astern, port and starboard about 50 to 75 yards back, and a single daisy-chain of ten hookless, plastic squids trailing in the wake amidships. Most beginners at this game troll too loud. The ideal engine speed for a single-screwed vessel after billfish is about 700 RPM. When marlin or sailfish rise to the teasers, the skipper slows to 500 or less, mainly to reduce the size of the wake and make the fly more visible when it's thrown,

It's the mate's job to spot the sailfish when he first appears, then excite him further by playing a bellybait back to him. He allows him to mouth the hookless bait, get a taste, then artfully plays the delectable morsel into casting range. While the sail's appetite alarm is clanging like a fire bell, its wild eyes big as softballs, the mate "disappears" the bait by whisking it forward and quickly reeling up.

Meanwhile the "on deck" angler takes his position in one corner of the sternsheets and readies his gear.

I was the man on deck.

I was fishing a 9-foot 12-weight Orvis rod, loaded with a shooting head, level line and a few hundred yards of 30-pound backing. The leader tested 16 pounds. At Joe's suggestion I'd stripped about 20 feet of line off the big DXR reel – the amount I'd probably have to cast – and coiled it carefully in a plastic bucket at my side. A couple of inches of water in the bucket would keep the line slick and tangle-free at the moment of truth, and the bucket itself would act as a stripping basket, preventing my nervous feet from tangling in the line-coils as they played out when a fish hooked up – a potentially embarrassing situation, as in "*Man overboard!*"

Eppridge had built the fly, a variant on classic designs originated by Harry Kime and Dr. Webster Robinson, the pioneers of West Coast saltwater fly-rodding for billfish. "I call it the Frank Perdue Special," Epp said. "It's just chicken feathers and Ethafoam, tied on a 6/0 Mustad hook." But Epp had carefully carved and tapered the Ethafoam body, glued eyeballs on it with irises that actually rolled, and then, for ultra-realism, added garish gill slots with a red Magic Marker.

"There he is," Joe said quietly.

Brownish-green and big around as a sawlog, the first sailfish of the day suddenly materialized behind the starboard bellybait. Curpin, our veteran mate, dropped the bait back to him and danced it enticingly, then swept it forward as if in escape. The sail was on it in an instant, slashing at the bait with Erroll Flynn-like cuts of its bill. He lit up as if someone had thrown a switch – bright, electric-blue stripes igniting the ultramarine water. Curpin teased him closer.

Bill and Joe brought in the daisy-chain and the other bait. Curpin glanced at me and grinned, then disappeared the belly bait.

"Now!" Joe said.

I flipped the Perdue Special to the spot where the bait had been. The dark blue dorsal was weaving from side to side in quick, nervous, searching maneuvers. *Where is that damned thing?*

I popped the fly once, twice . . .

He saw it and pounced.

I kept the rod tip pointed at him and when he turned, struck him hard with my line hand – *pow, pow, pow* – pulling directly back on the fly line in short, sharp pops. I could actually feel the hook bite home. Sails almost always jump at the sting of the hook, and with the rod tip low, I'd already bowed to his inevitable jump. What's more, if I'd struck him by raising the rod tip as most anglers instinctively do, I'd have been in a poor position to exert any further leverage on him.

So far so good.

But I reckoned without his catlike speed. He erupted from the water not fifteen feet away, a big strong fish climbing endlessly toward the sky, gillplates rattling, that slim, spiky bill flailing like a sabre, one big black eye locked on mine – water flew everywhere. Awed, I held on to the fly line just a nanosecond too long.

It felt like I'd grabbed a live wire.

Line burns smart.

When I brought him alongside the boat twenty minutes later, after two dozen jumps and a run that peeled nearly 400 yards off the reel, my lower back was aching, my wrists and forearms were stiff, and I'd sweated a gallon. My line-burnt hand still stung. But I never felt happier. Curpin grabbed the bill and worked the Perdue Special free, and we hoisted the 125-pound fish into the sternsheets for the traditional "grin and grab" photos. Back in the water a minute later he was still strong. He plunged away into the depths from which he'd risen.

Over the next few days, we all caught and released plenty of sailfish. Eppridge boated a 110-pounder in just nine minutes flat on his 13-foot Sage rod and a Billy Pate marlin reel that spools 600 yards of backing. Each dawn we'd be awakened by the hooting of howler monkeys in the flowering trees around the lodge. Breakfast was hearty: eggs, bacon, crisp homebaked hard-rolls, rich Costa Rican coffee. Then we'd pound out to the Bats and play with sails till the sun swung low. Home again, after a cool shower and couple of *piña coladas*, we dined on local fish, rock lobster or barbequed pork, then swapped fishing yarns till bedtime. I can think of no finer way to drive off the spleen and regulate the circulation. But there was more to come . . .

At 9 a.m. on July 28, 1968, Crater A of the five-cratered Volcán Arenál blew its top, killing the whole town of Pueblo Nuevo and all of its 600 inhabitants. The gases it expelled reached 2,000 degrees

Centigrade. Cows in the vicinity were cooked on one side, but remained alive on the other (temporarily at least). Early in the 1970s another crater popped a "bolus," a kind of volcanic mortar round of superheated lava. A Land Rover carrying four vulcanologists happened to be motoring along the unpaved road toward the town of La Fortuna. The bolus landed squarely on top of it, oxidizing the Rover and its passengers in an instant. *Phhht!* Like that. When Peter Gorinsky, our fishing guide at Arenál, told us these stories, I began to wonder if volcanoes weren't sentient as well as destructive. If so, the Roman god Vulcan is a hell of a shot with a mortar.

We fished Lake Arenál for an afternoon, evening and the following morning, under placid blue skies in refreshingly cool mountain air, catching gaudy, strong, slab-sided *guapote*, a.k.a. "rainbow bass" – close relatives of South America's peacock bass – on small, bright poppers and light fly rods, cruising the lake and watching for rises, plugging the weedy shortline with gratifying results. But every twenty minutes or so, Vulcan spoke. His voice was as loud as a sixteen-inch naval broadside. It raised the pucker factor a tad. Just when we'd forgotten him, concentrating on dropping the tiny poppers in the path of feeding fish, *Ka-boom!* There he was again, nudging our shoulders. But it kept us alert, on our toes, and if at night we dreamed of sudden scalding death, I'm sure it made better persons of us in the long run.

We were in for more of the Pacific Rim's rock-and-roll action at Casa Mar, though we didn't know it when we arrived. Casa Mar is one of the world's finest snook and tarpon camps. Located just south of the Nicaraguan border, it was then owned and operated by Bill Barnes, a short, bandy-legged fellow from Maryland who has followed the angling action wherever it's hottest in the Western Hemisphere. Billy runs the place like he would his own home: tiny, tidy, thatch-roofed cabins with overhead fans. A sprawling, fragrantly scented dining room. A well-stocked tackle shop. An open bar where the rum flows freely as the fish tales, and nobody frowns when you pour another or light up a smoke. Billy's gundogs – German shorthairs and English pointers – lope the grounds and poke their meaty noses up from beneath the tablecloths at dinner. When the fish are in, it couldn't be better.

The *terremoto* hit about 4 pm. It registered 7.4 on the Richter Scale. I'd been fishing outside the *barra* since lunchtime on that Monday, hooking and jumping and sometimes boating tarpon of 60 to 125 pounds. Pods of them came rolling through like silvery freight cars. All you had to do was cast the 12-weight line out there with a big, bushy orange-and-black Harry Kime streamer attached, strip it in a few times, and *wham* – they were skyborne. All afternoon we'd been following the clouds of birds – *tijeretas*, tropic birds, ospreys – and catching, then releasing, the tarpon beneath them. I stopped for a minute to replace a frayed tippet, and when I looked up the birds were gone.

"Que pasa?" I asked Tony, my boatman.

He shrugged. "Beats me."

The Caribbean sloshed dark and glutinous around us. Not a tarpon rolled as far as we could see. I threw and stripped for another twenty minutes, but not even a jack crevalle hit. The tarpon guides curse jack crevalle and they are indeed the plague of these waters, strong, tenacious fish that grab your fly with the ferocity of tarpon but never jump, and take nearly as long to subdue. A Casa Mar boat came squirting towards us. It was Eppridge and his guide, Ginder.

"There was an earthquake on shore," Bill said. "A bad one, according to the radio. Ginder thinks we'd better get in before the tsunami hits."

At first I thought he was kidding – Eppridge is a notorious jokester – but I saw he was dead serious. We raced the tsunami ashore at full throttle over the treacherous *barra*, where a boat had broached the previous year and a couple of fishermen were scoffed by the ubiquitous bull sharks that prowl these waters, and beat it narrowly – a five-foot comber that smashed docks at the Rio Colorado Lodge and totally rearranged the sandbars that guard the river entrance. When we wheeled into the docks at Casa Mar, all hands breathed a sigh of relief. In the dining room, shattered plates littered the floor and the fishmounts on the wall hung cockeyed. A waitress sat weeping quietly in one corner of the kitchen. Billy Barnes strutted in.

"The goddam thing threw me out of bed," he said, grinning. "I was taking a nap, and when I looked out the window the trees were swaying. All the dogs were howling like mad and the monkeys were screaming. I thought the lodge was going to fall down." He laughed uproariously. "How do you like that? Always something new in Costa Rica."

We went down to the rivermouth next morning to survey the damage. It was hot, airless, with great greasy swells crosshatching the boca. A big hunk of wharf from upriver was adrift, blocking the passage to sea. "I saw it come ashore about six o'clock last night," my guide Tony said. "Damn glad we got in ahead of it. It's the first time I ever saw a wave cause a *corriente* – a current – in the rivermouth."

At the seaport of Limón well south of us, and only about 25 miles from the quake's epicenter, the tsunami had sucked all the water out of the harbor, leaving the fishing fleet high and dry, then came crashing back in to smash docks, swamp boats, disrupt public services like water and power. The quake itself had destroyed bridges on the only highway to Limón from San José. In Limón alone, the death toll was placed at 23. Electricity was out throughout the country. Some *terremoto*.

When I got home to Vermont a few days later there was a foot of fresh snow on the ground. Down at the general store I bumped into a local meat fisherman.

"Where'd you get that tan?" he asked suspiciously.

"Down in the tropics," I said. "Fly fishing."

"You mean like you fish for them tiny brook trout around here?"

"Yep."

"Catch anything?"

"A few."

"Do them tropical fish eat any good?"

"Don't know," I said. "I threw them all back."

He smirked. Damnfool flatlander.

"Say, Bob," he asked slyly. "How deep did you have to wade to catch them tropical fish?"

"Deep enough," I told him.

In the Drowned Lands

Haunting short fiction about a man who, long removed from the world of gamebirds and gundogs, inherits a small shooting lodge and all its equipage – including a brace of Clumber spaniels – from an uncle who kept one foot in the 19th century. A multi-faceted gem from *Dancers in the Sunset Sky* (1997).

This is it?" Cargill asked. He hefted the antique firearm in his soft city hands and looked incredulously at the lawyer. "You hauled me all the way up here to the sticks – a whole day away from New York – just to tell me that I've inherited a . . . *a fowling-piece!*"

"You are his only heir," the attorney said patiently for the tenth or twelfth time. "Your uncle was an eccentric man, set in his ways. As I explained in my letter, his will required your presence, in person, at the reading if you were to inherit. Otherwise his estate would go to various charities. Besides, it's not just the shotgun, Mr. Cargill. There's also the land, the house and all of its contents."

"Yeah, right," Cargill said. "For what it's worth. Tell me, Counsellor, what is it worth?"

"Well," the lawyer said, clearing his throat, "to tell you the truth, Mr. Cargill, not a whole lot at present. We're too far from the interstate and the mountains for this property to interest any big-time developers. Mingo Mills, the nearest town of any size, is losing population. So's the whole region, as you must have noticed during our drive up here. There's no industry to speak of and even the farms are failing. I doubt you could find a ready buyer for the place in this current economy in less than a year's time, but if you were to hold onto the place for a while, who knows. At least the taxes aren't ruinous."

Cargill looked down at the shotgun. A bespoke pre-Civil War caplock, the lawyer had said, 14 gauge, made by W.W. Greener of London. *Actually it was rather a handsome piece,* Cargill thought. Long, slim barrels the glossy black of rich coffee, sinuous gooseneck hammers of case-hardened iron as bright as buffed nickel, the rose-and-scroll engraving on the sideplates elegant and finely cut, a diamond of ancient ivory embedded at the tip of its rosewood forearm, and two others of somewhat larger size on either side of the oil-finished, tiger maple stock. It had been years – decades – since he'd last held a shotgun, much less fired one. On a sudden whim he threw the gun to his shoulder. It came up light and smoothly balanced, a perfect fit, the ivory bead at the end of the tapering 30-inch barrels locked firmly on the amber eye of a woodcock mounted in frozen flight at one dim corner of the study . . .

Francis Edmond Cargill, an accountant, lived and worked in Manhattan. A widower now for some twenty years, ailing, dead at heart and childless to boot, he had little left to him but his profession, and that was dwindling away year by year as his clients passed on. Soon he would join them, of that he was sure. *Ho hum.* One day recently he'd received a letter from an upstate attorney advising him that he'd been named sole beneficiary in the will of a bachelor uncle whom he hadn't seen or talked to in nearly half a century. Indeed, he'd supposed that Colonel Elijah Cargill was long since dead, if he'd thought of him at all. The lawyer, whose name was J.G. Braithwaite, asked Francis Cargill to come upstate for the reading of the will. "The inheritance is substantial," he'd written. "I'm afraid I can't tell you just now what the legacy comprises. I suppose your uncle wished it to be a surprise. A codicil to his will, written shortly before his death, specifies that you must be present in the old man's house when it's read."

It was early autumn but still hot and humid in midtown, and Cargill was only too grateful for a chance to get out of the city for a day or two. That Friday morning he packed an overnight bag and caught the 10:15 train from Grand Central to Beacon where Braithwaite, a dry, soft-spoken, rather elderly fellow, picked him up in an equally ancient Plymouth station wagon. They'd crossed the Hudson River, then headed southwest on country roads into the foothills of the Catskill range.

It was a pretty drive through rolling, sparsely settled farm country with only a few small villages marking the way. They drove past marshes, alder brakes, abandoned barns and farmhouses, old orchards, stands of aspen and pine and mixed hardwoods, then drove a lonely two-lane blacktop road that eventually petered out into gravel.

"We're on the edge of what used to be called the Drowned Lands," Braithwaite said. "It was a huge, level tract of wild country, kind of a floodplain of the Walkill River – all brakes and thickets interspersed with bog meadow and grassland, with here and there a stand of open timber. Most of it's drained and cut over now, but your uncle kept his piece pretty much as it was in the old days. Are you a bird hunter, Mr. Cargill?"

"Used to be," Cargill said. "When I was a boy I sometimes shot with my uncle. But I drifted away from it when he moved up here and, later, I went to work in the city. Can't say that I miss it, though."

"Back in the nineteenth century this was splendid woodcock country," Braithwaite continued. "In 1839 an Englishman named Henry William Herbert used to shoot here with a friend of his from the town of Warwick – a huge fellow named Mr. Ward, who weighed three hundred pounds and shot a single-barreled Westley Richards. Even with those handicaps they often killed close to a hundred woodcock a day between them. A year or so later Herbert and another friend, probably shooting a double gun, bagged a hundred and twenty-five on one day and another seventy the following morning, not including forty or fifty birds their retrievers couldn't find."

"Game hogs," Cargill said. He winced and stretched his legs. Arthritis takes it toll. "Sheer waste. What could they do with that many birds?"

"Sold them on the New York market, no doubt. It was legal back then."

"More's the pity," Cargill said. "No wonder there's nothing left."

Braithwaite merely grunted.

It was late afternoon when they turned off the main road onto a rutted driveway winding through deep woods. A startled deer leaped ahead of them down the track, then broke into the forest, its white tail flagging. Farther on they flushed a small covey of ruffed grouse that had been dusting at the side of the road. They passed ponds etched with the rings of rising fish, on one of which Francis thought he saw a family of wood ducks, before coming to a stop before a small, slate-roofed field-stone cottage.

"Your uncle always referred to the house as his 'shooting box,' " the lawyer said. "An English country gentleman's term, I guess." Two great, feathery white pines, their upper branches sighing in a cooling breeze, flanked the north side at either end. "Grandmother and Grandfather trees, your uncle called them," Braithwaite explained, "planted ages ago to break the wind from the storms that sweep down now and again from the Catskills."

From somewhere behind the house came the anxious barking of dogs. "The kennel's back there," Braithwaite said. "I've been feeding and watering the dogs every day since your uncle's death." He cleared his throat. "Only two of them," he added quickly. "I hadn't really the heart to put them down."

The lawyer unlocked the door and ushered Cargill inside. "The Colonel didn't hold much with electricity," Braithwaite apologized, lighting a coach lamp mounted in a pewter sconce on one wall of the entry hall. "I misdoubt there's three lightbulbs in the whole place." English sporting prints lined the hallway, along with the large, spread fans of numerous ruffed grouse. "Your uncle was certainly a keen wingshot," Braithwaite said. "Even at the end, well into his nineties, the folks hereabouts would see him afield in all kinds of weather with his dogs and his gun."

Braithwaite led the way over lustrous, random-width pine floorboards through a cavernous living room sparsely scattered with throw rugs and a few pieces of overstuffed furniture upholstered in dark, well-oiled leather. The mounted heads of two big-antlered deer and a single black bear gazed solemnly down from the walls, their glass eyes glinting in the dusky green light from a leaded window. Again Braithwaite stopped, this time to light a pair of ornate kerosene lamps that stood on curly maple end tables beside an easy chair. A huge fieldstone fireplace dominated one end of the room. From it blew a whiff of cold ashes.

"In here, please," Braithwaite said, ushering Cargill into a book-lined study. "Your uncle called this his Game Room. If you could wait here a moment, I have to call my office." Cargill studied the bookshelves. Mostly sporting volumes from the nineteenth century by authors he'd never heard of. *British Rural Sports* by someone who called himself "Stonehenge," *Dinks on the Dog*, Maupassant's *Contes de la bécasse*, Frank Forester's *The Field Sports of America* in two volumes, and another by the same author entitled *The Warwick Woodlands*. *Ho hum*, he thought. The rear window of the Game Room looked westward into the backyard – to a handsome fieldstone barn with a cupola; a long, wire-enclosed shed, which he took to be the kennel; some other smaller outbuildings; and behind them, visible through the beginnings of the woods, what appeared to be a large pond or lake. Beyond it, nothing but flat, endless woodland broken here and there by expanses of bog meadow and dense stands of alder. Not a house nor another barn could he see, clear to the horizon. He turned back as Braithwaite entered the room.

"Let's get on with it," the lawyer said, suddenly all business. "The reading of the will." He pulled a sheet of foolscap from his briefcase and began: "I, Elijah Worthington Cargill, late Colonel, U.S. Army, being of sound mind . . ." It was as Braithwaite had suggested earlier – the land, the house and all the possessions within it, et cetera. Including the dogs and the Greener . . .

After Braithwaite left, promising to return on Monday morning to drive Cargill back to the station at Beacon, Francis poured himself a glass of sherry from a decanter he found in the Game Room and began to scout his new *pied-á-terre*. His stiff legs needed stretching. The house certainly appeared to be in sound shape – no leaks, no water stains on the beamed ceilings, no sagging floorboards or crumbling walls – though with nothing by the way of modern conveniences. The kitchen was dominated by a huge, old fashioned icebox – cooled literally by ice, great sawdust-flecked, opaque blocks of it, installed beneath the shelves, but it was well stocked, no doubt by Braithwaite, with fresh eggs, butter, milk, a pound of coffee, assorted vegetables and fruit, as well as some steaks and chops for Cargill's weekend meals. The sink faucet had to be charged by a hand pump, but the water was cold and sweet. The cupboards contained some fine blue-and-white china and a pebbled stoneware coffeepot. The stove, Cargill saw, was wood-fired, but there were plenty of kindling and split-hardwood chunks in a bin that stood beside it. He figured he could manage.

A kitchen table of solid oak stood on curved, hard-carved legs beside the west-facing window. On it stood another of the seemingly ubiquitous kerosene lamps. Was there no electric light in this house? Cargill circulated through the rooms, pausing to contemplate the bedroom with its brass four-poster and a tall armoire still filled with his uncle's clothing. Nowhere could he find a light switch, nowhere a single bulb. Nor a telephone. How could Braithwaite have called his office? Perhaps he'd had a cellular phone in his briefcase. Cargill went back out to the front door and peered down the driveway. He could swear he'd seen utility poles and power lines on the drive in. He must have imagined them. There were none, no power at all coming into the house from any direction. Well, it was a long way from the highway; no doubt the Colonel, a great believer in personal economies, had chosen not to foot the bill for installing poles and cables. *He was a parsimonious old coot*, Cargill recalled.

His sherry glass was empty and he went back to the Game Room to replenish it. Beside the decanter stood a humidor he hadn't noticed before. From it he took a long, thick, green cigar, not at all dry when he lit it, and as fragrant as any Havana he'd smoked when his wife would still allow him that pleasure. Puffing away grandly, he swung through the kitchen, found an icepick – God, it had been a long time since he'd used one – and chipped off a few shards of ice to add to his drink. He sat at the kitchen table and thought back on what he could remember of his uncle.

Cargill had found him to be a mysterious and romantic figure the few times he'd met the man during his boyhood. Uncle Eli – tall, slim, with dark, flashing eyes and a ready if somewhat cynical laugh – was his father's younger brother, the black sheep of the sober, God-fearing and industrious Cargill family. As a boy he'd run off to find his fortune in Mexico but had ended up in the Mexican cavalry instead, fighting Pancho Villa. When America entered the Great War, he'd enlisted as a common soldier; by Armistice Day he'd risen to the rank of captain. Between the wars he'd served in some hush-hush capacity as a military intelligence officer, traveling frequently to Africa, the Middle East, the South Seas, Asia and Latin America. On his rare visits to the family home in Oyster Bay, he told fascinating tales of Chinese bandits and big-game hunts in the Sudan, of diving for pearl shell in the far Paumotus or crossing the Empty Quarter of Arabia on camelback, of frozen toes in the heights of the sunny Andes and (sotto voce, over cigars and brandy after the ladies had left the room) of the smooth-bellied charms of those legendary Moroccan "dancing girls" called *ouled naïls*.

During World War II he'd returned to the infantry, commanding first a battalion, then a regiment, in North Africa, Italy and finally France. He'd been badly wounded in the Hürtgen Forest but never spoke of it. After the war, Cargill had seen him only once. He was a changed man. They'd shared a duck blind one sleet-slashed morning on Long Island Sound. A bleak, bang-up day, the sky close, cold and writhing as low as a snake's belly, ducks everywhere – *bluebills they were*, Cargill remembered, greater scaup, ripping suddenly out of the murk to cup unheeding into the decoy spread. From all around them came the banging of other guns, unseen in the fog. Cargill had shot well, with the hot blood of youth, the big Browning's jolt lighting a fire in his heart, dropping doubles on nearly every toll, once a triple, the ducks splashing dead, loose-feathered, wings all asprawl in the black racing chop, one, two, three and his uncle's fierce Chessie – yes, Rommel was his name – launching like a torpedo from the blind to fetch them back. But the Colonel had shot only once, killing a high single that was barely visible through the cloud scud; the bird tumbled end for end, like the footage Cargill had seen of flak-torn kamikazes over Okinawa, and splashed down close to the blind. It lay on its back, its broad black feet flailing weakly at the sky. "He's waving good-bye to life," the Colonel said. Cargill had looked over at him, amazed at this sign of sentiment in the heretofore laughing warrior.

"Too much death, too many people," Uncle Eli continued. There were tears in his eyes. "I'm leaving the army, Frankie. Leaving the whole damned twentieth century. It's time to call retreat." Rommel had lain his huge head on the Colonel's leg and groaned in sympathy.

As if reading Cargill's memories, the dogs in the kennel renewed their own whining. He walked out behind the house. There were two of them, as the lawyer had said, bitch and dog, but of a breed that Cargill had never seen before. They looked like outsized springer spaniels, but solid white in color, heavier boned and bodied, shorter in the legs, with longer ears, rougher coats and broader noses than any spaniel of Cargill's acquaintance. Their heads were huge, almost primitive looking, though their big, dark eyes were friendly, pleading for his company. He noticed that their water dishes were empty and, without thinking, unlatched the kennel door to refill them.

Immediately the spaniels bulled it open and lumbered off in the direction of the pond. Cargill hurried after them. But instead of drinking, the dogs aimed their big-bore muzzles earthward and began snuffling through the alder brakes that surrounded the water. Suddenly the bitch let loose a deep, plangent note. She froze in her tracks, looking back anxiously over her shoulder as Cargill rushed up. When he was twenty feet away, she pounced – and a woodcock whistled skyward in wild corkscrewing flight, followed an instant later by a second bird. Simultaneously the male spaniel made game, sounding off musically as his short tail buzzed with excitement, and as Cargill turned toward him, the big dog flushed yet another brace, no, a trio of woodcock. When no shots followed the flushes, both dogs gazed at him sadly, almost reproachfully, he thought. But they came in readily when he called them to heel. They both wore broad leather collars, on which Cargill noticed brass tags with the dogs' names elegantly engraved. The dog was called Sancho, the bitch Pansy.

"Good dogs," Cargill told them. "Tomorrow I promise I'll bring the gun." They grinned up at him, whining and nodding their heavy heads in eager approval. They knew the word "gun" sure enough.

Living in the city, Cargill had denied himself the pleasures of dog ownership for far too long, he realized. His wife, a fastidious if not indeed a fanatical housekeeper, had claimed to be allergic to them, and he'd never pressed the issue. Now he realized what he'd been missing. Rather than locking the spaniels back into their kennel, he brought them into the house, where over the next hour they proved themselves thoroughly housebroken. In the living room Pansy curled herself up on a throw rug at the foot of the easy chair while Sancho sprawled with a contented groan on the cool slates in front of the fireplace.

Cargill poured himself another drink and pulled *Dinks on the Dog* from the library shelf. Seating himself comfortably in the leather chair, he flipped pages until he found what he sought. Pansy and Sancho were Clumber spaniels, no doubt about it, the largest representatives of their sporting family, and also the slowest. Often called "the retired gentleman's shooting dog," the Clumber was of French origin, having come to England in the mid-eighteenth century as a gift from the Duq de Noailles to the Duke of Newcastle, whose manorial estate in Nottinghamshire was called Clumber House. The breed's period of greatest popularity in Britain was between about 1850 and the beginning of World War I. The Victorian Golden Age. The Clumber was the perfect dog for a retired military officer or civil servant on pension, well behaved in the house yet keen afield. A Clumber could be taken to the small coverts and truck-garden plots on the outskirts of London. While the elderly retiree sat dreaming of past glories on his shooting stick, his dog would nose about slowly among the bracken and turnip tops, seeking foot scent and throwing tongue whenever it made game, then retrieving whatever its master managed to shoot. *Sounds like the dog for me*, Cargill thought, flexing his stiff knees. *We'll see tomorrow.*

"Hey, guys," he called to the dozing Clumbers, "what say let's grill us a steak or two for supper?" He realized that he was slightly buzzed. Well, country air, unaccustomed cigar smoke, a few glasses of vino . . .

It rained that night, a steady, gentle susurration that stirred him from the murk of sleep into the cool dark blue of its shadows. But when he awoke refreshed the following morning, Cargill couldn't find his clothes. He'd folded them neatly on the chair beside the armoire before retiring. Perhaps the dogs had dragged them away during the night. Soft-heartedly, perhaps foolishly, he'd allowed the Clumbers to sleep on the floor at the foot of his bed. Well, he'd no doubt find the clothing somewhere around the house. In any case he'd brought no leisurewear with him in his small bag. He opened the armoire to see what his uncle might provide in the way of a shooting kit. In a few minutes he was clad in a fine, long-collared chambray shirt, fustian knee breeks, leather leggings, rough cowhide ankle boots, a long paisley-patterned waistcoat and a russet-hued shooting jacket of stout corduroy. On his head he clapped a low-crowned felt hat and studied himself in the full-length mirror mounted inside the armoire's door. Quite elegant, he decided. The perfect picture of a Victorian country gentleman about to embark on a day afield. The dogs agreed, yipping their approval as they danced clumsily at his feet. Oddly enough his own legs felt just fine today, no aches, no stiffness. Usually it took him half-an-hour to work out the kinks on arising. Now, still standing before the mirror, he executed a quick buck-and-wing in the mode of Fred Astaire, doffing his hat at the conclusion and bowing sardonically to his dim, rust-colored image.

After breaking his fast with a slab of crusty country bread accompanied by a thick slice of sharp, crumbly cheese – to hell with cholesterol nightmares – Cargill took his coffee to the Game Room where he examined the Greener more closely. On the desk he found a full powder flask and a shot pouch, both mounted with cut-off spouts that measured the appropriate charges for loading the gun. Strange he hadn't noticed them yesterday. But then again everything had been so new, in its old-fashioned way. In the roomy pockets of his jacket he found a nipple wrench, a box of shot wads and an oval capping device with a spring-loaded gate. He charged the Greener, tamping down three drams of fine-grained black powder with the brass-capped ramrod, then inserting a wad, a one-ounce charge of small birdshot, and another wad to hold it all in place, feeling somehow that he had done this before, though he couldn't recall ever having fired a muzzle-loader at any time in his misspent youth. He did not cap the platinum-lined vents that angled down into the barrels, however. He would wait for that until he was outside. At sight of the gun, and especially when Cargill began charging it, the spaniels had flopped down on the floor of the Game Room, whining in barely suppressed excitement.

"All right, my friends, let's get going," Cargill said. He slung the empty gamebag over his shoulder without thinking where it came from. The dogs lurched to their feet and led the way out of the house. A crisp morning, heavy frost on the green grass that still lay in shadow, a crust of ice on the black mire beside the pond. The swamp maples blazed crimson, the aspens gold, all muted by the purple of the alders. Mist rose from the pond and from the springs that laced the woodland. Music chimed somewhere, and he noticed that the small pewter bells on the collars of the dogs tinkled a marching rhythm.

Odd indeed, Cargill suddenly realized. He could swear those bells hadn't been there the day before. Nor during the night. He'd certainly have heard them when the dogs rolled over in their sleep . . .

But he had no time to ponder the problem. They were making game, down in the alders again. Ticking the hammers to half-cock, Cargill snapped a pair of copper priming caps over the Greener's vents and, with the gun at a high port arms, hurried after the dogs. At his approach Sancho flushed a brace of woodcock. Cargill found the Greener floating to his shoulder, his thumb drew the hammers to full cock, the heavy barrels swung up through the rise, then the touch of the slender, taut triggers – through billows of white smoke he saw the birds fall. Instantly his hands found flask and pouch, as if of their own volition, the ramrod was out, and as the dogs lay flat on their bellies, he began reloading. Then three more woodcock, startled by the shots, flip-flapped belatedly up out of the alders and flashed away, deeper into the covert.

"Good Sancho," he heard himself saying. Then, with a casting motion of his free hand, "Fetch dead, boy!"

And the dog hied into the brake, returning quickly with two 'cock, one after the other – warm, soft and russet-feathered, their long bills lolling, a bead of blood bright at the tip of one of them, their huge, dark eyes still wet and almost luminous. As he brought them in, two more woodcock flushed. Then another. Cargill laughed and watched them go. He raised the dead birds to his face, inhaling their hot, musky essence. The dogs gazed up at him in approval.

"Hunt on, my worthies," he said, and he was laughing as he hadn't in fifty years. "Hunt 'em up! Hunt 'em *all* up!"

Ahead of them lay the unspoiled mornings, crisp and cool and bright with the fire and steel of eternal autumn, punctuated only by brief white clouds of burnt powder, the slow cough of his smooth, steady barrels. Francis Cargill knew now that he would hunt all day, forever. The powder flask would never need refilling, the shot pouch would never go slack, nor would the birds ever cease to fly. It would rain only at night, of course. In his mind, as the mists blew clear, he could see the endless covert opening before him – the tight-laced woodcock brakes, the spongy snipe bogs, the sharp-thorned partridge lies, the grass-topped hills where he and his steadfast companions would pause to drink the cool breeze. Somewhere along the way, he was certain now, they would meet the Colonel. Together, dogs and men, they would push on into a world of blurred wings and broken rainbows.

Forever and ever, amen.

The Dead Man on Wendigo Brook

What trout fisherman, plunged into despair by hyper-selective fish that refuse all his imitations, hasn't wished for a "magic" fly? In this cautionary tale from the anthology *Seasons of the Angler* (1988), Jones reminds us to be careful what we wish for . . .

Perhaps it was only a trick of the water, a *trompe l'oeil* of the late summer light, or maybe just one of those hallucinatory visions provoked by hours on end of upstream nymphing. You know the feeling: cast, lift, reach, lift, cast again – over and over, always staring, until the world fades away, sun and bird song and roar of water, until all that's left is the endless downstream dance of the strike indicator. But in that moment, I saw the dead angler clear, down there in the depths beneath the floating red leaves.

I mean crystal clear, in detail. His waxen face with the hair floating vaguely in the current, pale eyes fixed upward on mine, the grizzled mustache trailing like eelgrass over a rueful smile, the blue collar points waving limply above the fishing vest. I could see it all in that mirror-light of underwater. A shattered black rod gripped in the stiff hand, forceps twisting silver from a retractor pin, the bulge of fly boxes in the buttoned pockets. A black-finished leader snips dangling from a D ring. Even the flies hooked into a fleece drying patch – dry flies – a Ginger Quill, an Adams, a Blue Dun and a fourth I didn't recognize, the brightest of the lot. All clear, all seen clearly in an instant.

As I looked, horrified, he rose a bit from the bottom – lifted, it seemed, by the hackles of those flies on his chest, by some heavenly Mucilin or mystical Gink that urged him free of the rolling current's downward grip. I grabbed for him, got hold of the slippery vest, arm-wrestled the current for a moment, felt the fabric slipping from my fingers, then a sharp stab of pain in my palm. I clenched. He broke away and down again. One hand rose, limply, as if in farewell, and he rolled back into the depths.

I staggered off into the shallows, stunned and disbelieving. Odd things happen to the mind on trout streams. Illusions and delusions are the bedrock of our sport. Maybe I'd imagined the whole thing. Maybe it wasn't a man but merely a waterlogged tree stump, or the carcass of a drowned deer. But I'd seen it so clearly. Then I remember the pain in my hand as I grappled with the body. Sure enough, there was a fly stuck in my palm, dead center. It was the fourth of the flies I'd seen on his vest, the odd one. Buried to the shank, I pulled at it tentatively, and it came right out – barbless, thank God. Absently, I stuck it in my own drying patch, then sat back on the bank, in the sun, to watch the pool for the body's reemergence, but mainly to think.

What I decided, when the body failed to show again, may seem heartless and inhuman, but remember that I am a fly fisherman and the season was winding down. I decided to fish on. What else could I do? The truck was a good five miles downstream, and it was another ten from there by jeep trail to the nearest highway. By the time I got out, it would be midnight – no time to organize a search party with grappling hooks for a man already dead and beyond help. I was fishing my way up Wendigo Brook, a little-known feeder of the Nulhegan River in the so-called Northeast Kingdom of Vermont. The region itself received little pressure from anglers – the locals are mainly "wormflangers" who fish near the bridges, and then only when the rivers are discolored from heavy rain – and this section was virtually trackless except for logging roads used seasonally and sporadically by the paper company that owns most of the land. I was packing in, light, with only a tarp for cover, and figured to be on the water for at least three days. There was a highway to the north where I could hitch a ride back to the trail, where my truck was parked. So far, the weather had been splendid – high, crisp, sunny September days; frosty nights full of owl hoot and coyote song and, toward midnight, a dazzling display of the aurora. The trout were fat brookies and cagey browns, bright and savage in their spawning colors. Why give that up for a dead man?

A fellow I know told me how he'd been fishing for spring steelhead up in British Columbia once when he came upon his partner, dead of a heart attack on the gravel. "I reeled in the fish that had killed him, released it, then laid him out with a stone for a pillow and his rod alongside him like a knight's lance," he told me. "Then I went back to the river. What the hell, the run was still on."

So I, too, fished on.

I t was getting toward evening, time to look for a campsite and kill a couple of trout for supper. Ahead, the stream wound down through a grassy meadow, one of those dried-out beaver ponds that stud the country up there, with plenty of standing, sun-cured drowned trees to provide firewood. I unslung my day pack and spread the tarp under a big white pine, built a ring from a fractured granite ledge, gathered enough wood for the night and laid a fire, then went down to the brook to catch supper.

Nothing rising yet, just the brown water coiling smooth and deep under the high banks. I pulled the dead man's dry fly from my patch and examined it. A strange fly, this one. It was hair-bodied, kind of like a deerhair Adams a friend of mine ties with a big, fat body resembling an Irresistible or a Rat-Faced McDougall. But this clipped hair was of a color I'd never seen before – all colors, it seemed, the more I looked at it. In that late-afternoon light, it almost glowed, refulgent and refractive at once. Blue and burgundy and mahogany, with glints of fiery green, as if copper wire were burning; a deep midnight luster in toward the hook shank, like the underfur of a fisher cat. It couldn't have been dyed, not with all those ever-changing colors, and I tried to puzzle out what sort of animal that hair could have come from. Not badger or moose or wolverine or skunk, certainly not squirrel or bear – not even cinnamon bear. Marten or sable, perhaps, but I doubled it. Hackle, wings and tail were clearly from the same animal, and equally deceptive as to their true colors.

The hook, too, was of a type I'd never seen. It was a size 12, I'd judge, sort of Limerick-bent with a turn-up eye, japanned in black lacquer like a salmon hook, but of course far too small for that purpose. There was something archaic about it that called up images of Hewitt or Gordon tying late at night by lamplight, with a Catskill blizzard howling beyond the windowpanes, or perhaps Dame Juliana herself in some echoing abbey chamber with rush torches guttering on dank gray walls. Could it have been tied before stainless steel came on the market? Unlikely – the fly was not a bit tattered. Or maybe it just didn't catch fish – that would account for its pristine state. But then why did the dead angler have it on his drying patch? What the hell, I'd give it a try.

I knelt in the bankside grass and worked the fly out toward the far bank with a few false casts. I still had a short leader on, the same I'd been using while nymphing, since this was just a trial run anyway and the tippet was heavy enough to turn over the big fly. The fly was traveling overhead in the higher light, and I could see it from the corner of my eye – glowing. A red-gold firefly, it seemed, above the oncoming dusk. I aimed to drop it on the deep run against the far bank, where a nice fat brookie ought to be lying, hungry and unselective as to his dinner menu. He would fill mine. But before the fly even reached the water, I saw a wake streak toward it. From my side of the water. Then another, from downstream. And another, from far upstream . . . . A huge dark golden-bellied shape leaped clear of the water and nailed the fly solid, a full foot above the surface. A big brown, by the look of him. He'd won the race. The other wakes turned sharply on themselves and chased after the brown, who hit the water like an anvil dropped into a lake.

Thank God for the heavy tippet. I was so stunned by the ferocity of the onslaught that I failed to drop the rod tip as the hooked fish jumped, then jumped again. The lesser trout jumped with him – half a dozen, it seemed, all in the same instant. All aimed at his mouth, where I could see the dead angler's fly glowing in the brown's hooked jaw. It was as if . . . It was as if they were trying to take the fly away from him.

I snubbed the brown around, took him on the reel and horsed him in, panic gripping my heart. I hadn't felt like this since I was a kid, fast to my first big fish and frantic that it might get away before I could land it and go running home to show my friends. But when I netted him and lifted him to the bank, he was too big to kill – a good twenty inches long, deep and thick and heavily kyped for the spawning run, far too big a fish for my supper, far too handsome to die. I slipped the hook and sent him back. The other trout were still there, in the bankside water, waiting as if for his return. As he swam off, they followed, darting at his mouth in puzzlement – where was that good bug?

What the hell was this? My heart slowed down and I moved upstream toward the head of the run. Once again I laid the fly out, once again the wakes appeared from all directions. Once again a big trout leaped clear of the water to glom the fly before it hit. Once again the other trout chased it.

Once again he was too big to kill. This was getting upsetting.

I took five more fish on five more casts as the light failed, each the same as the last. Now we've all had similar, or roughly similar, experiences at times, particularly at dusk, when almost any big bushy fly splatted on the water will take trout one after the other. I recall an evening on the South Platte, in the Cheesman Canyon, when I took eight nice Colorado browns on successive casts during a caddis hatch, without shifting a step from my position in midstream. But this night there was no hatch, not that I could see. And each fish took the fly before it hit the water.

I'd often seen brook trout chase one of their number after it was hooked, but brookies are notoriously naïve – some might say suicidal – in the face of danger. These trout, as best I could see, were browns – the Einsteins of entomological discrimination. And not little ones, still learning their Adams from their Baetis from their Coachman, but fifteen- and sixteen-inchers from the graduate school of Selective Sipping.

It was nearly dark by the time I wised up, cut off the dead angler's fly and tied on a mothlike Grizzly Wulff. It took me well into full dark, float following fruitless float on the now-still, apparently troutless water before a lone, ten-inch brookie foolishly gobbled the fly and sacrificed himself for my supper. I knocked him on the head and whipped his guts out, shamefacedly, then stumbled back through wet grass to light my fire. The dinner – fried trout, baked beans, cold cling peaches from the can – leaves no memory of taste behind it, but I must have eaten it, because I remember walking back down to the river to wash the pan. The water was strong and black as ice-cold coffee, but I needed whisky. I lay against the pine trunk in my sleeping bag, sipping Scotch from the peach tin, my mind dancing like a skyful of mayfly spinners.

You've probably wondered, as I do, why certain flies that bear absolutely no resemblance to anything in nature not only catch fish but, at certain times and places, are the only flies a trout will look at. The Royal Coachman, with its white wings, rusty hackle, bristly barred tail and three-segment body, is perhaps the best example. I've heard it argued that the segmented body makes the trout think "flying ant," while the white wings are there only to help the angler keep track of the fly in fast water. I've got another theory, and it came back to me that night as I lowered my Scotch supply and pondered the strange fly I'd found – a fly I'd started thinking of as *Ephemerella incognita*.

Trout have been around for millions of years on this planet, making a living largely off aquatic bugs, and during that time many insect species have come and gone, whereas the trout in its various forms has remained pretty much the same. Could it be that deep in the trout's racial memory, taped on its genes as vividly as its spots and fin rays and mating instincts, are images of insects long since extinct? Images that, when presented in a certain light or temperature of water, by a certain curl of current over a specific type of streambed – sand or boulder or pea gravel – trigger a strike as inevitable as a salmon's fruitless leap at a newly erected dam on its preordained spawning river? Maybe trout still feed on a long-dead past, just as men do on books long out of print but nonetheless still compelling. And perhaps this odd killer fly I'd come by, this *E. incognita*, by sheerest chance happened to imitate some splendid bug of prehistory, some trouty equivalent of braised sweetbreads or oysters on the half shell in an age of sawdust hamburgers . . .

By the time I sloped off to sleep, the Scotch bottle was down by a good three inches.

Fog on the water at daybreak – a pearly pea souper through which the spires of black spruce and the cracked, bone-white fingernails of snags poked, silent and dripping. Heading down to the stream for coffee water, I heard something splash away through the shallows. *Moose*, I thought. Their big, cloven tracks scarred the shore the full length of Wendigo Brook from where I'd entered it. After filling the pot, I went down to look for sign. I wish I'd never looked. There at the bottom of the run where I'd caught the big trout the previous evening were the carcasses of seven big browns. Clearly, they were the fish I'd hooked and released. But how could that be? I hadn't played any of them to the point of exhaustion. I'd hardly touched them in removing the barbless hook, and none of them had swayed even slightly onto its side before swimming off strong and swift to cover. Now, though, they were just heads and tails connected with bare bones. Whatever ate them had some appetite. The skeletons looked like cobs of sweet corn gnawed from end to end, machine-gun style. Big paw prints surrounded the spot, not the long, plantigrade prints of a bear or a bootless man, but round ones a good hand span in diameter, with sharp, deep indentations, as if from claw tips at the end of the toes. A catamont? If so, it was the size of a Siberian tiger – my hand span is nine-and-a-half inches. Thank God the thing had finished eating before I came up on it . . .

I hurried back to the fire and stoked it with my remaining wood. When the water came to a boil, I spiked my coffee with another inch of whisky, then waited for the fog to burn off. I dug the .22 Colt Woodsman out of my pack, checked the magazine, and jacked a Long Rifle round up the spout. Not that it would do much good against a creature the size of that one, but it made me feel better with the holster slapping against my thigh as I packed and headed upstream as soon as I could see a hundred yards ahead. I resolved not to joint the rod until I was at least a mile away from that place, no matter how good the water looked.

But as the day brightened and the sun shone down strong and jolly, my worry burned off like the fog. I felt a fool with the pistol on my hip and put it back in the pack. There were trout rising everywhere – in the pocket water, the riffles, along the undercut banks, in the long, slick, stillwater runs and the deep blue-green bottomless pools. Would *E. incognita* work its wonders under conditions like this, where every trout in the river was already glutting itself on the tiny blue-wing olives I now saw emerging? The naturals were no bigger than eighteens or twenties – a fraction of the size of the *incognita*. Even if I cast with the utmost delicacy, as fine and far off as I could manage, its impact on the water would probably put everything down.

I strung up, tied on and cast. At first nothing happened. The feeding trout continued to etch their endless, interwoven circles on the water, and I was about to breathe a sigh of relief – last night's events had just been another of those rare lucky moments in a fly fisherman's diary of strange happenings. But then another huge brown appeared out of nowhere and took the fly at the end of its float. In fact, the fly had been dragging abominably for half a minute while I stood there, falsely relieved that the mystery was explained. I played the fish fast but carefully, took great pains to insure that I didn't so much as touch it while pushing the hook with a fingertip out of the corner of its mouth. Again, it swam off in full strength, even splashing me with a faceful of water as it tailed away. Thus began, ironically, the most frightening, frustrating day of my angling life.

I tried the *incognita* in the most unlikely trout lies – in dead back eddies, in boiling currents too strong even for a tarpon, dapped it directly at my feet in seemingly fishless pools, even bounced it down a shallow gravelly riffle no more than ankle deep. Wherever I dropped it, trout appeared, often as if from the streambed itself, out of ancient redds long buried under glacial till, springing in seconds from alevin to parr to smolt to full-grown, hooked-jawed, bloody-eyed lunkers hellbent on suicide. One such – a broad-shouldered five-pounder at least – actually zipped up through water only half its own depth from dorsal to ventral, scooting along the gravel on its pectoral fins like some giant wind-up toy. I'd seen king salmon do that on the Salmon River near Pulaski, New York, when the water was down and the fish themselves were pursued by a horde of two-legged snaggers, splashing and falling down in their lust for kill. But never the dignified brown trout. It was sickening – ignoble, repellent, downright hoggish.

And behind me, as I fished and tried not to look back, I saw fish after fish – all carefully released as tenderly as possible – go belly up in my wake. Every one that the *incognita* bit died. Yet I couldn't stop fishing. Even as my mind shrank from what I was doing, as I cursed myself aloud, I kept casting, hooking, releasing, but inevitably killing trout – trout of such a size and beauty that if I'd seen some wormflanger catching and killing just one, a day ago, I'd have seriously considered shooting the bastard and leaving him for the ravens.

Poison, I began thinking. *Poison on the hook.* What I took for black lacquer is actually some kind of deadly venom – like that black tar the Wandorobo hunters use in Africa, boiled down from the sap of the Acocanthera, and smeared on their hand-forged arrows and spearheads, to kill even rhinos and elephants with the stuff. But I, too, was dying – going mad first, unable to stop what I hated doing, yet compelled by the poison to continue. Maybe in an hour, maybe not until tonight, I would gasp hopelessly for breath like those splendid fish dying behind me. Maybe I would roll belly up in my sleeping bag, eyes going white with death, and . . .

And what? Provide a midnight snack for that big, round-pawed carrion eater I'd surprised this morning by the riverbank?

That snapped me out of it. I looked at the palm of my hand where the hook had bitten me yesterday afternoon – less than twenty-four hours ago – but the wound was healed. As perfectly as if it had never been there. Nor was the flesh tender when I probed it. Oh, I felt a little woozy, but that might just be a touch of hangover from last night's Scotch, plus the belt I'd had instead of breakfast. And I hadn't eaten a bite of lunch. It was already late afternoon. No wonder I was giddy – too much fresh air, too much sun, too much adrenaline, too much imagination. When I looked back downstream, I couldn't for the life of me see a single dead fish, yet just moments ago it had seemed there were dozens. Maybe I'd imagined the whole thing.

But the *incognita* was still clinched fast to my tippet. And with a pang of horror I saw that, for all the big fish it had taken today, all the spiky vomerine teeth that had raked it, not a wing was tattered, not a hackle point bent, not a tail whisk frazzled or a strand of dubbing trailing loose. With a shudder, I cut the fly loose and threw it into the current.

Before it could hit the water, a huge brown surged head and shoulders up and onto it – snap, like a giant mousetrap and he was gone.

At that same moment, a wind kicked up and, under its sudden roar, I heard a low, throaty growl from downstream. I turned and ran . . . .

I slept that night on a rocky islet in midstream, wading out to it through currents that lapped over the top of my chest waders. There was ample driftwood jammed at the head of the island to build a huge, roaring bonfire. I kept the upholstered Woodsman beside me while I ate a frugal supper of beans, Spam and Bing cherries – no trout for me tonight. I'd killed enough in the hours just past to last a lifetime. I also reduced the Scotch level another few inches, trying to quiet my raging imagination. To keep my mind off the day's event, I dug out a book I'd brought along, as I always do on such trips, to read myself to sleep. Usually it takes half a page or less, after a hard, fine day on the water, but tonight I feared it would take longer. *Keys to the Kingdom*, it was titled, by Zadok Mosher. *Being a Compendium of Myths & Legends Peculiar to Northeast Vermont.* I'd picked it up in a fine little bookstore in Lyndonville that specialized in used books. No date of publication was given, nor was the name of the publisher, but clearly it was an ancient tome – glossy paper, antique typeface, faded leather binding, excellent drypoint illustrations, the sort of book no one makes anymore. I settled down into my sleeping bag, took a stiff wallop of Scotch and brook water, and opened the volume at random.

"The Monster of Wendigo Brook." Uh-oh. But I read on.

The Wendigo is thought to be a myth of the Cree Indians of the western boreal forests [Mosher wrote]. A murderous creature, half cat, half man, that stalks its human prey through the treetops. When it catches an unwary Indian, alone and deep in the forest, it swoops down and grabs him, lifting its hapless victim high into the air. Then ensues a pell-mell dash through the night sky, conducted at such speeds that when the Wendigo – dragged groundward by the weight and frantic struggles of its still-living captive – allows the victim's feet to touch the earth, the sheer friction sets his moccasins afire. The Wendigo, like a house cat, likes to show off its prey, frequently carrying it at chain-lightning speed around the camp from which the poor captive strayed. His kinsmen, huddled in their teepees, can hear him screaming all through the night: "Oh, my burning feet! Oh, my feet of fire!" In the morning, nothing is found of the victim but his scorched clothing and picked bones, usually under a tall tree at the top of which the Wendigo, like an owl, has made his meal.

Such, then, is the Wendigo of the Cree. But the Abnakis of northern New England have their own legend – that of the Water Wendigo. Like its western congener, this creature too is a man-eater, though it much prefers fish. It haunts the virgin trout streams of that luckless country, hoping to find a dupe to catch fish for it. To that end, it ties a lure on whatever old hook it can find, using swatches of its own fur to disguise the fatal implement. This fur, the Abnakis say, is irresistible to trout and salmon, some of which have been known to crawl on their fins from lake to lake in pursuit of a lure of such devising. No sooner do they taste of it, than they die. Whereupon the Wendigo dines on their corpses. But since the Wendigo cannot cast a fishing pole by itself, it needs a human intermediary to do its fatal business in its stead. This it handily finds, the Abnakis say, since what man would pass up the chance to catch a fish with every cast of his lure? Should the fisherman object to sharing his catch with the Water Wendigo, the Wendigo kills him along with the fish, then passes the lure on to another victim. No man has lived to tell how. Nonsense, of course. But when you hear a withered old Abnaki tell the tale, in a skin lodge of a still winter evening with the Aurora guttering overhead . . .

That was enough for me. I poured another Scotch and resolved, then and there, to fish no more on Wendigo Brook – tomorrow or ever. Total nonsense, of course, as Mosher said, but I would not press my luck. I was lucky to get rid of the fatal fly when I did. I unjointed my fly rod and slipped it into its case, finished my drink, stoked up the fire and went to sleep.

The sun was already up when I woke, so sound and dreamless had been my rest. It was a beautiful day, clear and warm with just an apple-bright bite of frost in the shadows, the brook tinkling and purling along its merry way over the timeworn rocks. I looked at my map and saw a quick way over the hills to the northwest, which would take me to the highway in a matter of a few hours. I'd have to bushwhack, and there might be a few bogs and beaver ponds along the way, but any amount of hard slogging was a cheap price to pay to get away from this cursed river. Still, I'd better get myself around a good breakfast first – a couple of chunky little brookies, caught on a human-tied, unmystical fly for a change. I went over to where I'd left my rod case leaning against a rock the night before.

The rod case was opened. The rod stood assembled. The line threaded bright yellow through the guides to the tip-top. The leader led down to the keeper ring. Cinched in it, snug and bright, was *Ephemerella incognita*.

Again I fled, to the limits of the island. I may well have been gibbering to myself as I ran. I skidded, half fell down through the sharp granite rubble to the water's edge. My reflection shone, unwavering, on the still, cold water. I looked down, dreading what I would see.

The face of the dead angler stared up at me from the mirror of Wendigo Brook. The grizzled gunfighter's mustache wavered, shimmered in the current, the pale eyes stared up into mine – dead at first, then with growing recognition. The face I saw was my own . . .

A Day Afield with the Wee Scot

A lesson in humility during a visit to the Beretta factory, with three-time World Driving Champion Jackie Stewart – a.k.a. The Wee Scot – chauffeuring Jones through Italy in a Ferrari V-12. From the Sept./Oct. 2002 issue of *Shooting Sportsman*.

I n the fall of 1969 I covered the Italian Grand Prix for *Sports Illustrated* to do a story on Jackie Stewart, who was about to clinch the first of three World Driving Championships. The race itself was exciting, replete with plenty of high-speed shunts, spin-outs and lead changes, and Jackie won it by only half a car length, but the most memorable experience of the whole trip was an afternoon I spent shooting clay pigeons with Jackie.

My wife and I had arrived in Italy a week before the race and taken a room at the luxurious Villa d'Este, on Lake Como, where Jackie and his wife, Helen, also were staying. With us was *SI* photographer Tony Triolo, a jolly, heavyset Italian-American who was great fun to work with on a story. It was Tony who'd nearly gotten me shot in Africa during a snoring match one night on the Tana River after a day of sand grouse shooting.

I knew that Jackie had been an Olympic-class wingshot before he took up motor racing, and I was delighted when he proposed that he, Tony and I should drive over to the Beretta works, in Gardone, where Stewart hoped to strike a deal for a matched pair of field guns in return for a personal endorsement.

"I've got a friend in Milan who'll loan us his Ferrari," Jackie said. "It should be a pleasant little outing."

J ackie was a speedy, quick-moving fellow – short and gnarled-looking, with hippie-length hair and a high-pitched Caledonian burr so thick you could cut it with a claymore. British sports announcers inevitably referred to him as "The Wee Scot," a term he disliked but had learned to live with.

On a day when there was no practice at the Monza track, we drove in a rental Fiat down from Como through the northern Italian countryside to Milan. The hunting season had just opened, and in every copse and field we saw men with shotguns – many of them firing at aerial targets so small that at first I couldn't see them.

"They're shooting songbirds," Jackie explained. "It's legal here, and ever since Roman times the Italians have been eating them. Quite a delicacy, it seems. Braised warblers on a bed of truffles, with thrush

117

tongues au gratin for hors d'oeuvres – yum, yum, hard to beat." He laughed. "But then who am I to criticize? I'm partial to haggis."

In Milan we picked up the Ferrari, which belonged to a businessman friend of Jackie's named Carlo del Ventisetti. It was a silver 365 GTB4 with a V12 engine, capable of top speeds close to 170 mph. Once we hit the Autostrada – which had no speed limit then – Jackie floored it and went into a casual, free-associational riff about his love affair with shotguns.

"I've been shooting since I was a wee lad," he said as the speedometer needle quivered at the far end of its range, "learning on the grouse moors of Auchentorlie and Eaglesham under the tutelage of my grandfather and father. Rough-shooting at first, behind pointing dogs, then driven grouse and pheasants. I love wingshooting – maybe even more than motor racing, as it was my first love. Both sports require good eye-hand coordination and quick reflexes, along with a steadiness of purpose and calmness under stress. There's nothing grander than the feeling you get from folding a driven pheasant high overhead, seeing it puff to the shot string, then tumble to earth stone-dead. When I retire from racing, I'd like nothing more than to set up my own shooting school in Scotland." [Which he did, years later, at the Gleneagles Hotel in Scotland.)

We were whizzing through traffic, changing lanes on an instant's notice, blowing off everything on the road. I glanced back at Tony. He was grasping the seat in front of him with white knuckles, eyes wide with terror, beads of sweat running down his face. I didn't feel too easy myself. Then from behind came another car, hell-bent on overtaking us. "Hmm," Jackie said with a glance in the side mirror, "looks like we've got a race on our hands. It's a Lamborghini Espada, a four-seater. He can't resist the challenge – it's a question of honor, both for the man himself and for the marque he's driving."

For about twenty miles, which unreeled behind us in less than ten minutes, we diced with the bronze Lamborghini. Jackie would let it come teasingly close, then pull away as if the other car were standing still. The driver looked to be a middle-aged Italian. His face was grim. This was a matter of machismo.

"Oh, well," Jackie said at last, "let's give him best. No sense risking all of our lives any longer." He eased off on the accelerator and the Espada whipped past. A few miles farther on we saw it brake and wheel into a gas station to refuel. Jackie pulled off the highway and parked behind the Lamborghini. He got out, smiling, and walked up to the flabbergasted Italian with his arms outstretched – "Bravo, Signor, for a race well run!" When the Italian recognized him, his knees buckled and he nearly fainted. Jackie was very famous already throughout Europe.

Back in the Ferrari, Jackie said, "That'll give him something to boast about for the rest of his life – he outdiced The Wee Scot!"

At the Beretta factory, a magnificent stone structure, parts of which date back to the sixteenth century, we were greeted by Signor Carlo Beretta himself. Beretta is not only the world's oldest gunmaker but also reputedly the oldest industrial enterprise of any sort in the Western world. It's been making superior firearms since 1526, when Bartolomeo Beretta, a contemporary of Leonardo da Vinci, produced 185 harquebus barrels for the Doge of Venice. The price of this order: 296 ducats. It was the start of something big. Since then Beretta has manufactured guns for European rulers ranging from Napoleon to Mussolini and is still going strong.

Signor Beretta led us out to a flag-stone-floored verandah where an array of foot traps stood ready. Servants offered us our choice of guns. We selected 12-gauge Silver Snipe over/unders. I'd never shot a Beretta, but the gun felt well balanced and a lot lighter than my old Ithaca side-by-side back home. We loaded and stepped up to our marks.

"Pull!" Jackie said. The clay had scarcely left the trap before he reduced it to dust. I managed to break my first bird, barely, but started hitting more solidly as I got used to the gun. But Jackie dusted doubles so fast that the shots seemed to blend together. I've never been particularly deft with doubles – not cool enough most of the time, too flustered to figure which bird to shoot first – though on this glorious afternoon I actually did hit them all. Or at least I flaked chunks off them, which Jackie graciously allowed to count.

By the final round Jackie and I were tied at twenty-four birds apiece. One more clay to go. I was up first. My throat was dry, my heart pounding, my fingers tingling. I took a deep breath and croaked, "Pull!" The bird soared out low, flat and fast, angling slightly to the right, and I swung with it . . . ad hit the trigger. *Pow!*

To my amazement, I smoked it.

"Well done, Robert!" The Wee Scot said. He grinned at me as he stepped up to his mark, "Pull!" The clay flew. I saw him follow it, then at the last moment purposely swing his muzzles just a tad to the left. *Pow!* A clean miss. By God, I'd beaten Jackie Stewart! But not really. He'd just done the gentlemanly thing. The only thing that really mattered to him was Sunday's coming race. Like the Lamborghini driver, I suddenly realized, I was now free to boast about this for the rest of my life.

Later, after tea and crumpets, we took a tour of the Beretta museum, then the factory itself and finally the proving ground – in a cliff behind the factory – where each and every gun produced by Beretta was test-fired, ten rounds apiece. The gent who performed this duty was a heavy-set, dark-whiskered fellow in a blue smock who appeared to be stone-deaf and perhaps a little bit punch-drunk as well. Well, no wonder, after so many years of gunfire with minimal hearing protection. When we arrived, he was just about to test an autoloader. He thumbed the shells into the receiver, then turned to look up the boulder-studded gulch that was his firing range. The rocks themselves were ragged and splashed silvery with lead from all the rounds that had been fired at them. The shaggy stubs of bushes protruded from both sides of the gully, and the trees overhead had been roughly pruned by nonstop hailstorms of birdshot. As he raised the gun to his shoulder, a lone butterfly came flitting down into the gulch, a pretty little thing, all black and yellow and tilting delicately on the breeze. The test gunner's eyes lit up. A real target! He laughed maniacally and raised the gun to his shoulder.

Ka-pow, ka-pow, ka-pow, ka-pow!

A torrent of birdshot went rattling its way up the gulch along with the endless echoes. A handful of butterfly confetti drifted down to the rocks below.

Ah, yes, indeed, it had been a pleasant little outing.

The Run to Gitche Gumee

Fifty years ago, Ben Slater and Harry Taggart ran the Firesteel River (a fictionalized Bois Brule) from its wilderness headwaters to its mouth at Lake Superior. Along the way, they trout-fished, bird-hunted, matched wits with murderous fugitives, and wooed sirenlike coeds. Now, with their mortality staring them square in the face, the old friends decide to reprise that trip – and, once again, what these aging knights-errant find on the Firesteel beggars the imagination. Here, in the novel's concluding section, they enjoy an idyllic sporting interlude before a final, terrible confrontation.

Heartbreak Rapids lived up to its name, but with unintended irony. There'd been no rain for close to a month and the water was bony. Ribs of granite reared around every corner, interspersed now and then with a grinning, glacier-scrubbed skull – new fields of hazard opening up at each swing of the Mad River's bow. We worked our minds and arms numb finding dodges to avoid them, scraping off lots of Kevlar in the process. In many places we had to get out and drag the canoe, waist and armpit deep in rushing water. Water travel had never been this tough in the old days, but then the human memory has splendid shock absorbers. It smooths out the ruts and frost heaves of the past so that, a year later, all you remember is the scenery. When we finally reached the bottom of the run, we were dead beat.

"We're five miles from Gitche Gumee as the crow flies," Ben said. "Maybe ten or twelve as the river twists and turns. And we've got a week until ducks are legal. Lots of time on our hands."

I studied the woods on both banks. It all looked like prime grouse and woodcock cover – popple, larch, alder, spruce. No posted signs.

"What say we find a good spot to make camp and just explore this country? Fish or hunt whenever and whichever the mood that strikes us, or just lie around and relax."

"Sounds good to me," he said. "This weather can't hold much longer and we could use a spate of rain to bring the salmon and steelhead into the estuary. Meanwhile, there's plenty of brown trout to keep us busy."

Half a mile downriver we spotted a clearing on the west bank, backed by an endless covert of quaking aspen. After we'd pitched the tent and collected an ample supply of firewood, we took a well-earned snooze. We'd been on the go for twenty-four hours straight, pretty good for a couple of geezers.

121

When I opened my eyes, the sun was clocking fast toward the western horizon. Ben was out in the river, working the far shore in the low sloping sunlight. His flyline traced long looping words against a yellow-green vellum of spruce and popple. I couldn't quite read them, but they had the grace of those Gothic scripts you see in medieval psalters. Illuminated manuscripts. Kate had a thing for miniatures. We'd traveled to Italy, Belgium, France and even New York City to see them. *The Book of Hours* of Catherine of Cleves. The *Trés Riches Heures* of Jean, Duc de Berry. The works of the Franco-Flemish Limbourg brothers, Pol, Jan and Herman.

And Pieter Brueghel the Elder, Kate's favorite, whose art drew from the Limbourgs' only a century later. She loved Brueghel's squat, thick-legged, red-cheeked peasants, the physicality of their lives, fishing boats foundering in the windspiked harbors, hunters in the snow returning with their quarry through gabled hamlets where magpies soar past welcoming pillars of woodsmoke. The Inn of the Stag.

"This is the real world," she'd say. "Those were *real* lives. You can almost anticipate the evening ahead, the songs and prayers and laughter, and smell the wild boar turning on a spit."

"Real lives," I snorted, but only once. "The Middle Ages, like the people who lived then, were short, brutal and ugly."

She looked at me with pity.

Of course, I thought, all lives are that way, even today. Nobody lives forever, though some may hope so. As my well-traveled daughter once said, "Europeans accept the inevitability of death. Americans think it's an option." Ah yes, death – it's patently undemocratic. But why does time have to accelerate with age? Why, when I was a kid, did the school year seem to last a decade, while I crept toward adulthood like a snail across a bathroom floor? Now you blink and . . . you're old.

Dear God, I prayed now, here on the bank of the Firesteel. Can't you put on the brakes, at least for this one last week? *Please???*

He must have heard me. The days that followed were full of slow riches. The weather held clear, hot during high daylight, the grass furred with hoarfrost as dawn. In the early mornings while the dew was drying we fished the river, upstream and down for miles, casting streamers to cruising browns. They were big fish just in from the lake and charged with the angry hormones of their spawning season, quick to strike at anything that dared to drift past them.

During the afternoons we pounded the endless covert for ruffed grouse. It was a vast stretch of aspen that had been cut progressively for pulp over the past half-century or more, so that every stage of growth was represented. Thick stands of doghair popple to provide grouse with safe cover in which to raise their broods. Long reaches of half-grown trees so close to one another that predatory goshawks could not interrupt grouse mating rituals. And tall islands of fully mature aspens with their craggy bark, branches drooping with the burden of catkins on which these birds relied for sustenance. Mixed in with the aspens were stands of hardhack and occasional volunteer apple trees. Partridges picked the seeds from the rotting windfallen fruit. It was ruffed grouse heaven. We hunted it hard, Jake sometimes flushing twenty birds in an afternoon. We'd pause every hour or so to let the dog cool off. Maybe eat an apple from one of the old-time trees or drink from an icy spring. Our legs grew strong, our eyes quick and we returned to camp each evening full of hunger and that wonderful sense of lassitude that results from a day spent on nothing but what pleased us most. At night we ate what we'd killed, never a whole lot and played music to the starlit river.

On our forays into the woods we found old cellar holes, family graveyards, an Indian mound, an ancient steam tractor from Paul Bunyan days flaking its hull into red dust, a nest built by golden eagles that contained the sunbleached skull of a coyote. *Change and decay in all around I see*. Deer bounced away from us but Jake never chased them. Once we encountered a bull moose, his neck beginning to thicken with the oncoming urges of rut, but he did not see us and we slipped away without incident. We found a giant white pine log full of carpenter ants. The blowdown had been ripped apart by a bear. Ants scurried around, trying to repair the damage to no avail. At the edge of a clearing one late afternoon we spotted a red fox stalking mice in the tall grass. Ben had Jake sit, and we watched for half an hour. The fox leaped high, tail plumed and black tipped, forepaws spread like a cat's, and never missed. He glowed in the sunset light. Then he caught our scent and *poof* . . . he was gone.

On the seventh morning we woke to the sound of rain on the roof. Drops splatted hissing on the coals of the fire. Ben peered outside. "At last," he said. "It's here for a while, and about time. This'll bring the big fish in from the lake."

"Ducks too."

"According to the regs you can't start shooting at migratory fowl until noon on opening day. That's not a duck hunt to me. Let's skip it today, let 'em move in and get used to the area. Then hit 'em tomorrow at the crack of dawn."

The rain was pelting down now, the Firesteel rising by the minute. The wind picked up from the northwest, the temperature dropped and we rigged a reflector for the fire with a sheet of corrugated iron Ben dragged up from the brush near the riverbank. We spent the day sorting through flies and shell boxes.

Toward evening I said, "How's about some *chai*?"

"Sure."

We boiled water and steeped a pot of Lapsang Souchong. Florinda's sourdough had gone stiff and stale but we toasted a few thick slabs of it over the fire. Ben spread the toast with the last of our butter and honey.

"Just like Winnie the Pooh," I said.

Ben looked at me, empty-eyed, then shifted his gaze. Glum weather always took him this way. Nowadays they call it Seasonal Affective Disorder. SAD. They've got a new acronym for every quirk or foible of the human condition nowadays, as if by merely renaming our woes they can cure them. Fat chance . . .

Or maybe it was the tea, with its Chinese name, had turned Ben's memories back to Korea. He stared at the racing river for a long while, then squared his shoulders.

"You want to hear about Chosin?" he asked.

"If you're ready."

As we ate and drank our tea, Ben told me about Chosin.

The teapot was down to cold dregs by the time he'd finished. We fed Jake a few leftover crusts of toast. Ben stared off into the rain.

"That tiger was really something," he said.

"Whatever happened to Sergeant Stingley?"

"I heard he died in Vietnam, during the siege of Hué in '68. It was all house-to-house fighting, not his style." He clammed up then, busied himself with a Rey del Mundo, the last of them. He lit up and took a deep toke. Then he coughed for a minute or two.

"Florinda packed a quart of bourbon in her care package," I said. "I think you could use a toddy about now."

He thought for a moment. "Naw, I'm through with that poison. Funny, just being out on the river again seems to have taken away my taste for it. Maybe I'll stay here forever."

We hit the rack early. Tomorrow promised action.

My dreams that night were of Gitche Gumee. The Shining Big Sea Water. But this was an inland sea gone weird and tropical. The Apostle Islands had become the Isles of the Blest. Coral atolls came and went over the horizon, waving the fronds of their coco palms to the beat of southeast trades. I was cruising this sea in a *pahi*, one of those elegant double-hulled sailing canoes carved from pandanus logs in which the ancient Polynesians made their stupendous voyages of discovery. Whales broached and blew and sang in the distance and I sat crosslegged on the deck between the hulls, playing my horn. I was riffing changes around the songs of the whales. We were approaching a high island with a lopsided volcanic cone rising above verdant slopes that were cut with quick rushing streams. The sound of distant waterfalls came to us over the billows. Shoals of wahoo and tuna quickened the surface, and dolphins sported alongside. The volcano puffed smoke rings that wafted out to us across the water. The smoke smelled like Ben's Rey del Mundos. Then as we neared the high island, I saw that the volcano *was* Ben, with a fat cigar clenched in his teeth. He was grinning at me and his arms were draped around the shoulders of two lava maidens. Kate and Lorraine.

We had to run the gap in the reef to reach Ben's island. The current raced through coralline jaws, twisting, eddying, surging and I could see fangs of bright coral waiting to rip our canoe. Across the lagoon a pair of young dogs frisked on the beach, awaiting our arrival . . .

CODA

It was still raining at 4 a.m. when Ben woke Harry. The rain was a steady thrum with the taste of sleet in it. Full dark, and a north wind rattling the tent walls. He handed Harry a cup of hot tea, black and bitter as the weather. Two hours until sunrise. "There's that little inlet downstream aways," he said. "Good spot to set out the blocks. I heard ducks moving awhile back, high on the wind, a big flock of 'em."

"What flavor?"

He shook his head. "Too dark to see, but from their talk I'd swear they were bluebills."

"Scaup? But it's way too early for them, isn't it?"

"Yeah, they usually don't show till November, when there's skim ice on the water. But with this freaky weather we've been having lately, who knows?"

"Global warming," Harry said. "It's fucked everything, even the seasons."

They ate another thrombotic breakfast – fried eggs, fatty bacon, toast slathered with butter and hunks of rattrap cheese to top it off, delicious – then broke camp, loaded the canoe and set off downriver. Jake could hear the ducks pass overhead. Silk slashed by a knifing wind. He looked up into the rain and shivered. He whined and mumbled to himself. Waiting.

Short of the cove they pulled ashore. Ben tied the canoe to an ice-sheathed popple trunk and they pulled out the bag of decoys. They waded down the bank to the inlet, skidding on shallow rocks. The water was cold through their waders. A small knot of ducks held against the northwest bank, heads tucked snug beneath the random wind. Redheads or canvasbacks by the way they swam, blocky and low slung, tails down in the water. It was still too dark to distinguish color.

"We'll have to move them out of here," Ben whispered. "That's where I

125

want to put the spread." He sent Jake around the inlet with instructions to spook the ducks. When they'd flown, the men moved. They waded out into the lee and placed the decoys, unwinding anchor lines stiff with frozen sleet. "Leave a nice-sized hole in the middle of the spread to draw new arrivals," Ben said.

"Yeah, Benjamin, this isn't the first time I've ever been duck hunting."

"Sorry, Doc."

Back on the bank they cobbled together a makeshift blind of juniper branches. Ben hacked them with his K-Bar and Harry stuck their butts in the mud, interwove the tough, soft-needled branches. Then they sat behind their dark green wall and shivered, waiting for first light. From time to time, eyes cocked skyward under the brim of his cap, Ben gave a come-hither purr on his call, alternating it with low throaty whistle or a loud, impatient *scaup! scaup! scaup!*

The sky overhead was shading from black to charcoal gray and then they could see streamers of low black ragged cloud wavering across it from the northwest. Fine weather for ducks. Shifting clots of them blew through, yammering at each other, too high and determined just yet to respond to the call's seductions. Then a band of pale light appeared above the eastern horizon.

They crouched lower in the blind. Ben called, two loud blats. Jake shuddered. Harry put his hand on the nape of the dog's neck and felt its warmth melt the sleet. "Easy boy." Ben's upturned eyes were fixed on something now, they circled, the call purred again, soft and happy. He nodded his head. They were coming. Harry kept his head down and listened, heard a rip overhead, the soft quick flap of slowing wings. The birds circled once, twice, then on the instant they were committed.

"Take 'em."

The old men stood and there they were, a dozen bluebills cupped and dropping toward the water, black chests and glossy dark green heads, white breasts and wings, scrubbing off speed, tilting from side to side, webbed feet the color of cold slate sprawled out before them like dive brakes. A perfect toll.

They fired and fired again.

Four birds hit the water.

Ben threw a hand signal. "Fetch dead, boy."

Jake was over the top of the blind and gone in a long, low racing dive, murmuring low in his chest. He'd marked the birds as they fell and surged toward them, ignoring the decoys.

The men broke their guns and pocketed the hot, still smoking hulls.

"Six ducks each is the limit," Ben said. "But I call this a day."

Harry agreed. "We can't eat more than two apiece."

By the time Jake had the ducks ashore they had torn down the blind, recovered the decoys and were ready to go.

"What's next?"

Ben looked out into the mainstream, the racing whitewater.

"Gitche Gumee."

A fast hard run with the power of the Firesteel fueling their arms and backs. Wind and rain slashed their faces. The salmon were running too, but against the current. The men could see them working along the bottom, dark bronze with the mating urge that would end in a tattered misshapen death. Brighter fish too, bigger and stronger than the kings and cohoes – steelhead. But a madness was in the men now, the fury of the river, and they could not pause for the cerebration required: fly selection, casting angles, knots and mends and retrieves. You move when the mood is upon you. All urgencies end in death. Upstream or down.

The river sweeps left, then right. In the distance the men can see the highway bridge and beyond it the combers of Gitche Gumee whitecapped and booming as they emerge from an endless fogbank. The canoe is moving fast on the strength of the Firesteel, closer, closer – a quarter mile to go now, two hundred yards . . .

Parked at the bridge is Ben's rust-scabbed Ford F-250. Men in camouflage slickers stand in its lee, huddled low against the rain. They carry rifles. Squatting on its skids beside the highway, Cardigan's helicopter, the color and shape of a wet sand dune. Its rotors are idling. Someone spots the canoe and points. His words are carried away by the wind. A figure emerges from the truck. Cardigan, dressed in a Barbour coat. He trots over to the chopper and climbs aboard. Little Ned reaches out from the cockpit to give him a hand up. The men with the rifles fan out, sprawl prone behind the riprap in shooting positions. The Huey lifts off, tilts sideways against the wind, and whupwhups its way toward the canoe.

"You men are under arrest." Baby Ned on the bullhorn. "You are fugitives from the law. You killed game out of season. You trespassed on posted property. You murdered a helpless and valuable research animal. You discharged a firearm within 100 feet of an occupied dwelling. Throw your weapons over the side and pull in to the bank immediately. Or we will commence firing."

The Huey hovers overhead now, the downdraft from its rotors further roiling the water. Gun muzzles protrude from the side hatch. Cardigan kneels in there, haughty and triumphant. The chopper veers off to achieve a better firing angle.

Ben flips Fritz the finger and the guns open fire. A gust from the lake

127

whirls fog around the chopper and tilts it off balance. Harry grabs his shotgun and fires a load of goose shot at the blurring rotors. One of the blades sheers off near the rotor cap and the helicopter veers landward. The rifles from the shore pop shots at the bouncing canoe but the bullets fly wide or ricochet off the water – they score not a single hit.

The debate is over. They've reached the twisted, rain-swollen stretch of raging rapids that nearly killed them fifty years ago. The Haystack looms out of the fog. They can still opt for an easy way out, leave the river and surrender, or hit for the far bank, split into the woods, elude Cardigan and his thugs, and hike to the highway, hire someone in town to drive them to Canada.

But they cannot do that. Boys will be boys.

They see Gitche Gumee glimmering cold and black as steel beneath the mist. It draws them on as it always has.

Beyond the fog bank, far far away, lies Canada. Or possibly death.

One last shot of adrenaline before they go.

"Fuck it," Ben says. "Don't mean nothin'. Drive on."

Jake thumps his tail in agreement.

The paddles dig for darkness.

It never ends in comfort.

Ramblings of A Dogman

Wit and wisdom regarding the canine race and our relationship with same, liberally spiked with amazing factoids, quirky anecdotes and Jones' usual pungent observations. From *The Hunter in My Heart* (2002), it first appeared in *Men's Journal*, where Jones was a contributing editor.

> *Outside of a dog, a book is man's best friend.*
> *Inside of a dog, it's too dark to read.*
> – Groucho Marx

Here's a dog story for openers. This guy comes home from work hungry and his wife's still out. But he knows that when she's going to be late she usually leaves something in the icebox for him. He peeks inside and sees a plate covered with waxed paper. It looks like a nice slab of meat loaf, so he spreads it on some saltines and eats it. His wife comes home, all embarrassed at having forgotten to leave him at least a snack.

"It's okay, honey," he says. "I had that meat loaf you left in the refrigerator."

"That wasn't meat loaf," she says. "That was leftover dog food from Fido's supper!"

"Well, I don't care," he says, "I like it. Get me some more."

Next time she goes to the grocer's she orders six cans.

"What's this, Missus?" that worthy asks. "You got a new dog?"

"No, but my husband ate some of this stuff the other night and says he likes it."

"I don't know, Missus," the grocer says. "You better be careful. Dog food's not for people – God only knows what's in it."

"Well, my husband is very stubborn. He says he wants more, and that's that."

The grocer shakes his head and fills her order.

This continues for about six months. Then one day the woman comes in and orders just one can of dog food.

"So your hubby finally wised up, did he?" the grocer says.

"Oh no," she says, "It's not that. The other night poor George was up on the couch licking his balls. He fell off and broke his neck."

Well, I don't care. I'm a dogman and proud of it. For more than half a century now I've lived with dogs, walked behind them over hill and dale, through alder hells and brier patches, swamps and prickly pear

129

deserts. I've taken them with me whenever and wherever I can. I've laughed at them and with them, and squirmed while they laughed at me. I've exulted in their doggy triumphs, been embarrassed by their gaffes. I've slept with them in cold, wet, miserable wilderness camps, and been warmed by them at home in the depths of a New England winter. I've mourned their inevitable deaths more keenly even than those of my own blood kin and been comforted by them in turn in times of distress.

I've even been known to eat dog food, though only on a dare, and it wasn't too bad apart from the aftertaste. And I haven't yet broken my neck, though I damned near did not long ago. In 1993, on Vermont Route 315 between Dorset and Rupert, while maneuvering at speed to avoid killing a partridge, I hit a patch of gravel and skidded head-on into a utility pole at thirty-five miles an hour. The chest strap on my seat belt gave way and I was thrown against the steering column. When I came to, the windshield was starred and my Jack Russell, Roz, was sitting in my lap licking blood from my face. My fogged brain was pleased with this: A dog's saliva is said to contain a mild antibacterial component, hence the old comparative "Cleaner than a hound's tooth." I looked around to check on my big yellow Lab, Jake, fearing he might have been injured in the crash. But no: He sat quietly in the backseat, concern writ large on his noble phiz. Dogs are fatalists. Yet when I turned to look at him he grinned with relief and wagged his tail as if to say: "Whew, I was worried there for a minute."

It's said that with time we grow to resemble our pets. Like my dogs, I love to wallow – though in facts and theories rather than mud, horse manure or deer droppings.

DOG NUTS

In *The Devil's Dictionary,* Ambrose Bierce defined the canine race thusly: "Dog. A kind of additional or subsidiary deity designed to catch the overflow and surplus of the world's worship."

Over sixty-seven years I've owned twelve dogs, ranging from tiny terriers and a bugle-throated beagle to rangy pointers and big, burly retrievers. That's really not many by the standards of the true dog nut, some of whom – people who ride to hounds, compete in dogsled races like the Iditarod, hunt raccoons or coyotes or mountain lions or bears – will own dozens at a time.

A woman who lives down the road from me – and it's a remote dirt road, five miles from the nearest hamlet – takes in any stray that wanders by. She does not hunt or herd with them, she just loves them. The word must have spread on the doggy internet because at any given moment she has anywhere from eight to twelve dogs living in clean, comfortable wire kennels around her doublewide trailer. They range from nondescript but healthy, well-fed mutts to a pair of beautiful Brittanies, with stops at such breeds as a spitz, a golden retriever, two basset hounds and a sprawl of Labradors. Their chorused voices ring out eerily on a moon-lit night when coyotes are singing in the surrounding hills.

In a wealthier town just over the mountain, it is fashionable among the doggy set to throw birthday parties for one's purebred pooch, replete with festive, conical paper hats, party favors and a huge birthday cake fashioned from Alpo, with beef jerky "candles" for the birthday "boy" or "girl." Little Tiffany, a charming bichon frise, had just turned two. She had fourteen sticks of jerky on her cake – one for each of her canine pals.

Even in death, some of us treat dogs as we would people. Pet cemeteries abound throughout the Western world. The Cemetery of Dogs, located on the forested islet of Asnières in the Seine River near Paris, was founded in 1899 by the French feminist Marguerite Durand to relieve that dulcet stream of its burden of dead, rotting dogs, thrown into it every day from the banks of the City of Light. Some forty thousand canines lie there today in eternal rot – I mean rest – some of those from the turn of the century in moss-grown marble mausoleums styled on the classical doghouse, while the graves of today's new residents are marked by machine-tooled headstones with laminated photos of the loved ones.

The biggest and oldest dog cemetery in the United States can be found in Hartsdale, New York, a suburb of Manhattan. The dog graves cover nine acres of meadow and willow trees, and on Memorial Day, according to Mary Elizabeth Thurston in her fine book *The Lost History of the Canine Race,* hundreds of people dressed in their mourning finery parade through the grounds carrying bouquets of flowers to place on the graves of their late pals. One woman, in keeping with her Jewish faith, waited a full year before placing a headstone on the grave of her Doberman pinscher, Apollo.

In their wills, many disillusioned humans leave their entire estates to their dogs.

That's a lot of dog biscuits.

ON GRIEF

Dogs die and break our hearts.

We die and they mourn us.

In his book *Dogs Never Lie About Love*, Jeffrey Masson, the former director of the Freud Archives and an unabashed animal lover, suggests that some dogs actually "commit suicide out of despair" over their master's death. He cites the case of a six-year-old boy whose cowboy suit ignited near a bonfire. While the boy lingered near death in the hospital, receiving eleven blood transfusions, his dog, whose name was Woodsie, refused to eat. The boy finally died, and the dog followed him two hours later.

Greyfriars Bobby was a Skye terrier sheepdog in Scotland. When his master, Old Jock, died in 1858, Bobby was still young. He followed the funeral procession to the Greyfriars cemetery in Edinburgh and after Old Jock had been planted, Bobby lay down on the grave. He stayed in that graveyard year after year, kept alive by the food people brought him once his story was known – little snacks at first, then leftovers from their own suppers, sometimes even whole roasts. Bobby lived there for fourteen years. He died in 1872. A statue on Candlemaker's Row in Edinburgh commemorates Bobby's vigil. It was donated by the Baroness Burdett-Coutts and stands above a drinking fountain built for wandering dogs.

A friend of mine, the best upland bird hunter I've ever known, gave up the pursuit of ruffed grouse and woodcock after his great dog Ruff died. Landy couldn't bear to go into the coverts again; the memories were too painful. For a few years he didn't hunt at all. Then he bought a beagle and began chasing cottontails and snowshoe hares. Now he's the best rabbit hunter I've ever known.

ON THE SENSES OF A DOG

"If you eliminate smoking and gambling," wrote George Bernard Shaw, "you will be amazed to find that almost all an Englishman's pleasures can be, and mostly are, shared by his dog." Dogs, though, are far more unbuttoned than most Englishmen. They're true voluptuaries, orgiasts when the opportunity arises, and like all consummate sensualists they have the senses to bring it off. Though dogs can indeed see color, if only in muted shades, because of the predominance of rods over cones in their eyes, they are far better at spotting movement in dim light than we are, and they can hear sounds far beyond our range (thirty-five thousand cycles per second to our twenty thousand). My dogs can distinguish the sound of our car when my wife is still half a mile from home, wherewith they begin their Happy Dance, singing at the top of their voices.

But the organ from which a dog derives its greatest pleasure is of course its nose. Any dog's idea of a great day is to walk its nose through the world, the wider the range the better. They're admirably suited for this work. Where we have only 5 million olfactory cells per human nose, the average basset hound has 125 million. Back in the early 1950s a meticulous German scientist named Walter Neuhaus designed an "olfactometer" and after extensive tests of both dogs and men, concluded that canine noses are one million to one hundred million times more sensitive than human beezers.

What's more, the dog has a secret weapon: the tiny (two and a half centimeters) Jacobson's organ, located between the roof of its mouth and its nostrils near the front of its face, which allows it to simultaneously sniff and taste everything it encounters. If what it encounters smells/tastes good enough, your dog will eat it, and is equipped to chase it for a good long way to do so. If the object encountered smells to a male dog like a bitch in heat, then chances are your male will want to hump it. If it smells like another male, he'll probably fight to establish dominance. If it smells like excrement, more often than not he'll roll in it – nobody knows for sure why.

ON THEIR INSOUCIANCE

"The great pleasure of a dog," says Samuel Butler, "is that you may make a fool of yourself with him and not only will he not scold you, but he will make a fool of himself too."

Dogs have a great sense of humor. As Turgenev says in *A Sportsman's Sketches:* "It is well known that dogs are capable of smiling, and even of smiling very charmingly." They love to have fun – especially at our expense.

We were hunting our way through a late-season blizzard, a mixture of sleet and big, fat flakes that cut visibility to about ten yards. My yellow Lab, Jake, of course had four-paw drive and studded snow pads, so the slippery going didn't bother him a bit, but with each step I was skidding on the brink of disaster. Every now and then I'd catch Jake looking back at me with what seemed a wicked, anticipatory grin, hindquarters wriggling and tail out of control. He knew where we were going, I thought . . .

We'd just topped a rise and were heading downhill toward a stand of dense young aspen whips – a patch of cover that had been good to us, grousewise, in seasons past – when my booted heel hit a buried slab of raw Vermont marble covered with wet, ice-crushed leaves. Sure enough, my feet went out from under me and I fell splat on my butt.

Jake's grin widened and he seemed to chortle at my embarrassment. He clearly said: *"Haw, haw, haw!"*

What I said was unprintable.

The dog was laughing at me, I was sure of it.

I'd always suspected it, and now it seems that it's true: Dog do have a sense of humor. A recent study by Professor Patricia Simonet, a psychologist at Sierra State College in California, detected not only canine laughter, but also subtle sounds that could be the doggy equivalent of human giggles, chuckles, cackles and titters. "To the untrained human ear," she says, "it sounds like a pant, a 'huh, huh.' "

Professor Simonet conducted her study by hanging around parks with a powerful microphone, taping the sounds made by dogs at play. It wasn't an easy task, she says. The dogs were willing to cooperate but the people often interrupted her recording sessions by asking what she was up to. Nonetheless, Simonet found that dogs use at least four sound patterns: barks, growls, whines and laughs. Only the laugh is reserved for playtime. When Professor Simonet studied her recordings, she found "a wide range of nuance and tone" – subtleties lost to humans, she says, since the frequency is beyond our ears. The key to her experiment was testing how dogs respond simply to the noise of other dogs laughing. Professor Simonet played the *huh huh* sound to a group of puppies, one by one. On hearing the broadcast they picked up their toys and jumped for joy.

Subtleties, hey? After reading of Professor Simonet's landmark work, I took my dogs aside and tested them with the subtlest dog story I'd ever heard.

"This fellow's bird dog has died," I told them, "and he's in the market for a new one. He sees an ad in the paper for 'good gun dogs' and goes out to a nearby farm. The farmer shows him a kennel full of pointers, setters and Brittanies.

" 'How about that big Gordon, over there?'

" 'Oh, he's not for sale,' the farmer says. 'He's my own personal bird dog – too valuable for me to sell.'

" 'Listen, let me at least see him work. I'd be willing to pay plenty for a good dog.'

"The farmer takes the Gordon out into a patch of likely looking cover on the back forty and tells him: 'Okay, MacGregor, find the bird!'

"The Gordon takes off into the brush, locks up on point, then barks once.

" 'That means he's pointing a single,' the farmer says.

" 'Oh, come on,' says the would-be buyer. 'Dogs can't count.'

" 'We'll see,' says the farmer. He goes over to the dog and kicks the brush. A single cock pheasant blasts out of the cover.

" 'That was just a fluke,' the buyer says. 'Let's see him do it again.'

"The farmer hies the dog on. A few steps later, MacGregor locks up and barks – four times.

"Same deal as before, but this time when the farmer kicks the cover, four pheasants flush.

"The buyer is sold. He forks over fifteen hundred dollars for the dog.

"A few weeks later the farmer has to go to town and decides to stop off at the guy's house to see how his dog is doing. Pulls into the driveway, no sign of the dog. The guy comes out of the house, looking kind of miffed.

" 'How's MacGregor coming along?" the farmer asks him.

" 'It didn't work out,' the guy says. 'You sold me a bill of goods. On

134

opening day I took him to my best covert. He got about two steps into it and started barking like crazy. Then he ran back and began humping my leg. Next he picked up a stick and started shaking it at me.' The guy shakes his head sadly. 'He'd obviously gone nuts, so I shot him.'

" 'You durn fool!' the farmer says. 'He was telling you there's more effing birds in here than you can shake a stick at!' "

I waited for the telltale *huh, huh*. No soap. Jake yawned. Roz, my Jack Russell, decided to chase the cat. Clearly this dog humor was more subtle than I'd figured. You can't expect to elicit a heartfelt whoop with a feeble joke. Man's best friend finds different things funny in different ways. Perhaps earthy humor was more to their liking, so I gave them my best shot – a bit of English doggerel:

THE DOGGIES' MEETING
The doggies called a meeting;
They came from near and far.
Some came by motorcycle
And some by touring car.

Each doggie crossed the portal,
Each doggie signed the book,
Then each unshipped his asshole
And hung it on a hook.

One dog was not invited,
Which sorely raised his ire.
He dashed into the meeting hall
And loudly shouted, "Fire!"

This threw them in confusion
And, without a second look,
Each grabbed another's asshole
From off another's hook.

And that's the reason why, Sir,
While walking down the street,
And that's the reason why, Sir,
When doggies chance to meet,

And that's the reason why, Sir,
Wherever they may roam,
Each sniffs the other's asshole;
To see if it's his own.

I waited for at least the equivalent of a doggy titter. Even a groan would have been welcome. Alas, no sale – though kindhearted Jake did indeed smile at me with what looked suspiciously like canine pity.

Next day we were hunting one of our favorite coverts, a hillside that usually teemed with woodcock and grouse. With my ear now trained, thanks to Professor Simonet, I listened for every subtle nuance of doggy humor. As we entered the top of it, I thought I could detect the two of them chuckling gleefully. Wickedly, it seemed. Or was I getting paranoid?

They led me down the slope through a stand of ancient apple trees where often, at that hour, we found a partridge or two feeding on the ground amid the windfallen fruit. It had been a good apple year, and the pomes lay on the ground like a carpet of outsized ball bearings. You had to duck to get under the lowest of the apple boughs, and of course keep your gun in one hand, ready to mount at the first flap of a grouse wing. I was just bending down to pass under one of these low sweepers, feet already skidding on the apples underfoot, when it happened. I heard the chain-saw rip of grouse feathers, stepped forward and raised the gun, and my feet went out from under me once again.

Thump!

I must have created a quart of applesauce when my tailbone hit the ground.

When I looked up, buttsore and humiliated by this pratfall, I saw both dogs not ten yards away, looking at me – eyes filled with glee, ears cocked, grins on their faces. Both of them were going "*Huh, huh, huh!*"

Then, as if to explain the joke, Jake shook his head, his flapping ears sounding just like a grouse flush. They'd set me up, the rascals. Led me into a spot where they knew my footing was unsteady, then faked the whole situation.

Yes, where humor is concerned, dogs prefer slapstick.

Fair warning: Be prepared.

They're totally lacking in inhibitions and unless taught otherwise (a rolled newspaper, a stern command, the repeated words: "No! Bad dog!" are good educational tools) will do whatever strikes their fancy, whenever the mood is upon them. They'll gladly copulate in the middle of Main Street at high noon, or in the nave of a cathedral during the sermon at Christmas services. Dogs will defecate in the park or in your living room if left to their own devices. Given the proper amount of rotten roadkill in his belly, a dog will redecorate the backseat of your car, or the front if you allow him up there, in the pattern our British cousins call "dog's dinner mauve." Only rarely, though, will a mature male dog urinate in either your house or your car. He's saving that valuable commodity for better things: to mark every tree, post, bush, weed or grass stem with his calling card. He especially loves to mark car or truck tires, seemingly aware that they will carry his byline out into the wider world – possibly fulfilling some deep doggy dream of immortality.

ON THEIR UNCANNY SENSE OF DIRECTION

Phrenologically and figuratively speaking, the Bump of Locality stands tall on a dog's otherwise flat-topped skull. Canine lore is full of stories about dogs slogging hundreds of miles to rejoin families that had moved far away, leaving poor Rover behind. My dogs have led me back to truck or camp through stygian gloom after many an evening's hunt. They have no problem finding their unerring way home on the rare occasions when we get separated in the woods.

But the best story I've read about this still-unexplained directional sense appears in a book titled *War Dogs: Canines in Combat* by Michael G. Lemish (Brassey's, 1996). During the Vietnam War, a U.S. Army scout dog named Troubles and his handler, PFC William Richardson, were airlifted out of An Khe into a landing zone some distance back in Indian Country. Richardson was severely wounded in a firefight soon after they landed and dusted off in a medevac chopper. The patrol they'd been working with left Troubles behind when they too were evacuated. As Lemish tells it:

"Three weeks later Troubles was found back at the First Air Cavalry Division Headquarters in Ann Khe. The dog, tired and emaciated, would not let anyone get near him. Troubles then slowly went to the tents comprising the scout dog platoon and searched until he found Richardson's equipment and cot. The dog then simply curled up alongside his master's belongings and fell asleep. If the pair had walked into the jungle, Trouble's return would be easy to explain: the dog followed his master's scent home. . . But the pair had been airlifted in, and Richardson left by helicopter, so no scent trail could possibly have been left behind."

Just how Troubles found his way home, and where he had been for three weeks, remains a mystery.

I've seen my own dogs do some amazing things. Last November, along the Blackwater River on Maryland's Eastern Shore, I was hunting ducks in flooded timber. Just before dawn Jake and I were huddled in a skimpy blind in the middle of a swamp. There was skim ice on the water, and we could hear the chortle of puddle ducks everywhere. My friend Stony Stonebreaker set out the decoys while I and Duke Cunningham, a Republican congressman from La Jolla, California, perched on a brace of upright two-by-fours driven into the mud with six-inch-wide blocks of wood nailed across the top. It might have been comfy to Stony, who's part

Indian, and for Duke, a former navy fighter pilot who was America's first ace in Vietnam, but for this overweight, sixty-something white man it felt more like a torture stake. Jake sat in hip-deep swamp water, his back to the decoys, watching my every wince. Just at legal shooting time, Stony said: "Here they come!" We heard the whistle of teal, the heavier rip of widgeon wings through the graying darkness, ducks circling the dekes. They cupped in, swift, dim shadows against the fading night. "Take 'em," Stony said.

As I stood to shoot, I saw Jake's eyes locked on mine. I fired twice, Duke twice, Stony three times with the pump gun – long, ragged lances of flame igniting the darkness. We could hear ducks fall, the crackle and splash of their bodies on the iced-over water.

Jake's eyes were still on me.

Stony gestured me to release him for the retrieve.

"Fetch, boy," I said. Jake rose, spun on his heels, and hit the water with a great cold splash. He hadn't seen a single duck fall. Not a one was visible from the blind – they'd all dropped behind hummocks of marsh grass and drowned trees – and the wind was at our backs, so he couldn't have smelled them. Yet Jake swam strong, unerring, without hesitation to each of the five birds on the water. He'd no sooner bring one back in than he'd turn and hit the water for another. We gave him no direction. After the fifth bird, he sat down in his icy hip bath again and began to groom himself.

How had he known where to go? I believe he could tell where they fell from the angle of my gun when I shot, and from the expression in my eye if I'd hit or missed. He may have also seen from the corners of his eyes the shots of my companions. Moreover, all dogs have an inner ear that can shut down to filter out extraneous background noises, so Jake may well have concentrated on the splashes of ducks hitting the water, and from those sounds gotten a rough idea of their range and direction. But did he actually count seven shots and know we'd killed five birds?

I have to believe he did.

ON TRAINING

The books available on dog training, in English alone, would fill a small library. The theories are even more abundant. But when it comes to hunting, I'm convinced that a dog's best coach is an older, woods-wise dog. For years I've always kept an older Lab and a young one for just that purpose. My yellow Lab Simba taught Luke all he knew about birds and cover; Luke taught Jake, and now Jake has converted my Jack Russell, Roz Russell, into, of all things, a bird dog. She can flush woodcock with the best of them. Sure, I can teach a pup – any pup – simple obedience: sit, stay, come, down, heel, fetch or kennel up. And most dogs, even nonhunting breeds, will quarter instinctively while running ahead of their master in field or woods. But an old dog that's learned the haunts and tricks of gamebirds, and that's amply rewarded with praise and head rubs when he finds game, will soon earn the envy and emulation of the younger one, thus shortening the hit-or-miss stage in a single pup working alone. Even a finely bred pointing dog, when he locks up on a pheasant or a covey of quail, will often compel a younger, untrailed dog to honor that point by the sheer force of his personality – coupled with fear of the disapproval the older dog will show if the pup dashes in and bumps the bird.

The use of shock collars in modern field dog training more often amounts to abuse. I've seen frustrated amateur trainers get so angry at themselves when their dogs don't do what they hope the pups will that they zap them again and again. By not trusting the dog's nose, they inadvertently teach the pup to avoid pointing a bird, and for a very good reason: It doesn't want to get zapped again. Not long ago a neighbor of mine who once played in the NFL strapped a shock collar around his neck and zapped himself to see what it felt like. Paul's a big guy – six foot five by 250 pounds. The blast, he says, dropped him to his knees.

ON MORALS

Dogs are nonjudgmental. You can be doing anything – driving a car, cooking, going to the toilet, hammering nails, typing, even making passionate love – and your dog will sit there watching with a mild, slightly quizzical look in his eyes. He's waiting to see what's going to happen next, and wondering – hoping perhaps – that it will involve him and the out-of-doors.

A dog doesn't even care if you're robbing a bank or stealing from the poor box, even committing murder, so long as you take him with you. He'll be by your side through thick or thin, willing to help if called upon, mourn if you fail. Bill Sikes in *Oliver Twist* is a cruel, warped man, a lowlife and criminal. He beats his dog without mercy, never even gives it a name. Yet the dog follows him everywhere, and when Sikes inadvertently hangs himself at the novel's climax, the dog – some kind of pit bull, judging by Cruickshanks' drawings – who's been crouching on the roof slates, watching events unfold, howls pitifully and leaps for his master's shoulders – only to miss and fall to his death on the cobbles below.

Mad Dog Roy Earle's dog, Pard, in the movie *High Sierra* insists on joining his master during Earle's last stand in the mountains. Roy puts down his Lewis gun and is reaching out to help the dog up the last pitch of rocks when a waiting police sharpshooter kills the man with one shot from a scoped rifle. Poor Pard whines in sorrow.

I'm sure even Hitler's beloved German shepherd Blondi, who died with him and Eva Braun on April 30, 1945, in the Berlin bunker, thought the world of the *Führer* even as the poison went to work.

DOGS AND FAMILY VALUES

Woodrow Wilson once said: "If a dog will not come to you after he has looked you in the face, you ought to go home and examine your conscience." Dog's are nature's true conservatives. They prefer the status quo and would like it to prevail. They want the men, women and children in their lives to remain together, never changing, never leaving, never growing older, always ready to feed them when suppertime rolls around, always loving each other. When my wife and I are working toward an argument, our dogs excuse themselves from the room. Our tones of voice must tell them what's coming: subtle changes of tone that begin before we're even aware that contention is brewing. Dogs, like us, would probably like to live forever. They want things to continue as they are – food, love, sex, sleep, warmth, other dogs and adventure. Can we fault them for such a dream?

If all mankind disappeared tomorrow, whisked from the earth without a trace, what would become of our dogs? Many would die, of course, having grown too reliant on us to feed them, too soft to deal with the hard truths of survival. It would, for a while at least, be truly a dog-eat-dog world.

But dogs breed twice a year. In six years, a single litter could produce sixty-seven thousand offspring. In perhaps a hundred or maybe a thousand canine generations, the distinctions we know as breeds would slowly meld back toward the dog's prototype. The animal that would emerge would be clever, yellowish tan, weigh about thirty-five pounds, with ears erect or perhaps tippy at the top: a marvelous sniffing machine ready at a moment's notice to mate, to eat, to fight or just to take a snooze. Maybe a grin now and then. Soon the nights would be filled again with howlsong.

I'd like to think that somewhere in that chorus a note would ring out in mourning for the bipedal fools whom once they loved and served so well.

The nineteenth-century French poet Alphonse Marie Louis de Prat de Lamartine once wrote:

"When man is lonely, God sends him a dog."

But what if a dog is lonely?

If you don't have a dog . . . well, think about it.

Kunst

From *Lost Soldier Lake*: During World War II, the sparsely populated cutover of the upper Great Lakes country was dotted with prisoner-of-war camps. This isn't common knowledge – but there was nothing common about the breadth and depth of knowledge possessed by Bob Jones. In this excerpt from an unpublished novel, an escaped German POW, Gerhard Kunst, explores a wild northern lake that seems lost in time, an impression intensified by his discovery of a ghostly abandoned logging camp.

Kunst had not yet explored the far northern end of the lake, a reach of weed-choked water where dead snags poked from the shallows like the sprung ribs of drowned giants. The woods at that end appeared to have been burned over sometime in the not-too-distant past. The skeletons of ancient white pines, their thick boles now charred and grown over with random blotches of yellow and purple lichen, rose above an impassable tangle of low, bushy spruce, jackpine and juniper. He was afraid that the rowboat drew too much water for the shallows, but one morning while crossing the lake above the chateau he noticed what appeared to be a narrow, crooked channel threaded through the snags. He moved to the rear of the boat and nosed his way into the mouth of the channel, at first sculling, then poling with an oar rather than rowing, so that he could see what lay ahead.

Small fish darted in and out of the weeds on either side of the channel. He could make out the long, dark shapes of pike, lying in ambush in the weedbeds. They began to sink when the shadow of the boat moved over them, retreating to denser cover. Open patches in the reeds and cattails that stippled the surface held many knots of migrant teal, which either paddled deeper into the reeds or sprang straight upward from the water with a frantic whistling sound. Kunst could not tell if the whistling came from their wings or was rather a vocalization.

As he moved deeper into the twisting channel, he noticed that a large hawk, attracted no doubt by the flushing ducks, was following him overhead, circling high on fixed wings, using the boat as a hunter might use a flushing dog. Twice the hawk stooped – Kunst recognized it as a falcon by the sweep of its wings – but the teal proved too fast and dodgy for it. *It must be a young bird*, Kunst thought, *on its own now for the first time in its brief life, just learning to make its way in the world. Not unlike myself*, he thought.

141

For some minutes now he'd been aware of a faint, distant rumble, like the warning growl of a bear his father had once shot on the high peaks of the Harzgebirge . . . but this sound was too continuous for anything animal. As he rounded a sharp corner in the channel, the rumble intensified to a muted snarl, and he saw ahead of him a low, roiling wall of thin mist. It swirled and sparkled above an array of huge, glacially-scoured boulders, themselves gleaming black and white in the intermittent sunlight. A rapids. And a big one by the sound of it, perhaps a waterfall. It must be the outlet of the lake. Already he could feel the current quickening beneath the keel of the rowboat. He sculled hard for the shore to his right but the outflow had him locked in its grip. He was being swept toward the lip of the rapids. Kunst jumped to the midships thwart, sat down, and fumbled the oar-pin back into its lock. He began rowing backwards as hard as he could. It was no good. He was going over. He would have to ride it out.

Ahead of him, through the mist, he saw the young hawk perched upright on a snag just back of the shoreline. It seemed to be watching him . . .

The water bulged black through the mouth of the rapids, then boiled to racing white froth, the swirls and eddies of chaos, with the snarl rising now to an outright roar. Kunst tried to steer between two huge rocks that rose like domed, misshapen skulls dead ahead. The boat would not respond. He caromed into the righthand boulder, the impact almost catapulting him from the boat. The starboard oar hit the rock and exploded in splinters. A quick, skeptical prayer flashed through his mind – *Dorinda Wakerobin, save me if you can!* Then the bow hit another boulder, a glancing blow that somehow straightened the boat out.

Kunst scrambled back to the stern, using the remaining oar as a rudder as he tried to read the vees of the racing water. The rowboat steered better this way. He crouched low to reduce his center of gravity, up to his hips in the water he'd shipped when the boat hit the boulders and came close to capsizing. Another right hand turn, then a left, another left – and then he was out of it, into a slower, broader run. It opened out into another lake. He looked back. The rapids rose steep behind him, a hissing, twisting brown and white cataract that writhed like a giant snake – some kind of sub-arctic anaconda, perhaps – down from the higher elevation of the lake above.

This new lake was huge. He sculled out into it, searching the shoreline for signs of human habitation. Nothing. No boathouses, no piers, no flagpoles or cottages rising back from the shore.

Good, Kunst thought. *If I have to retreat from the Claudel cabin, this is one direction I might choose.* No pursuer would be likely to follow him down the rapids. The rapids was why this larger lake was not inhabited. No one could get to it easily. Sooner or later someone would build a road into it from the highway, but for now it remained terra incognita.

The boat rode low in the water, heavy with all the water he'd shipped in his wild ride down the rapids. He sculled to a fingernail of beach, ran the bow up the sand, and tipped the rowboat to empty it. Farther down the shoreline he spotted what looked like the ruins of an old pier, its pilings rotted with age and sheared off at the water's surface, no doubt by the workings of ice over many winters. The twin ruts of an overgrown wagon road led up from the lakeshore into the woods, and Kunst made out the moss-grown, roofless ruin of a log cabin on the low bluff overlooking the lake. Perhaps a trapper's cabin, dating back to the last century? He walked up the shoreline, skirting tangles of driftwood, bleached and rubbed smooth as bones by the action of winter ice and summer waves over many years, then followed the old wagon road into the shade of the forest. What he'd taken for a trapper's cabin was an old, decaying boathouse.

Then through the second-growth pines in the fading light he saw a square gray structure in the middle distance. A building of some sort. He made his way toward it with quiet footsteps. It was a low shed, he saw as he neared it, with a rusted stovepipe protruding from the sodden wood-shingled roof. Other wooden buildings were scattered in the clearing around it. A great soggy mountain of time-blackened sawdust reared dim behind the structures. A rusted machine with tall iron wheels stood in the open near one of the sheds. Thick chains drooped from its axle. He recognized it from his reading as a logging device called a go-devil, used by the old-time timber crews to haul sawlogs out of the deep woods. The go-devil in its day had been pulled by teams of oxen. He noticed another long, low, barnlike shed with a rank of rotting feed troughs lining its inner wall – clearly a stable. A toolshed stood nearby, with a barrel of rusting, discarded sawblades beside the workbench. He rummaged through it, finding a broken file and a half-empty tin of gummy kerosene in the barrel.

This must be an old logging camp from the Paul Bunyan days. Abandoned now for many decades since the big trees were felled.

Kunst investigated the building he took to be the barracks, or bunkhouse as it was called. The windows, with most of the glass still intact, were thick with the dust of ages, but the door creaked open to his push. Inside were rows of short, wooden three-tiered bunks with pine slats to support the straw tick mattresses. Most of the mattresses had been ripped open by woodmice and the stuffing stolen for their nests. Straw lay scattered across the spike-scarred wood floor. Connected to the bunkhouse by a roofed walkway was the mess-hall, with three long, rough wood tables flanked by split-log benches. In the far end Kunst found a big cast iron wood-burning cookstove, fuzzy with rust. But it would still hold a fire, he could see.

The roofs of the old buildings had leaked in a few spots, amoeba-like cankers of dry rot spreading from the leaks, but for the most part they were still sound. He could repair the worst leaks, using boards and nails pulled from other structures. He rummaged around through the kitchen and found a hammer, its handle gnawed to a nubbin by porcupines but the head itself still sound. When he returned to the bunk room, he saw a woodmouse standing on one of the straw mattresses, gazing at him with dark, wet, worried eyes, its paws folded as if in prayer against its pale gray chest. The mouse shrieked when Kunst approached and sprang back into the mattress.

After exploring his way around the lake, it took Kunst the rest of the day to track his boat back up the rapids, using back-eddies wherever he could, hauling it by main force by the painter attached to the bow, sometimes chest deep in the cold, swirling water, boots skidding on the slick boulders of banks. He was exhausted and chilled to the marrow by the time he returned to the cabin.

Glorious Carnage

Twice in his life Jones visited "pheasant heaven": in the cornfields of South Dakota in 1948, and at the Hesketh Estate near Towcester, England, in 1974. The two experiences were as different as denim coveralls and bespoke Savile Row suits – but in memory they wore equally well. Originally written for the anthology *Pheasant Tales* (1995), it too was included in *Dancers in the Sunset Sky* (1997).

The sad thing about living through a Golden Age is that you don't appreciate it while it's happening. The label is only applied later, when whatever art or craft or wonder the age apotheosized has turned to lead.

By all accounts, the heyday of pheasant hunting in North America took place during the decade right after World War II, when I was in my teens. The birds had been thriving in the heart of the continent since the early twentieth century, enjoying the largesse of that great but already-doomed American institution, the family farm. With its woodlots and weedy edges, its corn and grainfields, its fallow ground grown in native grasses and seed-bearing forbs, its swamps and marshes and low soggy places as yet undrained and thus still unplowed, the family farm was approximately Pheasant Heaven. There the long-tailed birds could feed heartily, most quietly, hide from their natural enemies when danger threatened, and raise their broods in relative peace. Egg-weakening pesticides were not yet in widespread use, and harvesting techniques were cruder than they are today, so that enough corn, wheat, barley or rye was left on the ground after the combines went through for plenty of birds to survive even the harshest of winters.

The war itself had given pheasant populations a boost. The younger men who normally hunted them hardest each fall were off somewhere in military service. Gas and tire rationing and the scarcity of shotgun shells kept all but the keenest of the remaining gunners out of the pheasant fields and cast a cloak of peace over the midwestern countryside. In 1945 the pheasant population of North and South Dakota alone was close to thirty million. Today, the whole U.S. probably contains no more than that number of the birds.

I started hunting during that prelapsarian age of abundance, but of course I was unaware of the unique opportunities it offered. Growing up in southern Wisconsin, I was not all that far – maybe six hundred miles, at best twelve hours of two-lane blacktop and Burma Shave signs in those days before the interstates – from the epicenter of the pheasant quake: Sioux Falls, South Dakota. As soon as I was old enough to drive, I should have begged, borrowed or hot-wired a car, bidden sayonara to my kinfolk, and headed west to the Dakotas with naught but my dog and my gun. Yet I only went there once to hunt. A classmate and hunting buddy of mine was the son of a wealthy businessman who had standing invitations to hunt the big spreads northwest of Sioux Falls every fall, and in 1948, Jack and I went with him.

I t was my first trip away from home without my parents, and there must have been a thousand heady new sights, sounds, smells and ideas that impressed me as much as the hunting itself. But now all that remains in my fading memory is *The Clouds* . . . .

Yes, that's just what they were – whole cloudbanks of birds getting up from the cornrows after each drive, getting up all at once with a hell of a racket, a rattling, cackling, metallic rush of sound, a tornadic roar compounded as much of primary feathers thrashing against dry cornstalks as it was of irate birds screaming; big explosions of color separating and lifting like giant flakes from the yellow-green background of standing corn – *bronze/red/green/white/dun*-colored splashes enclosed in swirls of wing-fanned dust – and over it all the thumps of big-bore shotguns, ragged at first but blending finally into a steady crescendo. The same sounds came from cornfields all around us, as far as the ear could hear. I remember thinking later that this was what the Civil War must have sounded like during big battles – Chickamauga or Chancellorsville or Gettysburg – sporadic firing at first as the skirmish lines met and felt each other out, then halfhearted volleys while platoons came into the line, then the whole thing rising in intensity at last to a sustained drumroll of musketry. All that was lacking were the cannons – though some of those 10-gauge magnums banged nearly as loud.

The battlefield metaphor applied as well to the most effective hunting techniques employed in those days of abundance. The Drive. We hunted big fields, five or ten acres each of standing corn, maybe more. A couple of dozen men and boys would take part in these drives – half as "pushers" or drivers, the other half as "blockers," who got most of the shooting. The drives usually took place in midmorning or late afternoon, when the pheasants were busy feeding. Dogs were rarely used in these drives, though I recall that exceptions were made for a few well-trained Labradors and springers who could be trusted to stay coolly at heel until the shooting stopped. A whining or barking dog could ruin a drive early on by causing the alerted pheasants to leak out around the edges of the drive line before flushing. Any pheasant, wild born or pen raised, would rather run than fly – or so all the old-timers said.

While the blockers quietly took their positions at the bottom of the field, the pushers mustered at the far end, forming a shallow, cup-shaped line of men stationed no more than ten yards apart. Any wider a dispersal would allow birds to sneak back between the pushers. You wouldn't think so gaudy a creature as the ringneck – a bird, moreover, that weighs three pounds and measures three feet from beak to tail tip – could get so invisible so quickly. But it could.

At a signal from the drive-master's police whistle, the pushers started forward. They had to march at a slow, steady, almost military pace – no straggling or sprinting ahead permitted – to keep the line intact and properly dressed. They zigzagged slightly as they marched, covering as much ground as possible. Because pushing was less likely than blocking to produce lots of good, fast shooting, most of the pushers were boys or young men. The rich old guys with their beer bellies got to block. Jack and I did a lot of pushing that week.

Gun safety was always on everyone's mind. The local newspapers and radio stations wouldn't let you forget it: *Teen Killed on Fatal Pheasant Drive, Fargo Resident Blinded by Shotgun Blast*. Here you had two rows of armed men, one approaching the other at a slow walk. Nerves on both sides were screwed to the yelping point, as if in impending battle. When the birds started to panic, to run and then to fly, the temptation would be strong – almost overpowering – to shoot straight ahead, and to shoot far too low. No one wanted to collect a faceful of No. 5s at close range. Nor to be the one who delivered it. The rules were clear and firmly enforced: Shoot only at high birds, no hens and preferably only after they'd passed you, going away.

Here's what I recall of a typical drive near Slodeth, South Dakota, nearly half a century ago. A crisp, clear October morning, temperature in the low 50s, sky the blue of Betty Grable's peepers. The hollow banging of gunfire drums in the distance, all around us. Hendry Gobel, who owns the farmland we're hunting, stands in the middle of the drive line. He's a tall, fat, ruddy-cheeked farmboy-cum-entrepreneur in his early thirties, a decorated infantry veteran of World War II in Europe, now a big wheel in the Chamber of Commerce who doubles as the town's Chevy dealer and owns the local feed store as well. Wearing a flap-eared Elmer Fudd hunting cap and a red-and-black-checkered deer hunting coat over his Oshkosh-B'gosh bib overalls, knee-high lace-up leather boots caked with Dakota mud and cow dung, he totes a scarred but well-oiled Winchester Model 12, its 30-inch barrel extended with a bulbous Polychoke.

Hendry Gobel talks with a dutchy lilt. "Okey-dokey, poys, dere's lotza dem longtails in dis field today – see 'em in dere, down between da rows? When I plo da vissel, you guys *marsch!*"

"*Jawohl, Herr Obersturmbahnführer*," Jack mutters beside me. Yes, Hendry Gobel is a wee bit bossy.

But Hendry was right: We *could* see the pheasants down there between the rows, dozens at least, perhaps as many as a hundred of them, stalking jerkily, chickenlike, peeking at windfallen corncobs, the long-spurred cocks strutting in their gorgeous vanity while the drab hens scuttled humbly around their lords and masters.

Nervously I shifted my gun, a well-worn old 12-gauge Winchester Model 97 pump that Jack's dad had loaned me for this hunt. It was his old gun. He was now shooting a Belgian Browning. My own single-shot 28-gauge wasn't quite the ticket for these birds and I'd left it back home in Wisconsin. Most of the guys I knew shot long-barreled, unplugged autoloaders or pumps on pheasants in those days. You rarely saw a double gun in the fields where the longtails played. My loaner was choked modified, but most of the others wore Polychokes. The bulges on the ends of the barrels made them look like tank cannons. Blockers set their Polychokes at open cylinder – very effective at close range – while pushers preferred modified or even improved cylinder settings for the longer shots they were likely to get. Some of the better or at least more confident shots even set them at full.

A sharp blast from Hendry Gobel's whistle set us in motion. I could see a few pheasants look up at the harsh sound – the cocks with their feathery blue "ears" atip – and begin scuttling toward the end of the field. We walked steadily, our weapons at port arms, gun butts thwacking the dry cornstalks, Hendry muttering occasional orders to slow down or speed up, or to keep our intervals neat and tidy. I could see sunlight glinting off the gun barrels of the blockers. About halfway down the field a rooster panicked and flew off, left to right. Hendry Gobel upped on the bird and dropped it as it cleared the right side of the field – a fifty-yard shot, maybe sixty. He was one of the more confident shooters.

At Hendry's shot other birds got up and some flew toward the blocking line. The shooting began, ragged at first, then faster.

"*Schnell!*" Hendry yelled. "Move faster, poys! Ve gotta get 'em up right now!"

We dog-trotted down the cornrows, our blood up, whooping and yelling like the Iron Brigade at Antietam, slapping the dry corn with our free hands, and the birds flushed almost in unison. The gunfire sounded like nonstop thunder, and suddenly it was raining pheasants. A cock came cackling right toward me, the ripped-metal blare getting louder with each beat of his wings. I skidded to a halt and swung with him as he swept past me, seeing his bright black eye locked on mine, then took him going away in a flurry of tiny rump feathers. Another came blowing past me and I swung and hit the trigger. Nothing. I'd forgotten to work the slide. By the time I shucked in another shell, most of the birds were dead or gone. All across the bottom of the field, feathers filtered down through the still morning air. But then as we walked the remaining distance toward the blockers, a single skulking rooster flushed from beneath my feet – straight up. I nailed him at the top of his rise just an instant before Jack shot. When that once-beauteous bird hit the ground it was nothing but rags.

"I guess it's yours," Jack said.

"What's left of him," I said. "Thanks for nothing."

I think we bagged more than fifty cock pheasants on that drive alone – the number that sticks in my fading memory is fifty-six. Of course I'd killed only two of them, and Jack had three plus his spoiling shot on my last bird. Hendry Gobel dropped five, one for each round in his gun, as did some of the other more experienced shooters, Jack's dad among them. It was slaughter, no doubt about it, but what the hell, why not? The birds were there in abundance – no, in *over*abundance. In a way they were a cash crop. The more of them we killed, the less corn they'd eat from Hendry Gobel's fields, and thus the more money he'd realize from his harvest. Not only that, but Hendry charged the guests who stayed in his big, roomy farmhouse fifteen dollars a day for the privilege, which included delicious meals heavy on roast pheasant stuffed with apples and sauerkraut.

But the drives, though exciting and highly productive, weren't near as much fun as the hunts Jack and I made alone during the early afternoons. While the old guys swilled schnapps and beer, played sheepshead or took their sonorous siestas, Jack and I worked the edges of Gobel's swampland down near Tomahawk Slough for nooning roosters. Hendry's young black Lab, Mädchen, was only too glad to accompany us. In hip-boots and high spirits we slogged the marshes with Maddy porpoising ahead. It was fast, awkward shooting when she flushed a bird, with us standing ankle-deep in the muck, unable to shift our feet quickly, snap-shooting usually at big, fast-jumping cockbirds glimpsed only briefly through cattails and sawgrass against the hard blue sky. Sometimes we fell, knocked backward from the greasy-grass hummocks by the recoil of off-balance shots, but the water always felt good in that heat. I once emerged from a dunking with a mud turtle in my boot. We usually dragged back to the farmhouse before three o'clock, sweaty, flushed, reeking of foul-smelling swamp slime – but carrying at least half a dozen roosters between us. Gobel would *tut-tut* at our filth, grin fondly at our birds, sluice off the worst of the muck with a garden hose, and then it was off for another field drive . . . .

So that was my moment in Pheasant Heaven. I never thought I'd see its like again. But I was wrong, though it took a while.

Soon after the South Dakota excursion, I discovered girls. Then it was college, followed by a stint in the navy, marriage, fatherhood, a newspaper job in Milwaukee, then a move to New York and later Los Angeles for *Time* magazine. Then back to New York again for the Psychedelic Sixties – the Vietnam War, counterculture, assassinations, riots in the black ghettos and suchlike follies.

Not much time for hunting with all of that going on. But I finally got back to it on a serious basis in 1964, when my wife and I bought a house in northernmost Westchester County, about an hour by commuter train from New York City. Behind the house lay 900 unposted acres of hilly, undeveloped woodland and overgrown hayfields. It was prime cover for grouse and woodcock back then – alder brakes down low for the bogsuckers, lots of ancient but still-fruitful apple trees, plenty of white pines for grouse to roost in, wild cherries, fox-grape hells, hickories and big stands of sumac and doghair aspen up high, the whole of it crosshatched with miles of neatly built stone walls along which the partridge liked to skulk. But there were always a few pheasants hanging out in the uncut meadows that dotted the second-growth woods. I soon had a canine team to help me harass them – a big yellow Lab named Simba and a keen but slightly wacky German shorthair called Max.

These pheasants were the wild descendants of stock initially released before World War II, not pen-raised birds. They were fast afoot, veritable Roger Bannisters of roosterdom, and extremely reluctant to fly even when pinned dead to rights by the pointer. But Simba quickly learned that whenever Max locked up, his best bet was to circle out beyond the bird, then move back in on it. We got our share of flushes. I still remember one longtail that almost eluded us. It was a snowy day in November. We'd hunted the long wooded ridge at the top of a big meadow, then struck off down the brush-grown stone wall that bisected the field. From the way the dogs acted I knew there was a pheasant running ahead of them. Simba finally got in front of it near the bottom and the bird flushed – a rooster. But before I could mount the gun, the bird had lighted in the uppermost branches of a tall ash tree, from which lofty vantage point he looked down and gave us the raspberry in the form of a jeering, cocksure cackle.

What to do? I'd gotten religion by then and refused on principle to pot the bird out of the tree. We waited it out – five minutes, ten minutes – hoping he'd get nervous and fly. He didn't. Finally I leaned my gun within easy reach against the ash trunk, made a snowball and threw it at the pheasant. I zinged half a dozen snowballs at that cockbird before I threw a strike. He whirled and launched; I grabbed the gun, fumbled at the safety – and missed him twice. He soared back up the way we'd come down, finally landing at the top of the field a quarter of a mile away.

The dogs seemed amused at my bad marksmanship. "All right, lads," I told them gruffly, "let's start hiking." We plodded back uphill through the ankle-deep snow, halting near where I'd marked the rooster down. Up there, thanks to the wind, the snow lay thinner on the ground. The field had been mowed in the late summer and the grass was short, just the tips of it showing through the fluffy white cover. Any gaudy cockbird hunkered down in that stubble would have stood out like a zit on a teenager's face. No bird in sight. But then I noticed a straight line of taller grass, about a foot high, that grew along a fallen strand of wire, the remnants of an electric fence long out of use. I started walking the wire with the dogs just ahead of me. About halfway along, the snow suddenly erupted as the rooster took flight – from a patch of grass you wouldn't think could hide a field mouse.

I rolled him twenty yards out . . .

That's the way it was with those pheasants of the Near Northeast. I pretty much despaired of ever again seeing the kind of nonstop, slam-bang pheasant shooting I'd enjoyed in the heartland as a boy. Meanwhile, burned out on global violence, I'd quit *Time* and joined up with *Sports Illustrated*, where I covered the gentler worlds of pro football, motor sports and the outdoors. One of my beats was the Formula I racing circuit, and in 1973 at the U.S. Grand Prix in Watkins Glen, New York, I met Lord Alexander Hesketh. Then twenty-three years old, he was a plump, witty, wealthy and somewhat flaky Brit who had entered a new F-1 team into the lists. His driver then was the late James Hunt, a handsome, nervy young stalwart who went on to win the World Driving Championship but achieved greater name recognition when the actor Richard Burton stole his wife. Over dinner one night in Corning, New York, Alexander was telling me about his baronial estate, Easton Neston, north of London. "We got loads of pheasants," His Lordship said, "Why don't you pop over some time for a shoot?"

I pounced on the invitation like a springer on a covey of quail.

In January of 1974, the last month of the English pheasant season, I flew to London and then headed north, roughly a two-hour drive from Piccadilly Circus. Easton Neston occupies 7,000 acres near the town of Towcester (rhymes with "boaster"). The Hesketh manor house, built largely of marble, was begun in the late 1680s and completed half a century later. The ceilings in some of its rooms were thirty feet high. You could park a Rolls Royce in any of the downstairs fireplaces. Entering the house, I was first impressed by the sepulchral chill, then by the sight of a full-mounted brown bear rearing up in a dark hallway corner. Wintry lights glinted off suits of armor arrayed behind the bear. On the table in the entry hall lay a paperback copy of *M.A.S.H. Goes to Maine*, a huge bowie knife, and a guest book full of the scrawled signatures of Churchills, Windsors and Douglas-Homes. In the echoing dining room, a brace of Rubens paintings added a touch of warmth to the background behind the butler's eyes. The erect figure of a stuffed snowy owl glowered from one corner. I stood near the cracking fireplace, warming my bum as I sipped a welcoming glass of sherry, and admired the tapestries on the walls. Beyond the mullions of the rain-streaked casement windows I could see pheasants strutting haughtily on the putting-green lawns. I was a long way from Hendry Gobel's farmhouse in South Dakota.

At dinner that evening the rest of the guests assembled, and after a few minutes it became evident that what we Americans take for satirical novels of English country life are nothing more than straight reportage. Consider if you will the Lambton sisters, Anne and Rose. Anne was small and pale with the sharp-toothed grin of a dolphin. She affected a freaky air and a faux-Cockney accent – "wiv" for "with," for example – and feigned a total incomprehension of affairs in the "real world."

"Are vey still hafing vose 'orrible bombs in Londing?" she asked. "Oy 'aven't bean vare in mumfs. Oh pigs! Oy split me caviar!" She laughed with an oinking snort.

Her sister, Rose, was taller but even more out of touch, a whiter shade of pale with dyed, dark-red hair. She'd brought her pet dog along, a tetchy little Shelty bitch that lurked beneath the dining table nipping at ankles and whining now and then like a household ghost. Next to Rose sat Andrew Fraser, a younger son of Lord Lovat who led the No. 4 Commandos during World War II. A keen shot, dark, trim and amused, Andrew seemed very fit – except for his right eye, which he'd damaged quite severely not long before when he threw a firecracker into a bonfire. "The surgeons removed the lens," he explained, very cool and dispassionate, "but the rest of the eye is still sound. They say that perhaps I can wear a contact lens and regain part of the sight, but until then I'm afraid my shooting is a bit off form."

Across from Fraser sat Robert Femor-Hesketh, Alexander's younger brother. (A third brother, John, the youngest, was not present. An even keener shot than Fraser, John usually spent the bird season, from the Glorious Twelfth of August to the end of January, traveling around Britain in a car, complete with a built-in bed, shooting partridge, pheasants, grouse, woodcock and wildfowl wherever he could glean an invitation.) Robert Hesketh, or "Bobs" as he was known, proved a shorter, trimmer version of Alexander, who in those days at least stood six-four and weighed in at 240 pounds. Wide-shouldered and flat-bellied by contrast, Bobs sported a leonine mane and beard. Tough, bouncy and glowering, he too was a crack shot and competitor, as would be evidenced the next morning under the flighted pheasants of Easton Neston.

Dawn broke through a fine, cold rain – little more than a mist at first, but with teeth in it. I'd debated long and hard over dressing for the shoot in English style – Wellies, moleskin breeks, Norfolk jacket, ascot, Barbour coat, oiled cotton shooting cap, maybe even one of those classy fold-down shooting sticks. But no, I couldn't go that route – too phony, too foppish. Instead I dressed in my usual upland attire: scuffed but well-greased Russell boots, khaki canvas brush pants and game jacket, worn over a red-checked wool shirt, and topped off with a scuffy Jones cap replete with the requisite grouse tailfeather. Let them sneer their Limey sneers at the country-bred cousin from over the pond. I was a descendant of Natty Bumppo, by Gawd, and I'd shoot their eyes out . . .

Like hell I would.

We were eight guns that day, each man backed up by a loader to keep his matched pair of doubles primed and ready. My guns were slim, elegant, side-locked Bosses, long-barreled 12-bores, of course, courtesy of His Lordship (though only for the day, alas). My loader was a short, cheery assistant gamekeeper named Sid Atker, who chattered merrily as we slogged through a field of winter wheat to the first stand of the day.

"Ah, yes," quoth Sid, "most of the land is under cultivation, but His Lordship maintains about seven thousand pheasant on the estate, that he does, and shoots it only six or eight times a season, killing up to eight hundred birds a go. But today I reckon we won't kill no more than five or six hundred, not with the weather like this – watch your step there, sir, it's mucky goin', innit? – no, this rain will keep 'em from flyin', too heavy they get in the wet like this, they'd rather run than fly," – and where had I heard that before? – "but here come the beaters now, sir, you'd better get ready."

The beaters, some fifty men and boys and a few small girls from the neighboring village, pushed through the first patch of wood, trilling and chirruping and bellowing to frighten the pheasants ahead of them, thwacking the bushes and tree trunks with their clubs, now and then coshing a hare or rabbit as it tried to cut back through the line. The gamekeeper, a red-faced sergeant-major type who ran the shoot with an iron hand, directed the beaters with his police whistle (just like Hendry Gobel).

As the beaters neared the wood edge we could see the pheasants milling – tall, tan, scuttling figures, reluctant to approach the open ground. Then they exploded with a rattle of wet wings and lined out toward the guns where we stood a hundred yards away in the open field, each man fifty yards from his nearest neighbor. By the time the birds reached us, they were at full flight speed and thirty yards high.

Guns began slamming all up and down the line. Blue smoke hung suspended in the drizzle and drifted slowly in the light, cold air. The birds, when hit, seemed to double in size, their feathers puffing, then crumpled and fell with wings all askew. They thumped hard on the wet ground. Then again that strange phenomenon, only witnessed when clouds of birds are killed directly overhead. What appeared to be bronze snowflakes began to fall from the sky: pheasant feathers. Soon they were thick as a blizzard. I caught a glimpse, between shots, of James Hunt poking awkwardly at a high double and missing both birds. He had never shot before.

I saw Andrew Fraser, bad eye and all, center a cockbird, then with his left barrel knock feathers from another that sloped away to fall behind the shooting line. Not to worry, the dogs – thick-bodied, keen-eyed Labs that waited phlegmatically to the rear – would gather it up later with the other wounded birds. I watched Robert Hesketh just long enough to see him drop five doubles in a row, faster than it takes to write this sentence, all of the birds falling within ten yards of where he stood. None of them thrashed for even a moment. As for me, on that first drive, I killed some birds, but wounded or missed a lot more.

While the dogs collected the dead and the cripples, we guns moved to the next drive, a gloomy spot known as The Wilderness. My post was at the edge of the wood, in a cut among some pines. The birds came out of the trees fast and low, appearing in full flight only ten yards ahead of me as they bored through the feathery upper branches. It was snapshooting of the sort familiar to North American grouse and woodcock shooters, and my score quickly improved. I knocked down a clean double, then another, then a string of singles, mixed in with a few fretful misses, then a final double. Already my shoulder was aching. The Bosses, beautiful as they looked, were clearly too short for my length of pull.

Then a figure emerged from the stiffening rain. It was Alexander's mother, Kisty, the widow lady of the manor, a strong, handsome, friendly woman with a liking for America and Americans. Except for bright red knee socks, she was clad all in black – black breeks, black jacket, a wide-brimmed Andalusian-style hat, and a black eyepatch. She'd lost the sight of one eye as the result of a recent car crash, but the eyepatch gave her a jolly piratical look. Her good eye twinkled through the mist.

"I've been watching you, Yank," she said. "You shot well in this close covert. How do you like it so far?"

"Glorious carnage," I said.

She laughed, "Strange people, the English," she mused, knocking gobbets of clay from her boots with a gnarled walking stick. The mud fell with a sodden thump on a dead cock pheasant that lay at her feet. "They call this recreation."

154

The rest of the day was a blur of falling birds, my ears ringing with the hollow, ragged rage of 12-bore explosions, the hallooing of the beaters, the strident chirp of the gamekeeper's whistle. The whole world – black, gray, brown, green – smelled of blood and burnt gunpowder. At one point, a pure white pheasant flushed and swiveled its way through the barrage, miraculously escaping unhit. At another, a small, shaggy animal that resembled a long-legged pig emerged from the woods, did a double take on seeing the guns, and bounded back to safety. "Chinese barking deer," explained Kisty, who was strolling past at the moment. "A few of them wandered in here from an estate farther south. Ugly little things, though, aren't they? We don't shoot 'em."

The final tally for the day was 580 pheasant, sixteen duck (mallards that flushed from ponds in the fields), a dozen woodcock, and eight wood pigeons. Only a middling score for Easton Neston. "I'd hoped for at least twelve hundred," Hesketh told me later. This was not simply a matter of bruised pride: English landowners sell the game killed in such shoots to restaurants in London and elsewhere, using the money thus earned to defray the costs of gamekeepers, beaters, loaders and so on. A poor shoot is money out of pocket. The gamekeepers laid the birds out for us near the manor house, on the putting-green lawn. It was quite a sight. I asked Sid Atker if he'd kept count on how many I'd shot.

"You did right well for a newcomer, sir," he said. "I counted seventy-eight pheasant that fell to your gun, plus a couple of woodcock and a pigeon or two. Right well indeed, I'd say."

Later, back in my room for a welcome, blood-warming bath, I noticed that my shooting arm was black and blue from shoulder to elbow, the inevitable legacy of ill-fitting guns. But it was a small price to pay for the experience. Once again the heavens had blessed me with the manna of falling feathers. No, we hadn't done as well as the shooting party at Lord Stamford's park, which over four days in early January of 1864 had tallied 4,045 pheasant, 3,902 rabbits, 860 hares and 59 woodcock. Nor would I personally pose much of a threat to the shooting record of the late Lord Ripon, who between 1867 and 1904 settled the hash of 142,343 pheasant, 97,759 partridge, 56,460 grouse, 29,858 rabbits and 27,686 hares. Frankly, I doubt that anyone will. Yet I'm glad that I had at least two chances in my lifetime – in the South Dakota of 1948 and the English countryside of 1974 – to see and shoot at masses of flighted pheasants, wild clouds of them.

It was glorious carnage indeed.

The Leopard of Lorian Swamp

Fact, fable or a .577 round of both? Few writers could juggle the elements of good story-telling as nimbly as Jones, and in this harrowing, darkly comic tale from *African Twilight* (1994), his mastery is on full display. Many readers will recognize the legendary Col. Richard Meinertzhagen, whose exploits in Africa (and elsewhere) fascinated Jones, as the model for the casually haughty Brits – officers in the colonial Kenyan military – who find themselves being stalked by the leopard of the story's title.

> *And slowly answered Arthur from the barge:*
> *The old order changeth, yielding place to new;*
> *And God fulfills himself in many ways,*
> *Lest one good custom should corrupt the world.*
> – Tennyson, *Idylls of the King*

We had just finished a memorable safari in the Northern Frontier District of Kenya, one on which I had taken a very fine leopard in the eleventh hour of the final day. It was my first. A male, it pegged out at nearly eight feet from nose to tail tip, and we were celebrating the kill, relaxing at Bill Winter's home in Nanyuki before my imminent departure stateside. It was a Sunday afternoon, cool and cloudy on the slopes of Mount Kenya. We decided to run down to the Sportsman's Arms for tea. A British regimental band held forth on the hotel grounds that lazy evening, and we took our tea on the veranda to the strains of "The Colonel Bogey March."

You know the tune, but if not perhaps the words often sung to it will bring back the melody.

"It's horseshit – that makes the grass grow green . . ."

I sang them *sotto voce* between sips of piping hot Darjeeling.

"Look at that old gent, Bwana," Bill whispered after swallowing a bite of lemon tart. He cast his eyes briefly to my left. Seated near us at a wickerwork garden table, one gouty foot propped on a chair as he beat time to the music, was a splendid wreck of a fellow, mottled of cheek but bright of eye, with a hoary set of sidewhiskers and a magnificent if somewhat drinksodden moustache. He sipped at a rust-colored gin and bitters, no ice.

"Sir George McArthur Ponsonby, V.C.," Bill said. "A grand old ruin, hey? But he was a *dume* in his day, a real bull. Won the Victoria Cross at Passchendaele in the Great War, marched on Waziristan with General

Climo in 1919, exemplary Colonial service, both military and civilian, in Nyasaland, the Cameroons, and Tanganyika, a veteran of safaris *mingi sana* – many, many great hunts – back in the days when the word meant something, when they went in on foot, with porters balancing the loads on their heads. He can tell you a tale or two, old Sir George. What say we ask him over for a drink and a bit of a chin-wag?"

We did, and in due course Bill told Sir George about my leopard.

"Wasn't by chance wearing gold ankle bracelets, was it?" Sir George asked when I finished my modest story. "Graven with mystical writing?"

"No, sir," I answered, puzzled. Bill was grinning behind his hand. "Should it have been?"

Sir George chuckled and assured me most definitely that it should not have been. Not if I valued my health and sanity.

Bill winked, then tugged his left earlobe, a signal advising me to activate the small tape recorder I carried, locked and loaded, in the breast pocket of my bush vest.

Sir George ordered another gin-and-bitters. When it arrived, he proceeded to relate a tale of his own concerning leopards, the tale of a strange and dreadful hunt. It had occurred nearly half a century earlier, in the same reaches of the NFD from which we had just returned. Some years ago, he began, in the early 1920s he and another Englishman were hunting along the Ewaso Nyiro River, slowly following its sinuous route through that great game country to where it hemorrhages finally, as so many African rivers do, into the sands of an ever-expanding desert, leaving only a fetid marsh to punctuate its finish. Here then is his tale, abridged only slightly so as not to offend what is blithely termed a "family" readership . . .

I n the course of our trek down the 'Washo,' we happened upon a small *manyatta* – a village of shabby grass huts – on the edge of the Lorian Swamp, where that great blood-red river ends its career. The inhabitants, a degenerate breed of Marsh 'Dorobos, had never seen white men before. They fled weeping at the approach of our safari. Our porters, feeling superior to these rude savages, laughed long and hard at them, making jests in raucous Kiswahili that accused the poor savages of such bestial sins as snake worship and intimate congress with hyenas.

"The naked bums of these dusky Adams and Eves had no sooner vanished into the nettles than our lads began looting. We had already discovered, to our mutual dismay, that there was no controlling these boisterous hirelings once theft was in prospect, short of shooting a few of them. Twice thus far we'd been forced to do so, and both of us feared that yet another such episode would precipitate a full-scale mutiny. Our ammunition was running low. We might not be able to quell a concerted uprising without burning the rest of it, at which point our own lives would be forfeit. And even if we slew enough of the obstreperous rascals to bring the remainder to their senses, would the survivors fulfill their duties to us the rest of the way to the Coast, or decamp in the dark of moon with all they could pilfer?

"What to do, what to do . . . . My companion must have perceived my indecision. He smiled coolly.

" 'Heigh-ho,' said Rawley. 'I don't know about you, Sir George, but I fear my heart's all a-twitter.'

"The ball was now clearly in my court.

" 'By my troth, I care not,' quoth I, with what I hoped was an insouciance equal to the moment. 'We owe God a swoon, and let it go which way it will, he who swoons this year is quit for the next.'

"Rawley punched me lightly on the shoulder. *'Pukka sabib,'* said he.

"At that point, Kabiza, our burly headman, emerged from a squalid hut with a woman in tow. He crowed lustily. The other lads gathered round in eager anticipation. It was the old story. Nothing better enlivens a friendly afternoon of looting than a spot of jiggery-pokery! Though our gang would have been content with a withered old crone, this woman was young, nubile, and to some tastes, I reckon, quite lovely to gaze upon.

"She had something of the look of a Somali about her, a tall, lissome, coffee-colored wench with the poignant overbite and wide-set, almond eyes peculiar to Hamitic women. The women you see in those ancient Egyptian murals at the Victoria & Albert, you know, or among the Berbers and Tuaregs of contemporary Saharan Africa.

"Oddly enough, she didn't seem frightened, though she must have known how these sessions inevitably end. One of the bullies, his passion and interest spent, brains his sobbing victim with disdainful swing of his knob-kerri. Yet she stood there in the mud, the late, low sunlight mottling her golden skin, and smiled inscrutably into the distance.

"An innocent young savage, you ask?

"I wondered myself, even then. A brace of delicate, artfully wrought ornaments, forged from some precious metal, encircled her trim ankles, touches of a higher, perhaps forgotten culture. The anklets winked in the day's red decline. The girl's cat-like eyes impressed me as well, empty as they were of any recognizable human emotion. They had a classic, almost Pharaonic look to them, as if they had been carved from antediluvian amber and buried for centuries in some great king's tomb. Then she yawned, quite prettily it seemed to me, and turned to Kabiza with a playful smile.

"That worthy threw her to the ground, cast aside his *shuka*, the toga-like garb of the country, and with a low growl proceeded to cover her. The girl drew back her knees, whether in repulsion or acceptance of her fate, I know not. Kabiza's rowdy cohorts cheered. He thrust home . . .

"I averted my eyes in shame, then looked back suddenly as a hideous, soul-chilling cry split the air."

He paused to sip his gin-and-bitters.

"Who was it?" I asked.

"Kabiza, of course," he said, smiling wetly. "The headman's hips seemed to buck upward for an instant. He rolled to one side, on his back. his entrails spilled forth onto the mud in a welter of gore. His eyes bulged horribly, the scarred, ape-like face contorted in pain, his fingers clutching spasmodically at his innards as he tried vainly to replace them within his gaping abdomen. And Kabiza of course, disemboweled, shuddered and died a few moments later."

Again Sir George paused for refreshment.

"And then?"

He smiled once more.

"The girl was gone!" Sir George said triumphantly. "We stood dumfounded. 'My God!' Rawley suddenly cried. 'Look, there!' He pointed toward a narrow alleyway that led between the huts into the depths of the swamp. I saw the thing for only an instant – the sleek, sinuous form of a leopard, its hind paws and white-furred underbelly spattered with blood, disappearing swiftly into the man-high marsh grass. Or so it seemed.

"We sat long and late at the campfire that night. Rawley had broken out the medicinal brandy – Napoleon, 1813 if I'm not mistaken – and we slugged it back as if it were hock. Our rifles stood leaning against our camp chairs. The firelight played eerily on Rawley's manly features, aging him to a seamed simulacrum of himself, a feeble octogenarian if you will.

"Major Alistair Frederic Rawley-DePuis, D.S.O., V.C., late of Her Majesty's Coldstream Guards, was no stranger to the arcana of the African bush. Seconded at his own request to the King's African Rifles at the end of the Boer War, he had battled Kikuyu, Turkana, Suk and Nandi spearmen from Kirinyaga to the Nyandarua, from Lake Rudolph to the Kisii Plateau. By his own modest count, he had slain full three score or more of these swarthy adversaries, all of them in single combat. 'It's amazing,' he told me once, a sweet smile playing about his lips, 'how easily a bayonet slips into a man, and how difficult it is to withdraw.'

"He had fatally pistoled a laibon of the Kavirondo nation at point-blank range during a nefarious native ambush, wrestled a *rungu* from a crazed Maasai moran and killed him with his own warclub, been hexed by a

Turkana witch whose potion of spider venom and euphorbia sap had been slipped unbeknownst to him into his sundowner by a turncoat batman, survived countless life-threatening episodes of African mayhem and intrigue. After seventeen years of service on the Dark Continent, though, his good Dorsetshire common sense had been subtly altered. He had begun to believe in The Darkness.

" 'She's a Leopard Woman,' he said now. 'No doubt of it, Sir George.'

" 'Oh, I say, old son; I could not help but splutter. 'Isn't that putting, er . . . just a touch too much credence in the arcane?'

" 'Not at all, he replied. 'Though I've never come across it myself, the literature teems with eyewitness reports of such phenomena. Many of these African witchwomen have the power, one way or t'other, to change themselves at will into leopards or hyenas or aardwolves, even puff adders or mambas if they so choose, or so at least I've read. An old mess-mate of mine, Colonel Sidney Cartwright-Graham, reports witnessing just such a transmogrification in his book, *Nightdrums & Devilry in Danakil Land.* Chapter XIII, I believe. And Professor Woolworthy, the Cambridge myth wallah, devotes three whole chapters to the phenomenon, citing numerous examples in one or another of his swotty tomes – *Black Rites on the Blue Nile*, if I'm not mistaken.'

" 'But might there not be a simpler explanation?' I asked. 'The girl could have had a knife secreted about her person, and when Kabiza jumped aboard she gralloched him.'

" 'You saw the leopard as clearly as I,' Rawley replied. 'Where did it come from, and in broad daylight to boot?'

"He had a point, of course. Yet the eyes have a way of playing tricks on the forebrain, particularly at moments of sudden stress, when confusion reigns and events transpire too swiftly. The African bush, as I'm sure you chaps are well aware, provides an all-too-fertile ground for the sensitive European imagination. Fantasy runs riot.

" 'Well, at least the incident seems to have put a quietus to the porters' mischief,' I said. 'I noticed them just now replacing their ill-gotten goods, all of them meek as lambs.'

"We decided to break camp at first light the following morning. The sooner we were clear of this unholy ground, the better. Another five days of long marches through the Hothori and Sabena Deserts should find us on the verdant banks of the Tana River, where we could hire new porters and continue our hunt in a more leisurely fashion, downriver toward Lamu and the coast.

"The boys built a tall, strong *zareeba* of thornbush around the *manyatta*, fueled up their fires, and wrapped themselves uneasily in their blankets for the night. We too retired. About three hours later

Rawley and I were awakened by screams and shouts. Snatching our rifles, we leaped out of the tent clad only in our *kikois*. Total confusion reigned. Finally we were able to learn that the leopardess had returned, grabbed Achmed, one of our likeliest lads, between her jaws, then quick as a wink bounded clean over the top of the *zareeba*, back into that awful darkness. We could hear the poor boy screaming and bewailing his fate, the sound fading slowly into the depths of the morass. Then through the dark came an audible crunch, followed by silence. Rawley and I sat up the rest of the night, our rifles across our knees, but she did not return. No, no . . .

"No, she saved that for the morrow."

S ir George finished his gin-and-bitters, ordered another from the comely Meru waitress hovering nearby with her tray, then continued. "We were up before dawn, the boys gladly shouldering their heavy loads, our meager, dwindling supplies as well as an abundance of horns, hides and no small weight of ivory, for Rawley had slain a *tembo* whose tusks weighed more than 140 pounds each, and I one only marginally less toothy. Shunning a proper breakfast, we wolfed down a few pieces of biltong on the march.

"We gave the Lorian Swamp a wide berth as we skirted it, heading south by southeast for the Tana. Toward noon, just as we neared the end of the savannah, with the supposed safety of open desert visible dead ahead, the leopardness struck again. Creeping up through the tall grass, she nabbed the last porter in the long line. Nabbed him by the throat this time, so he could utter no more than a muffled shriek before she disappeared back into the waving grass, with him dangling crosswise in her jaws. Once more we were treated to the sound of The Queen of Darkness at table, harsh purrs of contentment emanating from her throughout her repast.

"We hurried on. Ironically enough, the Sabena Desert, one of the fiercest in the world, offered us our only hope of succor. Not even a spring hare could hide on its barren surface, much less a large, spotted cat, no matter how stealthy her approach. The pitiless sun, which dried us like so many pieces of that very biltong wherewith we had broken our fast, at the same time illumined everything under its gaze. We counted on it to highlight the leopardess, granting us at least enough law to get off a shot or two – from my 'best' gun, a .450 Rigby Nitro Express double rifle, or Rawley's .303 Lee-Enfield. Ah, but Old Sol let us down, that he did.

"At midafternoon she appeared out of nowhere – perhaps a small, unnoticed depression in the otherwise flat ground. She disemboweled two more porters with quick paw slashes, leaving her just time enough, before we came up, to peel away their faces with her remorseless jaws. This time we did not pause to bury the bodies.

"All day it went that way, and the next day, and the one after that. Our route across that ghastly wasteland was marked, and perhaps still is, with the bones of our dead. And with the loads they were carrying. Many fine trophies went to waste out there, eaten no doubt by jackals and hyenas.

"We tried, for the first few evenings, sitting up over the corpses of the newly slain in hopes of a shot at this demon leopardess. But she was too clever for us. While Rawley looked one way and I the other, she crept into camp unbeknownst and murdered a few more of our gibbering porters.

"Finally Rawley had had enough. 'The next time she strikes,' said he, 'I'm going after her.'

" 'But man!' I remonstrated, 'that's just what she wants. She'll do for you, mark my words!' All the rational explanations I had held of Kabiza's death had long since evaporated in the desert's dry air, in the unmitigated terror of that awful, endless trek. 'She's uncanny,' I cried, 'unkillable, the Devil herself, incarnate!'

"He smiled, rather sadly, I thought. As if he were resigned.

" 'I cannot sit idly by for one more hour without doing something,' he calmly replied. He picked up his Lee-Enfield and checked its fittings, tightening an action screw here, a sling swivel there, then applying a thin coat of gun oil to the parts he felt required it. Lastly he scrutinized his soft-point bullets for deformities, to ensure against jams. It was a work-worn weapon, that Enfield. It had seen service in South Africa, France, India and Africa, from Cairo to Capetown. It had dispatched more big game and more enemies of the Crown than any other dozen of its kind. Now it would pit its pluck, its English mettle (if you'll pardon the pun) against the dark, daft power of the Supernatural . . .

"Just then came an all-too-familiar scream and gurgle, trailing off into the night. Without a moment's hesitation, Rawley plunged into the gloom."

Sir George stopped. The regimental band had packed up its instruments and long since departed. Night had fallen, and with it a sharp, bone-biting chill. The old gentleman peered about, then shivered.

"Perhaps we'd best resume our conversation at a later date," he said. "It's getting a bit parky for these old bones."

"No, no, Sir George!" I said, nearby babbling. "I'm leaving for America in the morning; don't know when I'll be back again. Why don't you come inside and join us for supper? Be our guest. It would give me great pleasure."

"Hmm," he said doubtfully, knowing full well that he had his hook firmly planted in the corner of my mouth, through and through. The tippet would never part. "Perhaps just a small bite of something, a modest

Ploughman's Lunch, no more, but in from the cold, at any rate."

It seemed to take forever, what with our moving inside, waiting for a table to be readied. Sir George making a long overdue visit to the loo, then ordering drinks and dinner. But finally he was settled.

"Where was I?"

"Rawley had just plunged . . ."

"Yes, yes – into the gloom. I sat there alone for a minute, maybe more. Then my suddenly aroused sense of shame at being thought a coward propelled me after him. I pushed through the *zareeba* into the chill desert night. Rawley was nowhere to be seen, not even as my eyes adjusted to the dark. Nor could I hear him. Or anything, for that matter, save some jackals yipping far away, off in the back of beyond. I walked cautiously forward, the loaded Rigby at high port arms, my thumb on the safety for a quick shot, rather as if I were on a rough shoot for suddenly springing red partridge.

"Off to my left I could see the dark line of a *nullah* – a coulee or gulch, I believe you Yanks call it. Somehow I was instantly, perhaps instinctively, certain that the final act of this ghastly tragedy would unfold right there. I walked toward it with mounting trepidation. As I neared the edge, I heard a low whistle. It was Rawley, crouched in the ice of a boulder. I crouched low and made for him.

" 'She's down there,' he whispered. 'Eating our man, the good Baraka. You can hear her at it.' I listened. I could. 'But you must return to camp, Sir George. This is my job, by rights. I invited you on this safari, and thus I am in command here.'

" 'Tummyrot,' I answered. 'I outrank you ten ways from Sunday. The King says so. Now what shall we do?'

"His smile brightened the night. 'Good show,' he murmured. 'All you must do is cover me. I will work my way down to that next boulder, from which I should be able to see her. When I shoot, you must be alert to movement in any direction. She may flee at the shot, if I miss her, even if I hit her for that matter. Or she will charge. And leopards, as you well know, especially supernatural ones, are chargers. Stop her if she comes for me. Understood?'

"I nodded, and Rawley began to inch his way down the steep wall of the *nullah*, taking infinite pains not to disturb a single one of the many small boulders and stones that littered its tilting surface. The rattle of even a pebble would set off the leopard's fuse, causing her to explode in one direction or another. What felt like hours ticked past, lifetimes – spots crawled before my eyes – but finally he was in place. He looked back up the slope at me, raised his thumb, then slowly raised the Enfield . . ."

At that moment a steward arrived at our table with Sir George's entree. It was a smoking platter of *langouste*, flown up to Nanyuki at great expense from Malindi on the coast. With the lobster came a bowl of melted butter, a tray of capers and sliced lemon, a mammoth serving of rice, veggies and pickles and an iced magnum of champagne, Moet & Chandon "Dom Perignon," no less. Some Ploughman's Lunch. Bill and I were having bangers and mash.

"Enjoy," I said, with a touch of acerbity. "But please go on with your story. And don't hesitate to talk with your mouth full."

Sir George laughed.

"*Bang!*" he said.

"What?"

"*Bang!* Rawley fired at the leopard. I saw the long gout of flame from the Enfield's muzzle and perhaps it blinded me for an instant. All hell broke loose, as they say. A loud, high-pitched pantherine shriek. The clatter of violently disturbed rocks. A long swift dark shape momentarily eclipsed the stars above Rawley's boulder. Then his sudden, anguished cry of rage . . . All this in a heartbeat. The leopard had him, and he had her. I saw them for an instant, standing and swaying together like lovers, the leopard clutched in Rawley's strong embrace, her hind claws working at his abdomen. But of course I couldn't shoot for fear of hitting him. Then they toppled down into the *nullah*. I ran over to the edge and peered down, rifle at my shoulder.

"There she was – an elongate streak heading up the far side of the declivity. I swung with her and fired . . ."

The fork that Sir George had laden with lobster, rice and a tidbit of stewed tomato and held, poised at mouth-level, throughout this discourse, now disappeared into his maw. He chewed thirty times, maybe more, then finally swallowed. He muffled a belch behind his napkin.

"And . . .?"

"Where was I . . .?"

"The shot, you'd just fired the Rigby . . ."

"Yes, a right and a left, bang-bang, like two shots run together. The recoil and muzzle flash prevented me from seeing if either shot had told. I heard no scrabbling in the rocks, as from a moribund animal. Not a single cry from Rawley, not even a low moan. He was dead when I found him, poor chap. Disemboweled as completely as Kabiza. I dragged him back to camp by myself, the lads refusing to come beyond the *zareeba* until it became light. I sat by his body, waiting for dawn, thinking sad thoughts of Empire, and of the men who built it. They were heroes, all of them. Where is their like today?"

"And the leopard?" What happened to her?"

"Never found her," Sir George said in a cryptic grin. "Pug marks galore down in the *nullah,* but no blood, no hair, no scuff marks on the bare rock. I did find something, though."

"What was it?"

"These," he said, reaching into the pocket of his frayed bush jacket. The wrinkled old paw, covered with liver spots, trembled, then unclenched, palm up. In Sir George's hands lay two well-worn golden anklets, graven with strange runes or cuneiforms. They looked ancient – far older even than this husk of a man who sat before me, smiling gently but quizzically into my soul.

Old beyond time itself . . .

"The lads and I found these on the dessicated body of an aged woman, who lay near a boulder at the top of the *nullah.* Just about in line with my shots. She had been there a long, long time, mummified by the sun and the hot, arid winds so that her corpse was light as a feather. God knows why the vultures and jackals hadn't found her, or at least the driver ants. Her leathery body was clad in skins, dry as parchment now."

We sat in silence as Sir George finished his lobster. He stretched finally, yawned behind his hand, shot a cuff and looked at his wristwatch. It was a fine old timepiece, perhaps a Patek Phillipe, but its leather band had been mended near the buckle with duct tape. "Well," he said, "you lads will have to finish the champers. No heeltaps, mind you! I'm afraid I must toddle off to slumberland. Young children and old men, they both require an early bedtime. You two young stalwarts will learn the truth of that maxim, all in the fullness of time." He rose and smiled down at us, leaning his dropsical belly against the chair top.

"Thank you for my supper," he said, "not to mention the liquid refreshment. And pleasant dreams, both of you."

Sir George's tale had made my own leopard, killed from a blind as most are nowadays, appear rather hum-drum. All I could remember of the hunt now was the interminable waiting, the insect bites, the yearning for a smoke, the leopard's sudden appearance, as if from thin air, and then the shot that killed him. He dropped without a sound, stone dead to one touch of the trigger, one soft-pointed nip from the .375 H&H Magnum. Talk about anticlimax. Rather like modern life, really: hurry up and wait, then wait some more. Just about the time you're totally bored, bang, it's over.

"What do you make of it?" I asked Bill when the old man was gone.

He laughed and shook his head.

"This is Africa, Bwana," he said at last. "Anything can happen. But whatever the truth of the matter, it makes a nice bedtime story, doesn't it?"

Everything Your Heart Desires

One of Jones's "signature" pieces, this taut, bittersweet memoir of bird-hunting on safari in northern Kenya first appeared in the anthology *Seasons of the Hunter* (1985) and later in *African Twilight* (1994). The opening paragraphs, with their tensile lyric power and intimation of our own mortality, are among the finest he ever wrote.

In some strange way the birds we kill fly on forever. Perhaps it's the broken arc, the interrupted parabola, the high zig through the alders that never quite made it to zag – all those incompletions crying out to be consummated. But something is there that keeps them airborne if only in our hearts, their wings forever roaring at the base of our trigger fingers. The partridge that puffs to the shot string this morning at the edge of some frost-crisp apple orchard in the hills of Vermont is the self-same bird – but totally different, of course – as the very first dove we ever knocked down, a lifetime ago, over a Midwestern cornfield. And watched in disbelief the pale feathers spill slowly from a saffron sky.

Sometimes, drunk or dreaming, I see the world crisscrossed in a webwork of avian force fields, the flight paths of ghost birds winging on out as if they'd never been hit. In the end, of course, they will weave our own rough winding sheets . . .

The big Bedford lorries had arrived the day before, so by the time we wheeled into the campsite along the Ewaso Nyiro River, the tents were up – taut, green, smelling of hot canvas and spicy East African dust. It was a sandy country, red and tan, and the river rolled silently but strong, dark almost as blood, under a fringe of scrawny-trunked doum palms and tall, time-worn boulders. Sand rivers cut the main watercourse at right angles, and the country rolled away to the north and west in a shimmer of pale tan haze. The fire was pale and the kettle whistled a merry welcome.

This was the last camp of the month-long shooting safari through Kenya's bone-dry Northern Frontier Province, a hunt that had begun three weeks earlier at Naibor Keju in the Samburu country near Maralal, then swung northward through the lands of the Rendile and Turkana tribes to Lake Rudolf, and back down across the Chalbi and Kaisut deserts past Marsabit Mountain to the Ewaso Nyiro.

"I call it EDB," Bill said as we climbed down out of the green Toyota safari wagon. "Elephant Dung Beach. The first time I camped here the lads

167

had to shovel the piles aside before we could pitch our tents, it was that thick. *Ndovus* everywhere."

Not anymore. On the way in from Archer's Post, Bill had pointed out the picked skeleton of an elephant killed by poachers, and not long since, judging by the lingering smell. We'd stopped to look it over – vertebrae big as chopping blocks, ribs fit for a whaleboat, the broad skull still crawling with ants, and two splintered, gaping holes where the ivory had been hacked out.

"*Shifta,*" Bill said, and when we got into camp the safari crew confirmed his diagnosis. *Shifta* were even then the plague of northeastern Kenya, raiders from neighboring Somalia who felt, perhaps with some justification, that the whole upper right-hand quadrant of Kenya rightly belonged to them.

When the colonial powers divided Africa among themselves, they all too often drew arbitrary boundaries regardless of tribal traditions. The Somalis – a handsome, fiercely Islamic people related to the Berbers of northwest Africa and the ancient Egyptians (theirs was the Pharaonic "Land of Punt") – are nomads for the most part, and boundaries mean as little to them as they do to migrating wildebeest. But these migrants, armed with Russian AKs and plastic explosives, have blood in their eyes. They poach ivory and rhino horn, shoot up *manyattas* (villages) and police posts, mine the roads and blow up trucks or buses with no compunction.

Sergeant Nganya, a lean old Meru in starch-stiff Empire Builders and a faded beret, led us over to a *lugga* near the riverbank. In the bottom were the charred, cracked leg bones of a giraffe, scraps of rotting hide, the remains of a cook fire and an empty 7.62mm shell case stamped Cartridge, M1943 – the preferred diet of the Soviet AK-47 assault rifle. Nganya, who had been with Winter since their days together in the Kenya game department, handed the cartridge over without a word.

"I'm sure they'll leave us alone," Bill said as we drank our *chai* under the cool fly of the mess tent. "They know we're armed, and the lads will keep a sharp lookout around the *kampi*. Just to ensure sweet dreams for one and all, though, I'll post guards at night. Not to worry."

That evening we went out for buffalo. I still had one on my license, having killed a decent bull on the Tinga Plateau near Naibor Keju. He died in a splendid sunset.

Tonight's sunset was as gaudy as that one had been: a skyful of purples and mauves and lavenders shot through with ribbons of dying fire. Walking down the riverbank through those pyrotechnics was like strolling through a gallery of bad picture postcards. There were crocodiles along the bank, big ones that slithered off into the dark, fast water with a speed that belied their size; baboons yapped and snarled in the bush across the way.

Big, abrupt knobs of dark red rock thrust up through the trees and we scanned them as we walked, keeping our eyes skinned for *shifta*. And suddenly one was standing there – tall and skinny against the light, heart-stopping in his instant emergence from nothingness. Then I saw that it was Lambat, our head tracker, who only a minute earlier had been right behind me. He must have scampered up the hundred-foot kopje like a klipspringer.

"Ah," said Bill, following my gaze. "His Lordship's having a *shufti* – a bit of a look-see, as you'd say in America. Aha – and he sees something!"

Lambat had squatted and was peering intently upriver. It was almost too melodramatic, like a scene from a John Ford western where the intrepid Indian scout on the rimrock suddenly spots Geronimo's band. But this was real life and there was that high intensity about Lambat: slow, quiet, loose-jointed as a dead snake during times of inaction, he literally "lit up" when he spotted game, his dull dark skin suddenly glowing like polished mahogany, his muscles showing like well-wrapped cables, eyes bright as a gundog's on point. Now he raised his hands, palms forward, fingers spread. Ten. Then folded them, and opened them again.

And again and again.

"Christ," Bill said, "he sees forty, fifty – sixty or more."

"*Shifta?*"

"No," Bill laughed. "Buffalo. At least I hope that's what he means."

The herd was feeding a quarter of a mile ahead of us, along the riverbank. We could smell them before we saw them, that sweet stench of the cow barn that put me in mind of boyhoods in northern Wisconsin: trout streams and roast-chicken suppers in the big, comfortable lakeside kitchen after the evening chores were done and the herd milked, while bats flew over the flowering honeysuckle. But this was savage Africa: milkmen of doom, we bellied up to deal death to these wild bovines.

"That one on the right," Bill whispered beside me in the bush. "With his head down right now, near that group of cows: he's lifting his head up, chewing, now looking toward us. Shaking off the flies."

"I see him."

"He'll go over forty inches," Bill said. "He's the best of the lot. Hold on bone, Bwana, right on the shoulder. We want to break him down. But don't shoot until you're ready."

"Yes."

"We don't want to be going in after him now. Not in this light."

Pa-wham!

The bull dropped to the shot.

The herd broke and stampeded – bulls, cows and calves erupting like a giant black mortar burst as the dead bull hit the ground. "Oh, shit! Look at that!" Bill was beside himself with frustration.

Out of the thick bush to the right stepped a bull buffalo that looked, in the dying red light, to be half again as big as the one I'd dropped. "Oh, look at that big sod! He must have been crossed with a Texas longhorn. He's one for the book, Bwana, but we can't kill him now, can we? You've shot your limit."

The big buffalo and two smaller ones went over to the dead bull and hooked at him viciously, grunting and lowing.

"Crikey," Bill said, "aren't they bloody marvelous? Look at them, all scabby and thick and covered in shit, yet beautiful nonetheless. I've killed them in their hundreds over the years. Yet if I had my way, I'd put them all back on their feet just to see them galloping the plains again. Knee-deep through tall, sweet grass!"

His eyes shone noonday blue in the gathering darkness.

So blood can pall. This buffalo was the last of the big, warm, dangerous animals for that safari, and we would finish out the week at EDB with bird shooting. It was a welcome relief, a slow, leisurely cooling-out from the high tension and dark tragedy of big game, and for me doubly so, since bird hunting has always been my first love among the shooting sports. But this was a different kind of bird hunting.

I'd grown up on ruffed grouse, woodcock, sharptails and pheasants in the upper Middle West, and that kind of gunning meant cold mornings, iron skies, crisp wild apples, the crunch of bright leaves under muddy boots. It was all tamaracks and muskegs, old pine slashings, glacial moraines and ink-black ponds, the country peopled with tough little Finns and potato-faced Germans. In the one-horse logging towns, we whiled away the evenings on draft beer, bratwurst and snooker. The great unspoken fear in that land of Green Bay Packer worship weren't *shifta* but something far more fearsome: the Chicago Bears.

The contrast between American and African bird-shooting comes quickly clear. The morning after the buffalo hunt we are up before dawn. Even the coolest part of the day is tee-shirt weather, hyenas giggle downriver and a great fish eagle winnows the air overhead as we sip strong Kenya coffee at first light. There are lion tracks outside the tents, fresh ones – great, bold pug marks that circled the camp twice during the night. But our guards, the wry Turkana named Otiego and the big, slab-faced Samburu we call Red Blanket, report no signs of *shifta* during their watches. Yet they hadn't seen the lion either . . .

Not far from the river is a hot spring, a *maji moto* in Swahili, and we walk in quietly through a low ground fog, armed only with 20-gauge shotguns. Soon the sand grouse will be flying. Lambat leads the way, peering intently into the mist. He raises a hand: halt. We hear a huffing sound in the fog, then dimly make out two dark bulky shapes. "*Kifaro*," hisses Lambat. "*Mama na mtoto.*"

Either the fog thins or adrenaline sharpens my vision, for suddenly they come into focus, a big female rhino and her calf. The mother whuffs again, aware that something is wrong but unable, with her weak eyes and the absence of wind, to zero in on the threat. She shakes a head horned like a Mexican saddle and shuffles off into the haze, followed by her hornless offspring, which looks at this distance like an oversized hog. I'd often jumped deer while bird-hunting in the U.S., and once a moose got up and moved out of an alder swale I was pushing for woodcock near Greenville, Maine. But rhino are somehow different. If only for the heightened pucker factor.

The sun bulges over the horizon, a giant blood-orange, and instantly the fog is gone, sucked up by the dry heat of day. But then it seems to return, in the whistling, whizzing form of a million sand grouse, chunky birds as quick and elusive as their distant relatives, the white-winged doves and mourning doves I'd shot back home.

These are chestnut-bellied sand grouse, *Pterocles exustus,* the most common of some six species that inhabit the dry thorn scrublands of Africa. They fly to water each morning, hitting the available waterholes for about an hour soon after dawn, fluttering over the surface to land, drink and soak up water in their throat feathers for their nestlings to drink during the dry season.

I promptly began to miss them, overwhelmed and wild-eyed at their sky-blackening abundance. Then I settled down as the awe receded and I began knocking down singles and doubles at a smart clip. It was fast, neck-wrenching shooting with the birds angling in from every direction. I stood under the cover of an umbrella acacia, surrounded by shell husks, the barrel soon hot enough to raise blisters, shooting until my shoulder grew numb. Bill stood nearby, calling the shots and laughing at my misses.

"Quick, behind you, Bwana!"

I spun around to see a pair slashing in overhead, mounted the gun with my feet still crossed, folded the lead bird, and then leaned farther back to take the trailer directly above me – *pow!* The recoil, in my unbalanced, leg-crossed stance, dropped me on my tailbone. But the bird fell too.

"Splendid," Bill said with a smirk. "Just the way they teach it at the Holland & Holland Shooting School. The Classic Twisting, Turning, High-Overhead, Passing, Fall-on-Your-Arse Double. Never seen it done better, I do declare!"

Then it was over. The sand grouse vanished as quickly as they'd appeared. The trackers began to pick up the dead and locate any "runners." There were few wounded birds. I'd been shooting sixes, the high-brass loads we'd used earlier in the safari for vulturine and helmeted guineafowl. The heavy shot killed cleanly when I connected. You could use No. 7$^{1}/_{2}$ shot, perhaps even eights on these lightly feathered, thin-skinned birds, and increase the bag a bit, but there is really no need to. By using heavier shot, you ensure swifter kills, and there is never a dearth of birds.

Or so I was thinking. Just then one of the birds – a cripple, far out near the white-scaled salt of the hot spring's rim – scuttled away, trailing a shattered wing. Lambat stooped like a shortstop fielding a line drive, grabbed a stone and slung it sidearm. It knocked the bird dead at twenty yards. He picked up the grouse and brought it to me, walking long and limber, dead casual, a look of near-pity on his face as he placed it in my hand. Ah, the sorry, weak *Mzungu* with his costly firestick, blasting holes in the firmament with those expensive shells, when there were rocks right there for the picking. "His Lordship," indeed.

The camp was in an uproar when we returned. *Shifta* – four of them, scuffy little men with dirty shirts and heads wrapped in towels, accompanied by even scruffier dogs – had approached the camp. Ganya had driven them away with warning rifle-fire. No, they hadn't shot back, merely eased themselves into cover and out of range. They had faded southward, into the tangled vegetation of the riverbank. Everyone was excited. Even the old *mpishi* – the safari cook – was muttering and shaking his head as he poked at his perpetual fire. Normally the *mpishi* was Mister Cool.

After a lunch of oxtail soup, courtesy of the previous day's buffalo, and grilled sand grouse breasts, we drove up the river to Merti, the last town before the Ewaso Nyiro makes its great bend and loses itself in the wastes of the Lorian Swamp, hard by the Hothori and Sabena deserts. There is a police post at Merti and Bill wanted to check in, letting them know we were in the area. Along the way I kept seeing wrecked vehicles beside the twisting, twin-rutted road – fully half-a-dozen of them in the course of a thirty-mile drive. Some were badly rusted and nearly buried with wind-blown sand, but others seemed more recent. We stopped to examine one. The frame was bent like a steel pretzel, the hood ripped as if by a giant can opener. Even the wheel rims were twisted. The vehicle was barely recognizable as a Land Rover. But what could have torn the truck up so badly? On this barely traveled road, it could hardly have been a multi-truck collision.

"*Plastique*," said Bill. "C-4 or the Russian or Egyptian equivalent. A land mine did this work – the *shifta* use them all over the NFD."

Command-detonated?

"I doubt it. Probably a simple contact fuse. They don't use vehicles themselves as a rule, so why should they wait around to blow up a specific target when they can just plant a mine in a busy road and go about their business? They don't seem to care who they blow up. Whoever comes along will be a Kenyan or a tourist."

Merti, when we got there, had the look and feel of a besieged "strategic hamlet" in Vietnam. The police post was encircled ten feet high with barbed wire, its corners guarded by machine-gun towers. The town itself resembled the old, grainy sepiatone photographs of *laagers* during the Boer War, and you almost expected to see wide-hatted, leathery voortrekkers hung with bandoliers lounging outside the *duka* drinking beer, waiting for the order from Smuts or Botha that would send their commandos back into the field. But the Kenya police were definitely on the defensive in this undeclared war.

"Oh yes indeed, sir," the sergeant in charge said, smiling widely. "There are *shifta* about. Perhaps a hundred of them. Bad men, yes. *Mbaya sana*." But he wasn't doing anything about them. And rightly so, Bill pointed out later. If he sortied from the town, the *shifta* might lure him and his men deeper into the waterless thorn-scrub while others swung back to loot the *dukas* in towns and make off with whatever supplies and weapons they could lay their hands on.

"Well," Bill told him, "we're upriver in Block Seven near Kittermaster's Camp, hunting, and I'm sure they won't bother us."

"Oh no, sir." The sergeant smiled. "Of course not. Not with the police so close at hand." They both laughed heartily.

We stopped at the *duka* and drank a warm Tusker beer. The dusty, cool shop was pleasant but poorly stocked.

"I came off safari once, years ago, into a little *duka* like this," Bill recalled. "Back in my Anti-Stock-Theft days with the Kenya constabulary. I'd been chasing Turkana cattle thieves all over hell and gone. God, it was hot. What I wanted more than anything was a good, clean shave, and I'd run out of razor blades days earlier. I came into the *duka* and asked the owner what he had in stock. A big, happy, smiling chap he was, like that police sergeant we were talking to just now. 'Oh, Bwana,' he said, 'we have everything your heart desires!' He gestured around at his shelves. 'By chance would you have a razor blade?' I asked him.

" '*Hakuna*,' quoth he rather sadly. 'I have none.' "

Bill laughed.

"Everything your heart desires. Don't you love it, Bwana?"

In the evenings I was reading myself to sleep with a book from Bill's copious collection of Africana: a 1910 edition of a book titled *In the Grip of the Nyika*, by Lieutenant Colonel J. H. Patterson, S.D.O. The colonel had made his name by killing a pair of voracious lions that had stopped construction of the Mombasa-to-Uganda railway in the early years of this century by killing and devouring scores of Indian coolies who were laying the track. Patterson recounted those adventures in a best-selling book called *The Man-Eaters of Tsavo*.

This later volume, which Bill inevitably called *In the Grip of the Knickers,* is about a safari Patterson made along the Ewaso Nyiro, surveying the boundaries of the Northern Frontier District in company with an old school chum of his, fresh out from England, whom he identifies only as "B." Accompanying them is B.'s newlywed bride, a comely young Englishwoman called "Mrs. B."

Near the place where we were now camped, "B." had allegedly fallen ill with fever and one evening without warning, blown his brains out with a pistol. Patterson buried his friend, consoled the grieving widow, and got on with his survey. Later the colonel himself came down with fever and was nursed back from the brink of death by the brave Mrs. B., whom he later married.

"Makes you wonder, doesn't it?" Bill would say. "Maybe there was a little slap-and-tickle going on between the handsome White Hunter and his brave lovely little Clientess – it's been known to happen, Bwana. Picture the scene. Poor old B. wakes up sweating beneath his mozzie net, out of his head with fever. His wife is nowhere to be seen. The dank heat of the African night, lions coughing, hyenas cackling in the dark, and suddenly a girlish giggle from the White Hunter's tent – that sort of thing . . . Then, a shot rings out! 'The Short Happy Life of Francis Macomber' in embryo, wouldn't you say?"

But the book was fascinating and I would slope off into dreams of blood and illicit love, hearing the hyenas whoop, the crunch of their jaws on fragile bone and see looming up through the river mists the vague menacing shape of . . . Abdul the Abominable, the Power *Shifta*. He'd be lying there in ambush for us, to pay us for our sins. Never mind that the sins were undefined, we all had plenty to our name. Images of slow, bright knives, staked out covered with honey in the track of the *siafi,* the safari ants. Abdul standing there in the dark, cackling at our helplessness like a foul-breathed, rot-eating *fisi* . . .

I think I'll go out this afternoon with a shotgun," I told Bill at lunch on our last day at E.D.B. "A rough shoot – see what I can walk up. There must be plenty of birds right around camp."

"Sounds like a fine idea," Bill said. "I've got to stay here and organize the packing, though. You can take Lambat and Otiego along with you to push the birds up. There's no end of *ndeges* around here. I hear them calling in the morning – guineafowl, francolin, yellow-necked spur fowl, maybe even some button quail. You'll have a good time, I'm sure. *Ndeges mingi sana* hereabouts, birds galore."

And *shifta* as well, but we left that unspoken. It was too beautiful a day to worry about them, at least out loud. This was my last day afield, and the bird-shooting so far had been an alien form – there'd been the sand grouse, of course, and I'd shot driven guineafowl with Bill once, on an old coffee shamba that had previously belonged to Karen Blixen, a.k.a. Isak Diensen, the *Out of Africa* woman, and it had been good shooting but too formal, too much like an English driven pheasant shoot for my rough-and-ready American taste. The boys had formed a line at the top of a long, brushy slope and pushed the birds down to us where we stood above the jungly banks of the Tana River near where it rises beyond Thika, the guineas lurching into the air well above us, big dark birds heavier than pheasants but just as fast as they poured past, cackling, and we shot fast and furious, folding some nicely but seeing others slant down, heavy-hit, legs trailing, to land in the riverside tangle. When we went in to finish them, we found fresh buffalo sign: steaming mounds of shiny dung, trampled shrubbery.

"What do we do if they come?" I asked Bill, hefting the 20-gauge pitifully in my hands.

"Climb," Bill laughed. "*Panda juu*. There are plenty of trees at hand."

"I don't know if I'm still that arboreal," I said doubtfully.

"You will be, Bwana," he said. "Don't worry about it. Nature will take its course. I was in a situation like this with a fat old English nobleman once. He scampered up a thorn tree like a bloody *nugu* – just as agile as a monkey. Never even let out a yelp from the thorn stabs. Didn't feel them."

We'd gone in then and collected our birds, and the buff left us alone. Just as the *shifta* would leave me alone today. I hoped.

Yet deep down it was because of the *shifta* – the chance of them being there – that I wanted to do this. Every bird hunter knows the neck-itching feeling that crawls up from your kidneys when you walk into a good cover. As if something deadly were waiting there, silent in the mottled green dark. What's waiting, though, is no deadlier than humiliation if you blow the shot. Yet when the bird gets up with a rattle and a roar, it's as if some bogey man suddenly sprang out at you, heart-stopping, remorseless. Abdul the Objectionable in his final, fatal pounce. The adrenaline rush is beyond comparison. This would be even better.

The country upstream from camp was thick with wait-a-bit thorn and elephant grass, tough going as we pushed into it. Behind us the sounds of camp life – clanking pots, happy conversation in English and Swahili – quickly faded; ahead the doum palms and borassus swayed, their shadows shifting black on the bright grass. A heavy silence, broken only by the buzz of flies and bees, the rusty creak of nooning birds.

175

Otiego swung wide to the right and slapped his spear at the edge of a low thorn thicket. A bird got up with the forever-startling feathery *whirr* – a long brown bird, big as a pheasant – and I centered it, *pow*! Then another, and three more. I didn't hear my second barrel fire, but there were two birds down. Feathers still falling through the hot, hard light. Otiego brought them back – yellow-necked spur fowl, their throats pale orange, conspicuously bare, the wet dead eyes rimmed with bare skin, pebbly red.

We could hear others ahead of us calling back and forth, *graark, grak, grak*. They ran ahead of us as we approached; we could see them scuttling gray-brown through the scrub. Then from the left a different bird got up – darker, chunkier – and Lambat fell flat as he saw me swing past him, then shoot. The bird fell down. Its white throat and legs and mottled belly proclaimed it a Shelley's francolin, counterpart of the sharp-tailed grouse of my boyhood.

In the denser forest back of the riverbank, another variety abounded – Heuglin's francolin, dark-feathered and plump as a European partridge. They got up like ruffed grouse, with a great spooking thunder of wings in there under the confining forest canopy and had the same maddening habit of waiting until you were past, then lining out with a tree trunk between them and the gun barrel.

In the open, with the pheasant like spur fowl and the tight-holding, sharptail like Shelley's francolin, I couldn't seem to miss; now it was hard to score a hit. Otiego grinned wickedly and clucked his mock disapproval.

Back out in the open, we jumped a small covey of buff-colored, round-winged birds that buzzed off like outsized bumblebees. Button quail. I dropped two before they pitched in less than a hundred yards ahead. Lambat scooped them up on the run, but when we got to where the singles landed we couldn't trigger a single reflush. Yet there had been at least eight in the covey, perhaps ten – slow fliers at best – that landed in the tall grass. We could hear them scuttling, hear their frog-like *whoo-whoo-whoo* as they ran. We didn't see them again. The dead birds in hand looked vaguely like quail, but there was something odd about their feet. Then I noticed that they lacked the hind toes of true quail. It certainly didn't seem to hinder their speed on the ground.

For three hours we zigzagged through that wild, thorn-fanged riverside bush, a game-bird heaven, the trackers working like clever gundogs, spotting each possible hiding place, circling beyond it, then pushing through to put the birds out toward the gun. On some I shot nicely, on others I might as well have thrown the shotgun at them. But it was a Time Machine – no, a Time-and-Place Machine. At one moment I was back in a southern Wisconsin pheasant field, swinging on a fast-moving rooster with the corn tassels crunching underfoot; in the next I was kicking the soybean stubble for Georgia quail. Then I was up in Minnesota working the shortgrass prairie for sharptails, and in the next step jumping a partridge out of alder edges in Maine.

Yet at the same time I was aware that this was Africa: There could be a surly old bull buffalo just under the bank to my left, very angry at having his midday snooze disrupted; or a lion behind the next bush, sleeping off his midnight gluttony but not too lazy to get up and chomp a clumsy *mzungu*. And above all, there was Abdul & Company, with automatic rifles, plastique land mines and a total lack of compunction when it came to killing unwary travelers.

By the time we swung back into camp, Lambat and Otiego each had ten birds dangling from their hands and I a few brace more slapping my hip, their heads forced through my belt loops, their shot-loosened feathers sticking to my legs with a glue of dried blood, both theirs and mine, thanks to the thorns. The three of us were laughing as we came out of the *nyika*.

Bill was sitting outside the mess tent, having his afternoon tea. He looked up with a quizzical smile. "Did you have a decent shoot, Bwana?"

"It was everything my heart desired."

The Guinea Worm

From *The Diamond Bogo* (1976): In this hilariously off-the-wall *roman à clef*, the hard-drinking journalist Bucky Blackrod (a thinly disguised Jones) recruits poet and ex-race car driver Donn McGavern (a thinly disguised Dan Gerber) for a safari through some of the wildest, least-civilized country left in Africa. Bucky's constant companion is the Guinea worm, a foot-long parasite that inhabits his legs, pokes its head out for a look-see from time-to-time, but is too quick to catch. Get the picture?

Wait a minute!" said Bucky Blackrod. "I can feel it moving now. Get ready. Okay, nail the bastard!"

A group of drunks lunged at his hairy bare leg, propped on the scarred lip of the bar. Clumsy hands matched and groped. Irish curses blued the air.

"Missed him!"

The worm had emerged from the edge of Bucky's shin, waving up into the boozy light with its pointed eyeless head – a thin red ribbon fully a foot long. But at the attack, it had once again retreated.

It was a Guinea worm, *Dracunculus medinensis*, an African parasite that had plagued explorers ever since the days of James Bruce, the eighteenth-century Scot who had been the first white man to reach the source of the Blue Nile in Abyssinia. Bucky had acquired his unwanted passenger during a hunting safari in Central Africa three years earlier. Doctors could do nothing about it. The worm was impervious to drugs or medication of any kind. It lived in his legs, migrating from one to the other in a slow tingly crawl occasionally punctuated by a stab of pain, like a hot needle run through his veins. Toward evening, usually, it would emerge from his skin for a look around. But usually, toward evening, Bucky was halfway in the bag, too slow with drink to catch it. Thus the pursuit of the Guinea worm had fallen to his drinking buddies, who found it an amusing game. Unfortunately, most of them were slower than Bucky. Old men – retired cops, laid-off stevedores, elevator operators, cab drivers, just plain bums – they had been drinking since nine in the morning, when Clancy's opened. Clancy himself, a tall, cadaverous, big-knuckled man with a slab of patent-leather hair across his pale forehead, never drank. But even he could not catch the Guinea worm and had long ago given up trying.

"Maybe he's waiting to get back to Africa," Bucky said, ordering another shot to go with his beer. "I'll be over there by the weekend. Maybe he'll come out and go away. Go get himself a girl friend."

179

"Yes," said Clancy from behind the bar. "I suppose you'd call a female of the species a Guiness worm." He adjusted his leather bowtie as they laughed.

"I still say you should let me try this," said Riordan, the veinous ex-cop. He patted the .38 Police Special in the quick-draw clip at his hip. The butt of the gun peeked out from under a roll of fat in a dirty shirt. "He can't be quick as a bullet. We'd let him come out with the bar as a backdrop and I'd blow his soddin' head off."

"Clancy wouldn't care for that," said Bucky, tossing off his rye." And anyway, Riordan, you'd probably blow my soddin' leg off."

Riordan bridled, his red face going purple as the others chuckled.

"For thirty years I was the best pistol shot in my precinct," he growled. "From the Bowery to Fort Apache, from Harlem to Sheepshead Bay, I could do it. Bucko me lad."

"A sawbuck says you miss," piped Schultheiss, the crippled ex-elevator jockey. He slapped the ten-spot on the bar. Others chimed in, laying singles and fives on the pile, arguing odds and laying off one another's bets. Bucky peeled a twenty from the inside of his roll – expense money for the upcoming safari – and smoothed it atop the pile.

"Half the pot goes to Clancy, to fix the bullet hole," he said. "And the cops. All right, Clance?"

The bartender walked to the door, looked up and down the street, then pulled the shades.

"We can say it was a holdup man," he said.

"Shhhh," said Bucky, pulling up his pants legs. "He likes the quiet."

The other drunks staggered off away from the bar, Riordan drew the pistol and crouched on the hardwood floor, clearing a space for his shoes in the sawdust. He held the pistol in a double-handed grip, his elbows locked and lying across his knees, the muzzle far enough away from Bucky's bare leg to avoid flash burn. Clancy poured a shot for Bucky and another for Riordan. The Irishman shrugged it away. He wanted to be dead calm.

Silence fell over the saloon, apart from the odd hiccup – Maynard the onetime bicycle racer. They heard a siren go up Eighth Avenue. They heard two hookers giggle down the avenue. Flaherty, who had flown thirty-six missions as chin-turret gunner in a B-17 during World War II, struggled to stifle a beer fart. They waited.

The Guinea worm poked its head out of Bucky's knee. It swayed in the dim light, retreated a bit, then emerged slowly. It came out like a cobra from a fakir's basket, weaving to a music beyond the range of human ears. It was actually quite beautiful – slim, sinuous, graceful almost, a nearly translucent red, like a living thermometer. It hypnotized them with its dance.

Riordan shot.

They all jumped at the bark of the revolver. Bottles shivered on the bar. The clouded mirror shifted an inch to the left. Clancy's black leather bowtie took a ride on his Adam's apple. Flaherty cut his fart.

The Guinea worm, minus its head, whipped back into Bucky's knee like a snapped rubber band.

Later, walking up Eighth past the fag movie houses and the hooks and the muggers, who paid him no attention because of the blood and beer stains on his clothing, Bucky thought that the Guinea worm would either die inside his leg and rot there, or else grow a new head. It would probably grow a new head. It was that sort of animal. Anyway, he hoped it would. He had come to like it.

He was glad to be heading back to Africa. New York had gotten boring in the past few years. Everybody whined, or snuck around behind your back. Even the muggers were yellow. They cut first and took your money afterward. But they didn't bother him because he was too much of a slob. Only the grungiest of whores would have anything to do with him. He used to be a good-looking guy, but now he was getting fat and he didn't care about anything anymore. The job bored him: It was games. Politics put him to sleep. He liked to read, but he could do that anywhere. He carried his own music inside his head. His movies, too.

In Africa everything was strong and it changed all the time. Everything bit. He knew that inside his fat and his lethargy there was a thin, eager young man waiting to be unzipped. The Guinea worm had told him. He knew that once he got to Africa, the man inside would jump out and go running over the game plains, buck naked, with the Guinea worms waving a weird dance around his ankles.

He could see the buffalo ahead of him, through the heat haze, its huge black head shining, shimmering, waiting.

The Lost Fire

Although little-known compared to the much-smaller Chicago Fire (which happened the same day), the Peshtigo Fire was the single deadliest conflagration in American history. The story has all the elements that got Jones's juices flowing: nature at its most violent (and even vindictive); life and death balanced on a razor's edge; men and women enduring unimaginable horrors and displaying superhuman courage in the face of them. If the Peshtigo Fire weren't a matter of historical record, Bob Jones would have invented it. From the November 1999 issue of *Men's Journal*.

The fire lay all around them, a great drowsing dragon just waiting for a wake-up call, and the sky was an eerie yellow. The air, bitter with wood smoke, felt so dry that townspeople said, "If you touched a match to it, it'd burn." Even after full dark, the southern horizon would glare a sullen red. A woman returning home from church told a passing neighbor, "I'm afraid we shall all go to hell tonight."

Throughout that long, hot summer and well into the fall, the ground fires had smoldered, the red-hot coals cooking beneath beds of gray ash, eating deep into root systems, leaching sap from leaves and pine needles. There had been no rain to speak of since July 8. The cedar swamps flanking the town had dried out, and now the fire had invaded the peat itself. In the marshes where the Menominee Indians usually gathered wild rice each autumn, there was no longer enough water to float a canoe. Cranberries withered on the stem. The North Woods at that time was a climax white-pine forest – it was said that a squirrel could travel branch to branch from Sault St. Marie on Michigan's Upper Peninsula to the Minnesota line without touching the ground, 80 feet below. And now the boreal forest was a gigantic tinderbox – all it needed was a spark of ignition.

It came with an almost biblical fury on the night of October 8, 1871. A stiff breeze kicked up from the southwest, and people on the streets soon noticed what appeared to be snowflakes falling from the sky, though it was too warm for that. In fact, it was ashes. Suddenly, well after roosting time, birds began winging through town – migrant warblers, finches, jays, even ruffed grouse. Some watchers saw house cats, usually the most solitary creatures, slinking fast in a pack toward the river that ran through the town. Stabled horses began to whinny, then scream in panic. On the wind came "the confused noise of a number of cars and locomotives approaching a

183

railroad station, or the rumbling of thunder, with the difference that it never ceased, but deepened in intensity each moment more and more," as one witness, Father Peter Pernin, a Roman Catholic priest, recalled.

A swirling blizzard of ashes streaked out of the smoke, followed by a hail of burning coals. The red glare to the south intensified and the roar grew even louder. The entire top of a blazing white pine spun into the town and crashed on the sawdust streets, carried by a savage gust of whirling wind that knocked over wagons and buggies. The volunteer fire brigade, which had been clearing fire lines in the woods southwest of town for weeks with shovels, axes and hoes, came dashing back through the streets, their faces as black as minstrel-show sidemen, their clothing singed and smoking. "Get your wives and children! Forget about your homes! Run for the river! Run for your lives!"

What followed was America's closest approximation of hell on earth.

F ather Pernin was a newcomer to Peshtigo, Wisconsin, in 1871, the pastor of the brand new St. Mary's Church, and of another parish in neighboring Marinette, six and a half miles to the north. An energetic man of 46, stocky, dark-haired and cleanshaven, he had been born Pierre Pernin in France in 1825 and had served in communities from Quebec to Illinois to Oconto, Wisconsin, 14 miles south of Peshtigo, before coming north to the lumber town. He was the only survivor of the fire to write a book-length account of it. *The Finger of God Is There!, Or Thrilling Episode of a Strange Event Related by an Eye-Witness*. His narrative (retitled *The Great Peshtigo Fire: An Eyewitness Account* and recently republished by the State Historical Society of Wisconsin) is the first sustained report ever made from the heart of a firestorm.

Pernin had been aware that conditions were becoming dangerous for more than two weeks before the fire erupted. On September 22 he had visited some farms just west of town and found small blazes across the floor of the hardwood forest. This was slash-and-burn country. The area was known as the Sugar Bushes, a crescent of rich alluvial soil, rare to the region, supporting big stands of maples that are "sugared" to this day. Pernin decided to combine a little sport with his priestly house calls. "Whilst waiting," he wrote, "I took a gun, and accompanied by a lad of twelve years of age who offered to guide me through the woods, started in pursuit of some of the pheasants [more likely ruffed grouse] which abounded." The shooting was good, but as night fell Pernin and the boy found themselves lost and – worse – suddenly surrounded by creeping surface fires. Only by discharging his gun in the air a few times did he attract the attention of the boy's family, and even then their rescuers had to beat a path through the flames for the hunters to escape. A week or so later, traveling by horse and buggy between his two churches, Pernin was again almost trapped – this time by a wind-fanned flare-up of the dry brush flanking the dirt road. He whipped up his horse and raced into the wall of smoke and heat blocking his path, even though he had no idea how deep it was. He made it through.

On the morning of Sunday, October 8, Pernin had planned to say Mass at a country church in Cedar River, Michigan, well north of town, but the steamer that was supposed to take him there on Saturday evening couldn't dock in Peshtigo Harbor because of the pall of smoke enveloping the port. "God willed that I should be at the post of danger," he later wrote.

Torn between his faith and a gut-felt Gallic awareness of nature's indifference, Pernin found himself falling prey to a "species of mental torpor." Sensing the approach of doom and his own inability to forestall it, the priest was irritated by the high jinks of the patrons at a saloon across the street. Like most North Woods mill towns, Peshtigo had more saloons (some of which doubled as brothels) than churches – a ratio of 14-to-3 – and the paint was still drying on Pernin's church. "Toward nightfall," he wrote, "the greater part of [the revelers] were too much intoxicated to take any share in the anxiety felt by the more steady members of the community, or even to notice the strange aspect of nature . . . They quarreled, wrestled, rolled on the ground, filling the air with wild shouts and horrid blasphemies."

Still, despite his disgust with these sinners, Pernin took his pastoral responsibilities very seriously. His upbringing in France during Napoleon III's licentious Second Empire had made him all too aware of human frailties. He resolved to do his best to save as many of them as he could, saints and sinners alike, Catholic or Protestant or atheist.

In the years after the Civil War, America was booming westward at a breakneck pace, and fire was part of the process. There were towns to be built on the treeless prairies, railroad tracks to be laid, newspapers and books to be published – and most of the wood those endeavors required, from pulp to pine planking, maple, beech, ash, cedar and birch, necessarily came from the great climax forests of the Upper Midwest. Loggers, responding to the demand for lumber, wood products and paper, were working hard and fast to fell those trees, leaving their tops and slashings to dry on the ground, sometimes in piles 16 feet high that covered whole quarter-sections – 160 acres – or more. Loggers often could walk half a mile on downed tree trunks. Farmers in the North Woods cleared their land the fast way, with axes and fire. Railroad navvies cutting new rights-of-way customarily burned their slash as they moved along, leaving ground fires in their wake. Coal-fueled steam locomotives threw sparks from their

185

smokestacks and brake boxes. Little wonder that the *Chicago Tribune* dubbed 1871 "the black year," when almost simultaneous forest fires raged during the early fall from Illinois and Indiana through Michigan and Wisconsin and as far west as North Dakota.

The plank-sidewalk streets of logging towns like Peshtigo were covered with sawdust from the mills that sprang up by the hundreds in the north country. Built almost entirely of resinous, highly flammable pinewood, these were typical North Woods roughneck towns. With 60 logging camps in the vicinity, Peshtigo hosted barroom brawls galore, most resulting in nothing worse than black eyes, split lips and a bad case of "logger's smallpox," a condition caused by the spiked boots of one lumberjack landing hard on an opponent's prone body. But there were shootings and lynchings as well. And the whores were tough: Big Delia, of Muskegon's Sawdust Flats, stood six-foot-two, weighed 225, chewed Hiawatha brand chaw, and was said to have once knocked a logger clean out of his boots for not having removed them upon entering her bordello.

Peshtigo was more than a watering hole for lumberjacks and trainmen, however. It had at least four hotels, a sawmill, a large woodworking factory, a telegraph office, a jewelry store, several groceries and even its own pharmacy. A narrow-gauge railway ran seven swampy miles from Lake Michigan to Peshtigo proper. During the ice-free summer months on the lake, big, graceful schooners sailed in and out from Chicago and Milwaukee like enormous swans, loading up with the lumber that built the West. Three paddlewheelers made daily runs, carrying passengers and freight to and from Marinette on the Michigan border, and on down to Green Bay.

On the night of the fire, no schooners were docked in Peshtigo Harbor, the paddlewheelers were elsewhere, and the two coal-burning locomotives that might have provided a last-minute escape to Lake Michigan – at least for Peshtigo's women and children – stood in the town's engine house with their fireboxes cold, no steam up, no cars attached. And Peshtigo's population, normally about 1,700, had swelled to more than 2,000 that evening with the arrival of a thirsty crew of railroad laborers led by a burly former prizefighter named Big John Mulligan, who lived in town. Mulligan went home to his wife, but his workmen were among the hellraisers who angered Pernin.

At about seven o'clock that Sunday night, with the heat still intense, Pernin went next-door to chat with the "kind-hearted" Widow Dress. A breeze sprang up, and he "perceived some old trunks of the trees blaze out through without seeing about them any tokens of cinder or spark, just as if the wind had been a breath of fire." Pernin excused himself, ran home and began digging a trench, six feet long by seven feet deep, in the sandy soil of his garden. Into it he dropped his trunks, books, church ornaments "and other valuables, covering the hole with sand to a depth of about a foot.

"It was now about half past eight," he continued. "I first thought of my horse and turned him free into the street, deeming that in any case he would have more chance of escape thus than tied up in the stable."

When Pernin had finished, his housemaid came running up with a basketful of crosses, rosaries and religious medals. She carried a cage with her pet canary, but a sudden fire-tongued gust blew it away. The canary puffed into flame. The girl disappeared in the smoke. Pernin ran into the house to rescue the tabernacle, which contained the consecrated Host. Inside the house, he saw "a cloud of sparks that blazed up here and there with a sharp detonating sound like that of powder exploding, and flew from room to room."

His own pet bird, a blue jay, was "fluttering wildly 'round his cage beating against its bars . . . I grieved for its fate but could do nothing for it . . . I vainly called my dog who, disobeying the summons, concealed himself under my bed, only to meet death there later."

Over the din came the frenzied clanging of a church bell. The spire of the Congregational Church flared up, then cracked off and stuck upside down in the ground, aflame. Workers raced the town's Black Hawk pumping engine to the sawmill but were able to spray water on the roof only briefly before the canvas hose was burned through.

Dashing from his house, Pernin loaded the tabernacle into his buggy, then ran to open the gate to the road, only to see the gate and the fence whirl away on a blast of wind. He grabbed the shafts of the buggy and headed for the river. "The air was no longer fit to breathe, full as it was of sand, dust, ashes, cinders, sparks, smoke and fire."

Across the road, the drunks staggered into the tavern for shelter. "Without shout or word they re-entered the place, closing the doors as if to bar death out. A few moments later, the house was swept away."

The streets were jammed with people and wagons, racing toward the sanctuary of the cold, deep Peshtigo River. Buggies collided, men and horses blinded by the hot, blowing sand. Every building in town was on fire. "The neighing of horses, falling of chimneys, crashing of uprooted trees, roaring and whistling of the wind, crackling of fire . . . all sounds were there save the human voice. People seemed stricken-dumb by terror."

A burning roof whirled out of the sky. With it came despair. A man named C.R. Tousley, seeing his wife already dead and his way to the river blocked by flames, pulled out his pocketknife and cut his two children's throats and then his own. Another man, also preferring suicide to death by fire, stabbed himself in the chest but missed his heart. He staggered on to the river – and lived. A mother tied her toddler to her back, wrapped her two-week-old infant in a blanket, held it dangling from her teeth, then took two pails of water to douse her children and scurried safely to an open field.

"Farther on," Pernin recalled, "I was thrown down over some motionless object lying on the road; it proved to be a woman and a little girl, both dead." Out of the smoke appeared Pernin's horse, which he'd set loose half an hour earlier. "Whether he recognized me I cannot say, but whilst struggling anew to my feet I felt his head leaning on my shoulder. He was trembling in every limb. I called him by name and motioned him to follow me, but he did not move. He was found partly consumed by fire in the same place." Pernin pushed on through the smoke and flames.

With all the wood stacked in and around Peshtigo, coupled with the heat and aridity of the summer, a cataclysmic fire was almost inevitable.

Most forest fires begin, and end, as surface fires when they burn through the brush or understory, after having smoldered in the duff, peat bogs and root systems as ground fires. If a surface fire gets hot enough, though, it can vault to the treetops and blow up into a crown fire. And if there's enough dry fuel available, a crown fire can quickly reach catastrophic proportions. As weather conditions change, these fires can quicken, intensify and roil upward into a convection column. The blaze then becomes a mass fire, which acquires a life and movement of its own.

Conflagrations like the one that devastated Peshtigo generate internal winds, often in excess of 80 miles an hour – hurricane force – that fling fiery debris as far as 10 miles ahead and create spot fires that soar until they land on some kind of tinder. Then the whole process starts anew. At the heart of a mass fire, temperatures can reach 4,000 degrees Fahrenheit, burning in places at 22,500 BTUs per foot per second, the equivalent of a Hiroshima-class A-bomb's detonating every two minutes.

In such conditions, clothing, as dry as kindling from the heat, can combust at the lick of a tongue of flame. One deep breath of this superheated air will cause human lungs to char like paper bags. The fire consumes all the oxygen from the surface atmosphere and soon breathable air can be found only within an inch of the ground – if even there.

When Pernin reached the river, he discovered that it had proved no barrier to the fast-moving flames. Houses, mills and stores on both banks were already ablaze, and the town's sole narrow wooden bridge, clogged with panicked people crossing from both sides, was itself in flames. People spilled into the water, many to drown, others to be seared by the ignited timber drifting downriver from the sawmill. Cows and draft horses, dogs and hogs, even deer and a lone black bear stampeded down

Oconto Avenue, the town's main thoroughfare, headed for the river, some of them on fire, screaming. Their frantic rampage knocked women and children sprawling into the fiery, sawdust-covered dirt.

A logger named John Cameron watched a pretty girl he knew, Helga Rockstad, racing down the plank sidewalk of Oconto Avenue with the flames at her heels. The fire touched her streaming blonde hair, it flared up, and she dropped to the ground like a wing-shot bird. The next morning all Cameron could find of Helga was two nickel garter buckles and a mound of white ash.

Not everyone ran for the river. Some jumped into shallow wells, where a few lived but more suffocated or were boiled alive. Anywhere from 40 to 100 people locked themselves into the Peshtigo Company House, thought to be the sturdiest structure in town. No sooner had they closed the doors than the pinewood boardinghouse blazed up, to be consumed in a matter of minutes. The shrieks were short-lived. It would prove impossible to identify the victims, whose number remains uncertain.

The woodworking factory exploded like a giant Roman candle sending a cascade of burning tubs, broom handles, clothespins and pails out over the river. Huge, glowing logs blown out of the sawmill twirled skyward and fell on the people clustered on the riverbank. Clouds of oxygen-starved but still combustible gases and soot, which some survivors described as "black balloons," drifted out of the 100-foot-high wall of flames. Once recharged in the open air, they blew up overhead like artillery. Just such a balloon found Charles Lawrence and his family where they were huddled in an open field, bursting over their heads and incinerating them all. A young husband who'd become momentarily separated from his wife in the smoke found her again and made it to the river – only to discover in the glare of the flames that the woman was a stranger.

Pushing his buggy with its sacred cargo into the shallows, Pernin found himself in a scene worthy of a Hieronymus Bosch painting – hundreds of men, women and children, some horribly burned, skin blackened, huge blisters of raw flesh red and ragged, all of them standing "motionless as statues, some with eyes staring, upturned towards heaven, and tongues protruded." They were waiting like sheep for the end of the world. Why didn't they take to the water? In a moment the fire would be on them.

With a roar of rage at their stupidity, Pernin started shoving the men beside him into the river. "One of these sprang back again with a half-smothered cry, 'I am wet!' "

That's the least of your worries, thought Pernin. He grabbed the man and wrestled him into the water, then dragged him in deeper, "At the same moment, I heard a great splash along the river's bank. All had followed my example. It was time, the air was no longer fit for inhalation."

By then, it was 10 p.m. Injured cattle swam bawling through the millpond above the bridge. A young girl named Carrie Heidenworth was knocked loose from the log she was clinging to by a fire-maddened cow but managed to grab one of its horns and was carried back to shallow water. People wet their heads with both hands or covered them with soaked blankets and quilts, chin-deep in the icy stream for nearly six hours. In perhaps the saddest irony of that night, a railroad engineer named James Mellen got his son George, 14, and daughter Ella, 4, into the river, only to find them still there at dawn, dead from hypothermia.

Pernin and the others crawled out of the river at 3:30 a.m. Their hair had been burned off, their faces and eyes swollen from the heat. But now they faced another danger. "The atmosphere, previously hot as the breath of a furnace, was gradually becoming colder and colder," wrote Pernin. "Though close to a large fire, arising from heaps of burning fragments, I was still convulsively shivering." The beams of the woodworking factory were still flickering. All around lay piles of red-hot barrel hoops, and Pernin watched men lie facedown on the iron to warm themselves.

The topsoil for miles around had been scorched. The sand on the riverbank, fused by the heat, crackled as people walked over it. As the sun rose through a roiling, acrid sky, those left alive saw only the stonework and brick smokestack of the mill still standing. Barrels of tenpenny nails had been welded solid, and in the ruins of one store they found 60 dozen ax heads that had melted like butter into a candent lump of steel.

For Father Pernin, the only good the fire had wrought was to consume the saloons and brothels that had angered him. But even he must have wondered if the punishment fit the crime.

The townspeople gathered around a huge mountain of coal that was burning brightly. There was nothing to eat until someone found a few dozen blackened cabbages in a charred garden, the outer leaves charcoaled but the insides raw. Corpses filled the streets, many just heaps of ash and identifiable as human only by the melted rings and necklaces they had worn. Some bodies appeared untouched by the flames, but the coins in their pockets had melted.

Sometimes the jewelry and small change were still intact, though, and one looter took advantage of it. An outraged posse caught him in the act. The ad hoc trial was swift, and the jury unanimously sentenced the man to be hanged on the spot. Naturally, though, every rope in town had been incinerated. The lynch mob found a logging chain and looped it around the offender's neck, but there was not a single rafter or tree limb from which to hang him. "Whilst the preparations dragged on, the miserable man loudly implored mercy. The pity inspired by the mournful surroundings softened at length the hearts of the judges, and after having made him crave pardon on his knees for the sacrilegious thefts, they allowed him to go free."

By this time, Pernin's face had swollen to the size and color of a ripe pumpkin, and he couldn't see. And as far as anyone knew, no help was on the way.

When the fire had started, Big John Mulligan – the boss of the railroad crew that had been cutting the new Chicago & NorthWestern right-of-way – put his wife on his back and "galloped like a quarterhorse" to the river. Though Mrs. Mulligan's nightgown was burned off during the run, she still had a fragment of a woolen shawl to cover her in the river. They made it through the night. At dawn, the foreman set out alone on foot to Marinette, some six and a half miles north, for help.

It was a ghastly hike. Skeletal trees stood everywhere, limbless and wreathed in flame. Blazing windfalls blocked the roads. All around lay the seared carcasses of deer, bears and game birds. Parched by heat, smoke and ash, Mulligan stopped at the ruins of farms along the way but found no water.

And no survivors.

Marinette and its sister city of Menominee, Michigan, had been largely spared by a crescent of sand dunes just to the south, which diverted the fire. While men fought the flames, women and children had been evacuated to the lake by the paddlewheelers moored in the Menominee River. The fire had vaulted the river with ease and burned its way to Birch Creek, in Michigan's Upper Peninsula. It was still raging to the north when Mulligan located timber baron Isaac Stephenson, Marinette's town leader.

"Can you get us something for the folks at Peshtigo to eat?" he asked.

"Why, what's the matter at Peshtigo?" Stephenson asked, exhausted by a night of firefighting.

"My God!" Mulligan said. "Don't you know? Not a stick of the village is standing."

Stephenson quickly arranged for relief teams with blankets, tea, bread and bandages to head south by wagon and steamer.

By the time they got there, the cold front Peshtigo had been praying for, accompanied by heavy rains, had hit the area – 24 hours too late.

Though it occurred on the same night as the better-known Great Chicago Fire, the disaster in Peshtigo took far more lives – at least 1,200 versus Chicago's 250 – and still ranks as America's deadliest conflagration. All told, the Peshtigo fire burned an area of 2,000 square miles, 1,280,000 acres of some of the finest pinery in the world. Two billion trees were destroyed. Simultaneous fires burned out at least four hamlets in

Door County, across Green Bay from Peshtigo, stopping only when they reached Sturgeon Bay. No one will ever know the exact death toll, but fully a third of the residents of Peshtigo died that night, and as much as 75 percent of the smaller farming population of the Sugar Bushes to the west. Estimates of the total range as high as 2,250, including the fatalities in Door County towns like New Franken, Robinsonville, Rosiere and the sawmill hamlet of Williamsonville. Williamsonville was never rebuilt, and local historians today can't even agree on precisely where it once stood. Nor can they pinpoint how many of its citizens died – approximately 75 or 80 is the best guess. In the booming, freewheeling nineteenth century, Americans didn't carry driver's licenses or ID cards. A man could change his name at will. Most of the laborers were newly arrived immigrants who spoke little or no English, and the ones who filled the tough logging camps and mills of the North Woods came mostly from Scandinavia, Germany, French Canada or Eastern Europe. Businesses kept poor employee records, if any. Death was so commonplace in that era of unchecked epidemics and mass disasters that few of the survivors cared whose reeking, bloated body they were shoveling into the ground, unless it was family. For the most part, the dead were quickly forgotten. The living had business to attend to.

The dead are still remembered in Peshtigo, however. Today, mass graves mark the peaceful, neatly maintained burial grounds in what were the Sugar Bushes, and Peshtigo's main graveyard alone holds the unidentified ashes of at least 350 victims. Saddest of all, though, are the single tombstones standing over the graves where as many as 12 members of the same family are buried – in the case of the Newberry clan, ranging in age from 2 years old to 32.

"All lost in the calamity," the markers say.

No further details are necessary.

Along with other horribly burned townspeople, Pernin was taken to Marinette by wagon later that day. He had already learned that though most of it had been spared, his church property had not. "Ah!" he wrote. "And I had promised the poor unfortunates of Peshtigo to bring them to Marinette and shelter them in those very buildings. Thus I found myself bereft in the same hour of my two churches, two presbyteries and schoolhouse, as well as of all private property belonging to them and myself."

On Tuesday he was recovered enough to return to Peshtigo. Most of the town's dead who could be found had already been buried. What remained was black, reeking ashes. "A few calcined bricks, melted crystal, with crosses and crucifixes more or less destroyed, alone pointed out where my house had once been, while the charred remains of my poor dog indicated the site of my bedroom. I followed then the road leading from my house to the river. There, the carcasses of animals were more numerous than elsewhere, especially in the neighborhood of the bridge." Near the river, not far from where he'd last seen his horse, he found its bloated remains "so disfigured by the fiery death through which he had passed that I had some difficulty in recognizing him . . . Human relics could [scarcely] be distinguished from those of horses."

Pernin crossed the river via the scorched, wobbly beams of the bridge, where he received the surprise of his life. "I had barely reached the other side when one of my parishioners hastened to meet me, joyfully exclaiming, "Father, do you know what has happened to your tabernacle?

" 'No, what is it?'

"Come quickly then, and see. Oh! Father, it is a great miracle!"

They ran to the point on the riverbank where Pernin had pushed his wagon into the shallows. The buggy had been knocked over by the ferocious wind, but the tabernacle itself had somehow lodged on one of the big logs that had broken loose from the raft above the sawmill. "Everything in the immediate vicinity had been blackened or charred by the flames; logs, trunks, boxes, nothing had escaped, yet there rose the tabernacle, intact in its showy whiteness, presenting a wonderful contrast to the grimy blackness of the surrounding objects. I left it in the spot where it had been thrown by the tempest for two days, so as to give everyone an opportunity of seeing it."

Very few stopped to bear witness. They were too busy looking for their dead and rebuilding the town.

No accurate count was ever made of the dead in the 60 outlying logging camps that had served the mills of Peshtigo. Hundreds of nameless immigrant "choppers-in-the-woods" were cremated in their bunkhouses, others fled into the burning timber in terror, hoping to find a lake or a swamp to dive into. Few found one. Lumberjacks who had escaped knew that dozens of savvy timber cruisers had been camped out in the woods that night, estimating board feet and marking individual trees for the winter cut. Search parties combed the ghost forest, hoping to find a few survivors or at least a handful of bones to mark the demise of their comrades. Mostly they found dead deer – hundreds of them.

Six days after the fire, as one group passed under a tall, blackened pine, the charred body of a young camp foreman came crashing down at their feet.

"Why in the world did he climb that tree?" one asked. "Didn't he know that fire burns upward?"

What difference did it make?" his friend answered. "It was hell on earth that night . . . and hell in heaven, too."